The Imago Dei

The Imago Dei

A Priestly Calling for Humankind

JOHN THOMAS SWANN

Foreword by Rick Johnson

WIPF & STOCK · Eugene, Oregon

THE IMAGO DEI
A Priestly Calling for Humankind

Copyright © 2017 John Thomas Swann. All rights reserved. Except for brief quotations in critical publications or reviews, no part of this book may be reproduced in any manner without prior written permission from the publisher. Write: Permissions, Wipf and Stock Publishers, 199 W. 8th Ave., Suite 3, Eugene, OR 97401.

Wipf & Stock
An Imprint of Wipf and Stock Publishers
199 W. 8th Ave., Suite 3
Eugene, OR 97401

www.wipfandstock.com

PAPERBACK ISBN: 978-1-5326-0406-5
HARDCOVER ISBN: 978-1-5326-0408-9
EBOOK ISBN: 978-1-5326-0407-2

Manufactured in the U.S.A.   JUNE 7, 2017

Contents

Foreword by Rick Johnson | *viii*

Chapter 1   Introductory Matters on the Examination of the Image of God as a Priestly Calling | 1

     Articulation of Research Problem of Understanding the Image of God
     Definition of Terms surrounding a Priestly Interpretation of צלם אלהים
     Scope and Limitations of This Study
     History and Review of Relevant Research on the צלם אלהים
     Presentation of Thesis
     Warrant for Research of the צלם אלהים as a Priestly Commission
     Research Methodology for Interpreting the Divine Image
     Summaries of Chapters

Chapter 2   Biblical Study on the Image of God | 29

     Establishing the Interpretive Paradigm of Genesis 1
     Establishing a Theological Crux for the Image of God: Exodus 19
     Primary Exegesis of Genesis 1.26–28
     A Proper Understanding of the Image of God and Creation in a Priestly Context

Chapter 3   Examination of Biblical Compatibility of the צלם אלהים as a Priestly Calling | 87

     Examination of Selected Passages from a Priest Paradigm
     Alternate Creation Passages and Their Connection to Priesthood
     Selected Apocalyptic Passages on the New Creation and Priesthood
     Occupational Passages and Suggestions of an Expanded Priesthood
     Reflection on Biblical Passages for Priestly Intention

Chapter 4   Examination of Theological Compatibility of the צלם אלהים as a Priestly Calling | 138

> The Purpose of and Selection for Theological Comparison
> Reflection on the Compatibility of Theology with a Priestly Emphasis

Chapter 5   The Significance of a Priestly צלם אלהים within Biblical Theology | 153

> Summary of the Significance of a Priestly Image of God in Old Testament Theology
> Examination of the Idea of a Priestly Image within New Testament Theology
> Conclusions on the Priestly Calling of the Image of God for Biblical Theology

Chapter 6   Concluding Matters on the Interpretation of the Image of God as a Commission to Priesthood | 172

> Future Studies Impacted by the Priestly Designation of the Divine Image
> The Impact on Theological Thought
> Contemporary Applications of the Image of God as a Priestly Calling

Selected Bibliography | *189*

Foreword

A detailed and sustained theological presentation that takes seriously a wide range of biblical texts is a joy to encounter. John Swann's thesis is just such a book. It is also a timely contribution to a continued and growing interest in the field of biblical theology. Many have concluded that the various writings in the Bible are too diverse to treat as representing any kind of unity of thought. By identifying an important concept at the beginning of the Bible, exploring its location in the structure of ideas in the creation narrative, and then following the implications of what he discovers there, Swann is able to illuminate a range of texts throughout the rest of the Bible and suggest important new directions for church theology and practice.

This book is an excellent example of exegetical study that penetrates beyond surface investigation of the text and vocabulary to the thought world of the various parts of Scripture being considered. Swann's discussion takes some of the contemporary work done on the creation narratives and uses it to present new ways of understanding other parts of the Bible.

The concept of the image of God figures heavily in the doctrine of humanity in theology, but the term occurs very rarely in the Bible itself. This fact has left a vacuum for interpreters to understand its significance in a striking number of ways. Without explicit biblical definition, interpreters have been free to exercise quite a bit of imagination in making sense of the vocabulary in Genesis 1:26–27, specifically the words "image" (*tselem*) and "likeness" (*demuth*).

In the early Christian centuries, the presence of two words to convey the idea led to the view that the text refers to two components of the human constitution. Irenaeus understood the image to refer to reason and the likeness to refer to certain supernatural attributes of a moral nature.

Humanity was like God in being able to think and in the capacity to exhibit traits of character. After the fall, humans retained the image, the ability to reason, but lost the likeness, the additional moral qualities. Irenaeus's view remained influential for centuries.

Old Testament interpreters generally agree that the language of image and likeness in Gen 1:26 is an example of hendiadys, naming a single reality by two terms. Since the word "image" frequently refers to a physical representation such as a statue or idol, it can be understood as signifying the connection between humanity and God, and the word "likeness" would be intended to emphasize the difference or distinction between them. Humans are somehow like God without being the same or identical. The problem still remains to identify wherein they are alike.

The context in Genesis 1 provides the basis for the claim that the image is the exercise of dominion over the creation. In Gen 1:26 immediately after God's statement of his intention to create humans in his image and likeness, he adds the intention that they will rule over the creatures of the sea, the sky, and the earth. The point is repeated in v. 28 in the divine blessing and command after creating the humans. As God is the creator who sustains all, so humans were created to be God's agents in ruling the animal world.

Since the text does not explicitly say the image is the exercise of dominion, however, other interpreters have responded that the image is not equal to dominion but rather is some aspect or quality that allows or enables the humans to fulfill that role. Defining the image in terms of relational capacity offers a possible solution. Creating humans as creatures capable of relationship means that they have the ability to respond to other relational beings, including God and other humans. God can then address them with a word of command, and the humans have the potential to respond in obedience or disobedience. Exercising dominion over the other creatures is part of that response. This view sees the image as personhood. Just as God is a personal God, so also humans are personal beings with intelligence, will, and moral capacity. The fall did not destroy the image, but it can be understood to have distorted it making relationship with God and others problematic. Such a view has a natural affinity with Trinitarian thought that sees human relationships as mirroring the relationships between the members of the Godhead. A variation of this view is that of Karl Barth, who found particular significance in the relation of the sexes as reflecting the Godhead. Genesis 1:17 explicitly notes that in making mankind in God's image he made them male and female. Such views make use of the I-thou language of certain strands of modern theology. It also accounts for the reason Gen 9:6 cites the image of God as a basis for the punishment for murder.

A different approach to the image draws upon the use of statues in antiquity to serve as signs of the rule of a monarch. Just as kings would set up images of themselves as representations of their dominion, so God set humans on the earth to manifest his dominion there. This model addresses the connection with the divine commission to rule the earth, but leaves open the question of what it is about humans that makes them fit to serve as divine images. As such it could be combined with other views that define the image as personhood, reason, or other spiritual or mental qualities.

Whatever definition is given to the image has important consequences for theology and ethics. Identifying the image as rational capacity which is unaffected by the fall easily leads to a kind of theology that is overconfident in its understanding of its grasp of truth and God. Proofs of the existence of God can be presented as conclusive. If human reason is understood as subject to the effects of the fall, however, then human systems of thought must be defended with some humility. Identifying the image as the exercise of dominion provides a platform to remind humanity of its responsibility for ecology while also warning of the tendency of humanity in its fallenness to despoil God's good creation. These views also raise important questions for understanding how Christ as the image of the invisible God restores fallen humanity in the New Testament.

Swann's proposal likewise has far-reaching implications for theology and ethics. He integrates his exegesis of the Genesis texts with the address of the Word of God to the people of God in the rest of the Bible. It is a fresh approach that builds on the work of biblical scholarship in more recent times and applies it broadly. In so doing Swann shows his strong interest in using the results of technical scholarship to address the community of faith. He writes with a pastor's heart following many years of serving in that role, like many of the greatest theologians throughout history. The challenge he issues is broad and comprehensive and deserves a wide hearing.

Rick Johnson
March 11, 2017

Chapter 1

Introductory Matters on the Examination of the Image of God as a Priestly Calling

ARTICULATION OF RESEARCH PROBLEM OF UNDERSTANDING THE IMAGE OF GOD

The primary account of biblical creation in Genesis 1 describes humankind in terms of the image of God (צלם אלהים).[1] While there are multiple creation accounts distributed throughout the Hebrew Scriptures, Genesis 1 serves—both on the basis of its canonical placement and its comprehensive scope—as the foundational account for the understanding of both biblical cosmogony and, perhaps more importantly from a scriptural standpoint, biblical anthropology.[2]

---

1. It should be noted that throughout this chapter, any reference to Gen 1 refers to Gen 1:1—2:3 unless otherwise noted. The Creation event of Gen 1:1–31 is incomplete without Gen 2:1–3, demanding a consideration of the first verses of Gen 2. However, insisting on Gen 1:1—2:3 for each reference to Genesis 1 seems pedantic when the first three verses of the second chapter can simply be considered as a part of the story of the first chapter.

2. Cameron, "Introduction," 53; Van Wolde, *Stories of the Beginning*, 1; Kessler, *Old Testament Theology*, 132; Middleton, *Liberating Image*, 60; cf. Balentine, *Torah's Vision*, 60–63; Firmage, "Genesis 1," 101; McKeown, *Genesis*, 375. This statement can be—and obviously has been—disputed; however, it is declared here not as an undisputed fact but rather to provide appropriate context for the research problem. Specifics on why and how Genesis 1 serves as a foundational account will be dealt with as appropriate in the course of the study.

Since Genesis 1 serves this foundational role, a proper understanding of the divine image assumes significant importance.[3] The problem for theological studies, however, is while the image of God is critical for theological anthropological reflection, the specific data surrounding the צלם אלהים is relatively limited.[4] The precise phrase occurs only twice in the whole of the Old Testament (Gen 1:27; 9:6), and its closest match (דמות אלהים) only once in Gen 5:1. With a cursory reading, the immediate context of Genesis 1, and even the larger context of Genesis 1–9, provides an ambiguous illustration of how to interpret the divine image and what it entails for humanity.

However, while a precise interpretation of the image of God can be elusive, the implications of the divine image are nonetheless extensive.[5] Minimally, the use of the divine image in Gen 9:6 provides the foundational authority underlying the prohibition against homicide and therefore serves as an essential aspect of the valuation of (human) life. This then provides a basis for not only the criminal laws but also the purity and hospitality laws of the Torah.[6] The social aspects of the prophets' oracles also revolve around or serve as extensions of the image of God, as does the Christians' adoption of the image of Christ (Rom 8:29; 1 Cor 15:49; Col 3:10–11) in the New Testament.[7]

The importance of the divine image becomes even more distinctive when the association between Creation theology and the theologies of call/election and covenant are considered. Notably, the first covenant proper in the Old Testament—the Noahic covenant (Gen 9:8–17)—occurs during the re-Creation period following the flood and directly follows the ascription of the divine image and the reiteration of the command issued to Adam to multiply to Noah (Gen 9:1–7; cf. Gen 1:26–31).[8] While it lacks the direct reference to the צלם אלהים, the connection between Creation and covenant at Sinai is perhaps even more important. The establishment of Israel as a "treasured possession" of God and a "kingdom of priests" (Exod 19:5–6)

---

3. Garrett, *Systematic Theology*, 1:392; Grenz, *Named God*, 361.

4. Boer, *Ember*, 3; Childs, *Biblical Theology*, 112; Ware, "In the Image," 2–3.

5. Bray, "Significance of God's Image," 201; Cairns, *Image of God*, 18.

6. Kessler, *Old Testament Theology*, 126–27; Craigie, *Book of Deuteronomy*, 157; cf. Dempster, *Dominion and Dynasty*, 73; Keil and Delitzsch, *Commentary*, 1:97.

7. Strine, "Ezekiel's Image Problem," 270; Cairns, *Image of God*, 28–29; Brunner, *Man in Revolt*, 96.

8. Cross, *Canaanite Myth*, 296; Rendtorff, *Canon and Theology*, 127. Dumbrell emphasizes this point even further, suggesting that the connection between Salvation/Deliverance and Creation and covenant in the Noahic covenant served to bring humankind back into the Sabbath rest of Creation. The connection between Creation theology and covenant in the Noah narrative also somewhat mitigates Cross' observation that the Creation account does not include any specific covenantal terms. Dumbrell, *Covenant and Creation*, 34–36.

effectively serves as an act of divine creation as the Pentateuch itself interprets the Sinai covenant as a re-creation of the fellowship that existed between God and Adam.[9] This interpretation is most easily and directly seen in the comparison of Exod 20:8–11 and Deut 5:12–15, where the saving work of YHWH is directly equated to the Sabbath of Creation.[10] This is also further in accord with Philip Davies' observation that the narrative does not have to declare what "*must* have happened, but . . . [what] *could* have happened."[11] The gap between the descriptive and the normative—an issue present within biblical theology since Gabler's inauguration speech—is largely a false one.[12] Historically, there may have been a difference between the Creation and the exodus and Sinai event; theologically they were equivalent acts of deliverance and creation that should be read synchronically rather than diachronically.[13] The connection between Genesis 1 and Sinai should be easily accepted, since it is functionally identical to the already accepted connection(s) between soteriology and eschatology and between the (initial) Creation and the final re-Creation that will occur in the Day of the Lord.[14] The recognition of these connections and the synchronic nature of biblical creation theology is critical to proper understanding and interpretation of the image of God and respect for the extent of its importance.[15]

While specifically nuanced interpretations of the divine image abound, all of the interpretations of the divine image can be divided largely into two broad views: either the צלם אלהים is a characteristic/condition of humankind, or it is a commissioning/commandment for humankind.[16] The interpretation of the divine image as a condition has been prevalent for much of the church's history, being explicated by Justin Martyr and Origen as a capacity for reason as early as mid-second century AD and upheld in subsequent

---

9. Stuart, *Exodus*, 422.

10. Craigie, *Book of Deuteronomy*, 157; Merrill, *Deuteronomy*, 150–52.

11. Davies, *Memories of Ancient Israel*, 37.

12. Pierce uses softer language, but his observations surrounding his pursuit of a "middle ground between the descriptive and the normative" are broadly applicable and demonstrate the points rendered here. Cf. Pierce, *Enthroned*, 8.

13. Rendtorff, *Canon and Theology*, 128–31.

14. Ibid., 134.

15. Calloud, "A Few Comments," 139.

16. Obviously, a commandment assumes certain characteristics and a characteristic expects certain obligations or outworking. The two broad categories used in this discussion are perhaps best considered to be *termini* of a spectrum that expects both elements are present to some degree. However, for purposes of the greater discussion, this consideration is best left assumed and only the primary categories/poles of the spectrum emphasized.

centuries by both Catholic and protestant scholars.[17] The alternate interpretive position is to recognition that the image of God is not a condition, but a calling or a commissioning describing the expected activity of humankind. While they do not advocate this position in these exact terms or explicitly, the majority of the writings of the early church fathers reveal essentially this mentality. Both Clement and his pseudonymous imitator directly link the idea of the *imago Dei* with the "work of righteousness" and suggest that living out a righteous life serves as the expression of the צלם אלהים (*1 Clem.* 33:8; cf. *2 Clem.* 9–11).[18] Their concern was not so much to define the *nature* of the image of God as it was to capture the *presentation* of it. This approach has found something of a resurgence in modern interpretations of the divine image that often focus on the relationship between the image and the aspects of dominion in Gen 1:28.[19] While the right to dominion might be a characteristic, the exercise of dominion is a commission.

In assessing the nature of the commission of the image of God, it is useful to recognize that within the Old Testament the image of God is always used in a context of worship.[20] As the Creator of humankind, God has assigned his creatures the task (and privilege) of exalting and worshiping him.[21] The recognition of this assignment suggests that it is reasonable to interpret the צלם אלהים not primarily as a condition or even in terms of a mandate for sovereignty, but rather in terms of worship and—in light of the development of the Israelite faith—cult.[22] Notably, this understanding accords well with the scholarly consensus that there was considerable priestly influence on the formation and writing of Genesis 1. Any study of the צלם אלהים therefore should begin with a consideration of the cultic or priestly

---

17. Burns, *Theological Anthropology*, 10–12; Zachman, "Jesus Christ," 46–48.

18. It should be noted that although the interpretation of the divine image as a condition has prevailed in much of the history of the church, the Early Fathers' approach that describes the image as a calling or enactment actually predates Martyr, particularly if the traditional dating of *1 Clement* in the last decade of the first century is accepted.

19. Grenz, "Jesus as the *Imago Dei*," 621.

20. Van Wolde, *Stories of the Beginning*, 26–29. While the worship context might be muted—or perhaps better said, missed by contemporary readers—the introduction of the צלם אלהים establishes the creation of humankind as an essential part of the overall temple-building exercise of Genesis 1 and therefore inherently related to a cultic and/or worship environment in at least a broad sense. Smith, *Priestly Vision*, 3.

21. Cameron, "Theological Anthropology," 54; Ware, "In the Image," 8.

22. Cf. Pierce, *Enthroned*, 27–28. The use of the word "primarily" is important: both conditional holiness and the expression of sovereignty in whatever form it takes have important relationships to the צלם אלהים. The present concern, though, is not whether the image of God relates to holiness or sovereignty, but rather whether or not the commissioning of humankind for worship is the dominant emphasis of the divine image.

concerns; however, this has not always been the case. It is necessary to rectify this situation. And while efforts have been made to examine Genesis 1 from a cultic standpoint and emphasize the Temple of Creation motif, those efforts largely have failed to fully associate the meaning of the image of God with the overall temple-building imagery of Genesis 1 and instead continue to subvert the cultic understanding of humanity to a royal understanding emphasizing dominion. It will be useful instead to expand on the cultic aspects of God's commissioning of humankind. The question(s) of why the image of God is best interpreted as a commission to priesthood and how that commission is expressed in Genesis 1 and throughout the Bible is the concern of this study.

DEFINITION OF TERMS SURROUNDING A PRIESTLY INTERPRETATION OF צלם אלהים

A proper understanding of the צלם אלהים naturally requires an understanding of the independent lexical meaning of צלם. Similarly, since Gen 1:26 parallels צלם with דמות the latter term could directly impact the understanding of the divine image and therefore also demands study. Secondary terms that relate to the interpretation of the image of God—including ברא, כבש, and רדה—are dealt with contextually in the following chapters of this study. Only צלם and דמות demand particular lexical attention from the outset of this inquiry. On the other hand, while a lexical examination of כהן is unnecessary, the importance of priesthood to the present study demands a proper overview of what constituted a priest or reflected priestly interests within the ANE generally and the Old Testament specifically. Therefore, a brief discussion of the primary attributes of priesthood is also warranted.

צלם

Etymologically, צלם derives from the word "shadow." This seems to reflect the idea that just as a shadow is indicative of a larger or greater object, so too does an image represent something greater than itself. Generally, צלם and its cognates in other ANE languages indicate statuary figures of some sort, with the most common referents in both Hebrew and comparative writings being idols. It is not a common term; within the Old Testament צלם appears a total of seventeen times in fifteen verses.[23] Of the six occurrences in the

---

23. Gen 1:26–27; 5:3; 9:6; Num 33:52; 1 Sam 6:5, 11; 2 Kgs 11:18 (2 Chr 23:17); Ezek 7:20; 16:17; 23:14; Amos 5:26; Pss 39:7; 73:20.

Pentateuch, five relate to the Creation in some way; either directly (three occurrences in Gen 1:26–27) or indirectly as a point of reference or reiteration (Gen 5:3; 9:6). These occurrences will be further detailed in the course of this study. The remaining use of צלם in Num 33:52 clearly describes Canaanite idols. Similarly, 2 Kgs 11:18 and the parallel story in 2 Chr 23:17 both use צלם as a description of pagan idols.

Within the Latter Prophets, only Amos and Ezekiel use צלם in the context of pagan idols (Amos 5:26; Ezek 7:20; 16:17). Ezekiel also uses it an additional time to describe a view—or perhaps a portrait or ostraca—of the Babylonian soldiers whose apparent virility enticed Oholibah (Jerusalem) into infidelity. Considering the clear use of infidelity as a metaphor for spiritual unfaithfulness and the visionary aspects of the context, this use of צלם also seems primarily to indicate idolatry—if not the idolatry of actual idol worship, then at least a metaphorical idolatry of worshipping human prowess.[24]

צלם is used in the Writings only twice, both times in the Psalms (Pss 39:7; 73:20). Neither of these poems indicates any overt idolatry, instead focusing on the more primitive "shadow" aspects to indicate humankind's ephemeral nature. Considering the frequent use of archaic meanings and language in poetic materials, this is not entirely surprising, though the frequent reliance on Creation theology within the psalms may illustrate this usage as the finitude of humans as mere images of God contrasts with the infinitude of YHWH.[25] Regardless of whether צלם is being used archaically for poetic purposes or theologically as a reflection of Creation theology, neither use detracts from the general sense that צלם indicates primarily an idol of some form.

The final incidences of צלם are found in 1 Samuel 6 and describes the "tumors" and rodents cast by the Philistines. These require a more involved examination. On the surface, the images constructed by the Philistines were not for the purpose of worship. Iconic tumors do not represent any known ANE deity. On the other hand, while the icons were not representative of a deity they were nonetheless formed in a distinctly cultic context: the Philistine priests directed the construction of the icons with the purpose of acknowledging the God of Israel (cf. 1 Sam 6:2–3). It is almost certain that some form of sympathetic magic underlay the shape of the images. Within the ANE context, magic in general and sympathetic magic in particular were linked to spiritual realms that fell directly under the priestly purview.

---

24. Block, *Book of Ezekiel*, 760.
25. Goldingay, *Psalms 1–41*, 71.

Therefore, while the צלמים in 1 Sam 6:5 did not indicate idols intended to be worshipped, they were clearly cultic objects of some sort.

Considering the preceding analysis, it is reasonable to suggest that the most natural understanding of צלם in the Hebrew Bible is as a cultic representation meant to connect with a higher plane or deity. This is important, since it establishes the fact that nowhere in the Old Testament does צלם indicate a royal figure of any kind.[26] Even the ambiguous uses of צלם in the Psalms—disconnected from the concept of a cultic icon—fail to indicate any sort of royal ideology. This pattern of usage stands in contradistinction to the tendency to emphasize the צלם אלהים in royal terms. Based on the actual pattern of use within the Bible itself, the צלם is best understood in terms of cultic importance.

דמות

There has been considerable debate regarding the relationship between צלם and דמות. This debate has specifically revolved around whether the terms are essentially synonymous in Gen 1:26 (and subsequent texts such as Gen 5:1) or whether דמות is synthetic and intended to add an additional layer of anthropology to the passage.[27]

While theologians focus more on the image (צלם) of God rather than the likeness (דמות) of God, דמות is actually more prevalent within the Hebrew Scriptures than צלם. It occurs twenty-five times within twenty-two verses, most prominently in the book of Ezekiel.[28] Ezekiel pairs דמות and צלם synonymously in Ezek 23:14–15. דמות is used in Ezek 8:2 to describe the Spirit as similar to a human, but yet very clearly *not* human. There is an overt distinction made between the essential supernatural aspect of the visitor and the general anthropoid form that the being assumed as Ezekiel

---

26. This is not to deny the possibility that the צלם could indicate a royal image. Both Egyptian and Akkadian writings use their cognate of צלם to associate their kings with deities, though the interrelated aspects of monarchy and cult in those nations leaves it open to argument whether the "images" are more reflective of royal authority or divine empowerment. But regardless how other ANE nations used "image" in their writings, there is no demonstrably royal usage of צלם within the specific theological framework of the Old Testament. Miller, "In the 'Image,'" 294–95.

27. Boer, *Ember*, 2. Presently, most scholars support a synonymous interpretation of צלם and דמות; however, it is worth noting the past dispute over this issue—particularly during the Reformation—for the sake of thoroughness.

28. Gen 1:26; 5:1, 3; 2 Kgs 16:10; Isa 13:4; 40:18; Ezek 1:5, 10, 13, 16, 22, 26, 28; 8:2; 10:1, 10, 21–22; 23:15; Ps 58:4 [MT v. 5]; Dan 10:16; 2 Chr 4:3.

presents the condescension of God to Ezekiel's limited ability to comprehend him.²⁹

Ezekiel's use of דמות to juxtapose a higher or supernatural essence with a comprehensible human form is consistent in chs. 1 and 10 where fourteen of the twenty-five occurrences of דמות are found. Chapter 1 contains the majority of the references in connection with the theophany of the wheel. Considering the overall vision involved, Ezekiel's use of דמות seems to be an attempt to describe something beyond his capacity of understanding and present an analogy with a clear indication that the true vision of God is greater and more glorious than the prophet could properly describe.³⁰ Overall, Ezekiel's use of דמות serves to express some form of *limited* similarity between the likeness and its object.³¹

Isaiah's use of דמות is similar to Ezekiel's use and reflects the same understanding. When he compares God to pagan idols (Isa 40:18), Isaiah essentially challenges his audience to ask, "What object is not of such limited similarity to YHWH that it might possibly represent him?" Isaiah's other use of דמות in Isa 13:4 is connected with the theophonic mustering of the heavenly host for battle. Just as Ezekiel would later do, Isaiah describes the divine activity in a manner comprehensible to human listeners, but only with a caveat that any human activity pales in comparison to the divine work.³²

The emphasis on the limitation of similarity is not particularly blatant in the use of דמות in 2 Kgs 16:10 (describing the model of the altar) and 2 Chr 4:3 (describing the molding of the gourds on the temple furnishings), but neither is it absent. In both instances the term is used in the context of representation without equivalence. The model altar is a nonfunctional reflection of the actual altar; the gourds are symbolic but obviously not real fruit. Similarly, Psalm 58 is obviously symbolic; however, the more interesting aspect of the use of דמות is that the comparative use ("venom like the venom of serpents") serves to specify or delimit the type of poison from a general toxin to venom specifically associated with snakes. This both suggests a limited similarity and a specific application of connotations to

---

29. Daniel duplicates this method of using דמות in Dan 10:16 when attempting to describe the "man" of his vision.

30. Block, *Ezekiel 1–24*, 98.

31. Gentry and Wellum, *Kingdom*, 192. Ezekiel 23:15 is the only possible exception to this use; however, considering that the portrait or inscription that Oholibah viewed was itself a secondary or delimited depiction of the actual reality of the Chaldeans—both physically and metaphorically—it is reasonable to aver that Ezekiel's use is wholly consistent.

32. Konkel, "דמה," in Van Gemeren, *NIDOTTE*, 969.

the poetic phrase; this is not simply venom, but venom from the deceptive snake.

In a closer context to Genesis 1, דמות occurs only in the תולדת of Genesis 5. Notably, Gen 5:3 uses both צלם and דמות in essentially the same manner as Gen 1:26 and establishes a consistent interpretation. On the other hand, דמות appears without the accompanying צלם in v. 1, where it indicates the likeness of God. This is suggestive of some form of synonymy between the image of God and the likeness of God, though it is interesting to consider Gen 5:1 as a contrast with God's creative activity rather than a statement of consistency with it.[33] By contrasting acts of human procreation with God's acts of creation, the תולדת ultimately shows the limitations of humanity before God. This interpretation remains consistent with the overall examination of דמות as a statement of limited representation.[34]

Ultimately, while דמות is not specifically a cultic term, the biblical distribution of the term favors contexts of theophany (Ezekiel and Isaiah), temple (2 Kings and 2 Chronicles), or worship (Psalms). Further, while genealogies are not cultic, the תולדת are typically ascribed to priestly sources or interests. This pattern of distribution suggest that the most common understanding of דמות within the Old Testament itself is simultaneously as a cultic delimitation of humankind's ability to portray or behave as YHWH and yet as an affirmation of the similarity or relationship between humanity and God—another cultic interest.

כהן

There were a number of terms for priests/priesthood in the ANE; however, כהן is the standard word used in the Old Testament. The verbal use always occurs in the Piel—perhaps as a denominative form, or alternately a factitive idea of bringing something to a certain state—while the nominative form seems to be or derive from a Qal participle. This pattern of use makes it difficult to assess the exact etymology of כהן. However, while the specific etymology of כהן is unknown, the frequent use of the word in the Hebrew Scriptures allows for a reasonable understanding of the nature and role of priesthood.

In all cases, priests assumed a role as intermediaries of some sort between the divine and the mundane. This mediation essentially serves as the connection between God and the Created order.[35] However, while

---

33. Hamilton, *Book of Genesis*, 255.
34. Ware, "In the Image," 2.
35. This is not to suggest that God could not enter into Creation except through

the general function of the priesthood in establishing the divine-human communion is accepted, the specific emphases of that communion are widely disputed. While it is impossible to examine and argue for specifics in the scope of the present study, the broad categories are consistent and can be considered without demanding any particular prioritization of the priestly roles. These broad functions of the priesthood can be summarized as the consecration of people and objects, the curation of the holy place and implements, the edification of worshipers through direct teaching or some form of divination (such as the אורים ותמים), and the mediation of sacrifices and other cultic rituals.[36]

Priestly Responsibilities of Consecration

YHWH's קדש nature demands that his worshipers themselves reflect some form of holiness. The entrance into priestly service expects an immediate act of consecration, and the frequent changes in clothing and washing of the body surrounding the priests' movement from, to, and within the holy place all serve as smaller acts of consecration.[37] This idea of consecration and cleanliness is not limited to the priests, but extends—in Israelite society—to the people, explaining the numerous purity laws of the תורה.[38] Besides the need for personal purity, priests also served a role in ensuring the overall ritual cleanliness of their society.[39] To be a worshiper of YHWH demanded not only that the people abstain *from* certain worldly activities, but also that they become holy *to* God.[40] It was the priests who were responsible for the evaluation and pronouncement of cleanliness (Lev 10:10, et al.).[41]

---

priestly activity, but rather to recognize that God has ordained the priesthood as the ideal means by which he is to be approached and a consistent means through which he conveys his will to humankind at large (whether that conveyance is through the teaching of תורה, priestly divination, or other methods). Cf. Nelson, *Raising Up*, 2–4.

36. King, *Realignment*, 67; Nelson, *Raising Up*, 15.
37. Kessler, *Old Testament Theology*, 358–59; Nelson, *Raising Up*, 37, 49–52.
38. Stuart, *Exodus*, 423; Nelson, *Raising Up*, 43; Eastwood, *Life and Thought*, 72.
39. King, *Realignment*, 61–62.
40. Kessler, *Old Testament Theology*, 344–47.
41. Cross, *Canaanite Myth*, 299; King, *Realignment*, 171.

Priestly Responsibilities of Curation

Priests are consistently linked with holy places in both Israelite and the surrounding ANE ideologies.[42] The communion between the human and the divine, while possible anywhere, was intended specifically to occur in the temple(s) of the deity.[43] Since the temple itself needed to be consecrated into holiness, and the people entering the temple grounds to worship required consecration and intercession, it was necessary to have designated people who cared for the holy environment.[44] Biblically this care extended beyond the line of Aaron to include the tribe of Levi as a whole (Num 1:47–53), but the inner temple areas and the specific instruments of the temple remained the sole responsibility of the priests.[45]

Priestly Responsibilities of Edification

Whether priestly oversight of the תורה is a function of their curation of the holy things or an aspect of their mediation between God and humankind, the Israelite priests were entrusted with the preservation and instruction of the תורה.[46] Just as they were to discern between the holy and the profane, so too were they to teach the nation as a whole what YHWH required of his people.[47] Similarly, the divinatory aspects of the priesthood—most clearly expressed with the Urim and Thummim, despite the general lack of information on the exact practice involved—served to enlighten the nation of God's will and therefore fall under the didactic responsibilities of the priesthood.[48]

Priestly Responsibilities of Mediation

If the knowledge to approach God is found in תורה, the place for that approach manifested in the temple, and the ability to approach a holy God manifested in the cleanliness rituals of Israel, then the sacrificial system and

---

42. Nelson, *Raising Up*, 27–28.

43. Cross, *Canaanite Myth*, 298–300; Zevit, "Prophet versus Priest," 200.

44. King, *Realignment*, 170; Nelson, *Raising Up*, 61; Pleins, *Social Visions*, 63.

45. Routledge, *Old Testament Theology*, 185; cf. King, *Realignment*, 41.

46. Garrett, "Biblical Doctrine," 139–40; Garrett, *Systematic Theology*, 2:552; Nelson, *Raising Up*, 11; Torrance, *Royal Priesthood*, 3–5.

47. Nelson, *Raising Up*, 87.

48. Blenkinsopp, *Sage, Priest, Prophet*, 73, 81–82; Nelson, *Raising Up*, 39–44; Routledge, *Old Testament Theology*, 184.

other cultic activities of the nation served as the actual means by which YHWH was approached.[49] While the priests did not necessarily—or even likely—perform the actual slaughter of most of the animals sacrificed, they did facilitate the practice to ensure it was acceptable before God.[50] This facilitation of sacrifices, along with the priestly leadership in other cultic activities and the issuance of blessing, served as a form of mediation by which the Israelites could safely approach God.[51]

Summary Comments on Priestly Responsibilities

It could be argued that consecration of the holy place and the edification of the worshipers served as products of mediation, or that the curation of the holy place necessitated the consecration of the people and the proper conduct of sacrifice and liturgy.[52] Either of these approaches illustrates the interconnectivity of the different priestly duties and suggests that they are better considered *in toto* toward the overall purpose of bridging the world of the divine with the created world.[53] The different aspects of connecting God and humankind can be outlined separately to provide a workable model for evaluating the presence of priestly functions in different passages of Scripture, but should not be considered autonomous from one another.

SCOPE AND LIMITATIONS OF THIS STUDY

A fundamental question for the pursuit of Old Testament theology is whether the text is best interpreted synchronically or diachronically.[54] However, the question itself is a bit misleading as it casts the two options in terms of opposition when it is perhaps better to consider them synergistically in terms of *both/and* rather than *either/or*. While certain portions of Scripture, such as narratives, will naturally favor a diachronic approach, a synchronic approach might be wholly valid for certain studies focused on the overall presentation of the Old Testament.[55] Since the study of the image of God—a

---

49. Cf. King, *Realignment*, 70–73; Stuart, *Exodus*, 423; Patton, "Layers," 167.
50. Blenkinsopp, *Sage, Priest, Prophet*, 80; Routledge, *Old Testament Theology*, 185; Nelson, *Raising Up*, 59–60; Zevit, "Prophet versus Priest," 200.
51. King, *Realignment*, 69; cf. Nelson, *Raising Up*, 44–46, 85; Garrett, *Systematic Theology*, 2:552–53.
52. King, *Realignment*, 67.
53. Nelson, *Raising Up*, 15, 52.
54. Sailhamer, *Introduction to Old Testament Theology*, 31–33, 184–94.
55. Ibid., 192.

fundamental part of biblical anthropology—must necessarily accord with the entire biblical presentation of humankind, a synchronic approach is somewhat necessary. Anthropological conclusions must be synchronically consistent not only with the whole of the Old Testament, but also with the New Testament. At the same time, individual passages must be treated with appropriate concern for their individual (diachronic) concerns and audiences. Therefore, the present study will seek to present a valid interpretation of the צלם אלהים that adequately spans the entirety of the biblical portrait of humanity without compromising the individual integrity of any given passage of Scripture.

This examination places primary concern on the text and interpretation of Genesis 1. The study of additional passages from both the Old and New Testaments ensures synchronic compatibility. Since it is impossible to examine every passage relating to humanity in the scope of this study, the supplementary passages are limited to those that reflect the divine-human relationship in the context of Creation theology or that demonstrate a commissioning of humanity into a priestly calling.

The focus on the two aforementioned types of Scripture provides certain guidelines for the scope of the present study. Further, though this study is concerned with biblical theology, the primary concern is Old Testament theology; reflection on the New Testament is provided to demonstrate consistency rather than to serve as an exhaustive treatment of New Testament anthropology. Likewise, deuterocanonical works and rabbinic writings will be considered, but only to a very limited extent in order to ensure accuracy to *biblical* theology. Instead, they will be referenced for possible insight into earlier interpretations but not as primary or indisputable sources of interpretation.[56]

HISTORY AND REVIEW OF RELEVANT RESEARCH ON THE צלם אלהים

Review of Premodern Interpretations of the Image of God

While the earliest Christian theologians did not write theologies *per se*, their writings cannot be discarded as the first examples of biblical theology. These writings reflect deep theological reflection and development of thought, and bridge the proverbial gap between exegetical theory and ecclesiastical praxis.

---

56. Rendtorff, *Canon and Theology*, 19–24.

First Clement is the earliest known noncanonical Christian document, and directly addresses the image of God. Clement introduces the divine image, but does not pursue a theoretical agenda or ascribe characteristic qualities to it. Instead, he uses it motivationally as an impetus for good works and righteous living (cf. *1 Clem.* 33:8, et al.). This use limits a proper analysis of Clement's position, but it does suggest that the image of God served in some capacity as the ability to live righteously. The close temporal proximity between Clement and Paul's statements concerning the imitation of the Christ (cf. Rom 8:29; Eph 4:22—5:2) suggests that Clement's silence assumes familiarity with Paul's Christology (and anthropology) that likens the imitation of the Christ to the image of God.[57] Similarly, *2 Clement*, while not delving into the divine image as *1 Clement* does, further indicates that the physical activities of humankind can express the image of God.[58] In fact, the majority of the first and second century writings that express interest in the image of God do so without concern for the *nature* of the image so much as the *presentation* of it through righteous activities. The earliest theology of the image of God was one of activity: the image is expressed in holy living.

The later clarification of this theology arose through necessary reaction to gnostic heresy and Greek philosophy.[59] While other challenges arose and were addressed, these two broad categories provided the greatest impetus for and threat against the development of Christian theological thought since they infiltrate the orthodox praxis of the church by the mid-third century AD.

The ascetic movement of the early church lent itself toward a quasi-gnostic diminishment of the value of physical life in favor of spiritual growth. Irenaeus' late second-century *Against Heresies* is possibly the most important early defense against the intrusive gnostic influences, and presents one

---

57. This approach to interpretation is further strengthened if the Johannine corpus is also considered. First John 1:3 describes the role of Jesus in salvation in terms of κοινωνια directly before calling the reader to practice truth and walk in light "as he is in the light." This combination affirms the connection between the imitation of the Christ and the pursuit of righteous living in a manner not dissimilar to either Paul or Clement.

58. Lightfoot and Harmer, *Apostolic Fathers*, 65. Lightfoot and Harmer take this statement further, and actually compare the exhortations of *2 Clement* 9–11 to the ethical imperatives of the Epistle of James.

59. This statement is somewhat redundant, as Greek philosophy was one of the foundations of the gnostic movement itself. The two threats are kept separate here to reflect that the developed gnostic system was something unique from the philosophy that helped originate it. It became a system of thought separate from the "pure" philosophy of the Greeks. Also, while the term "gnostic/gnosticism" is used above, the earliest encounters between Christianity and gnostic thought patterns would have occurred in a proto-gnostic phase that would have owed its development to elements beyond Hellenistic thought.

of the most cogent orthodox Christian theologies of the period. What is significant about this approach for the present study is Irenaeus' understanding that humanity retained the image of God not as a material or immaterial status, but as the determination and freedom to resist sin according to one's choices.[60] In other words, it continued to be perceived with a direct connection toward Christian activity, even in more spiritualized contexts.[61]

Christian Platonism continued to develop out of the works of Justin Martyr and Origen throughout the third and fourth centuries. Rather than counter philosophy as Irenaeus did with Gnosticism, Christian Platonism assimilated Hellenistic paradigms of thought into a Christian perspective. This approach shifted the interpretation of the image of God from one of activity or the self-determination that produced activity into one of reason and the ability to analyze the world.[62]

These earliest anthropologies did not tend to debate the loss of the *imago Dei* but instead assumed that it remained within humankind. Further, the core of the image of God was acknowledged to be found in righteous living. Irenaeus' self-determination and Origen's appreciation for reasoning both looked to righteous living for their contexts. Self-determination meant humanity could choose to live righteously. Irenaeus anticipated the (much later) arguments about the depravity of man preventing this choice by insisting that it is humankind's obstinacy that interfered with the choice rather than a loss of divine attribute (*Against Heresies*, book IV, 38.4). The issue becomes one of unwillingness rather than inability. This not only expresses the image of God as self-determination, but also anticipates the interpretation of the Christian Platonists. To Origen and the later Christian philosophers, rationality allowed human beings the ability to discern the correct course in life. Failure to live a righteous life was rooted in irrational thought born of

---

60. Burns, *Theological Anthropology*, 6.

61. It must be acknowledged that despite its importance, *Against Heresies* is not necessarily a reflection of the normative theology of the time. However, while the thesis that Creation was immature and progressive may have been (at least somewhat) unique, the perception that the overcoming of sinful living was a necessity for true virtue was nigh universal.

It may also be pertinent to note that while the conflict between interpretations of divine sovereignty and human freedom is frequent in modern theological debate, the church fathers apparently had no qualm accepting both elements with little anxiety.

62. Ciulinaru, "Anthropology," 185. This philosophy may also contain certain gnostic vestiges as well, since the ultimate result of this interpretation denigrates the human body into little more than a vehicle for the soul. Even the eschatological resurrection of the human body existed simply to "spiritualize" the flesh for its eternal position of spirit-container.

sin.[63] The righteous man considered things rationally, which—since the image of God is interpreted as the capacity for reason—supports the continued presence of the divine image within humanity.[64]

The earliest theology of the image of God therefore appears to have been the ability to live in a manner that follows God's / Christ Jesus' own example of life.[65] Since every person is formed in the image of God, there was a universal expectation for Christians to conform to the image by producing righteous acts.

Review of Reformation and Enlightenment Era Interpretations of the Image of God

The movement toward philosophical models moved the primary means of theological thought from biblical theology toward systematic theology, which dominated the medieval period and did little to directly expand upon Early Fathers' work regarding the *imago Dei*. However, during the medieval period the *activity* of righteous living that the Early Fathers emphasized was increasingly associated with the *condition* of holiness. This reinterpretation, when combined with theology of the fall, effectively removed the image of God from humanity. Fallen humankind is unholy; at least a part of the image of God must have been lost.[66]

The Reformers who caused a resurgence of biblical theology had two primary motivations for accepting and elaborating the medieval doctrine(s) advocating the loss of the divine image. The first motive, emphasized by Luther, was the grace of God. The second, exemplified by Zwingli and Calvin, was the sovereignty of God.

Luther asserted that it was impossible to understand pre-fallen humanity since the corruption of humankind in the fall destroyed any possibility of comprehending what it would be like to hold the image of God.[67] He also asserted that if the patristic association of the image of God with

---

63. Xintaras, "Man," 53.

64. This attitude toward the image of God opened the path of righteousness to those who may not know God but are paragons of rationality. This is the origin of the conceit that philosophers and artists—from Aristotle to Virgil—had a place of reward. In the Middle Ages, this place was not heaven itself, but a paradise for the "unsaved righteous." While the present examination lacks the scope to address the theological issues surrounding this development, it is pertinent to note that even in the philosophical understanding the divine image serves more as a directive than as a characteristic.

65. Cairns, *Image of God*, 108.

66. Calvin, *Genesis*, 26.

67. Chaney, "Martin Luther," 17; Cairns, *Image of God*, 126.

reason or self-determination were accepted then Satan—more intelligent than humanity and equally free-willed—would by default hold the image of God.[68] Using this argument, Luther bolstered his position declaring humankind's loss of the image of God and the need for even regenerate people to constantly petition God for continued grace to obey the divine will.

Ulrich Zwingli, like Luther, considered the image of God lost. Rejecting any possibility for secondary causes, Zwingli noted that humankind's creation was entirely contingent upon God. He therefore interpreted the image of God as humanity's association with the divine. With the fall and the dissociation of human beings from God, the divine image was lost. This interpretation explains human inability to follow divine commands; without the image of God humanity is doomed by original sin to depravity.[69] Zwingli therefore preserved God's sovereignty: humankind cannot act for good of its own accord. Only God can produce good works. At the same time, Zwingli's method somewhat aligns the image of God with the Early Fathers' emphasis on righteous living: God's power working through Christians manifests the *imago Dei*.

Calvin features the image of God with greater prominence than either Luther or Zwingli, continually emphasizing the divine image as a reflection of God's sovereignty. Calvin's approach elaborates upon the others' theologies by emphasizing the Christ's unique embodiment of the *imago Dei*.[70] God's image is manifested in his activities, and since one of God's activities was the creation of human beings, humankind was originally created with the image of God (*Inst.* 1.5). When humankind sinned, it violated the purity of God's activity and thereby "obliterated" the heavenly image (*Inst.* 2.1.5).[71] This position juxtaposes the *sola fide* emphasis of the Reformers with the

---

68. Cairns, *Image of God*, 125. Luther's argument is at least weakened and perhaps wholly invalidated by the fact that he seems to ignore the patristic emphasis that the self-determination embodied in the image of God was one that enabled obedience to God and that Satan, the Father of Lies, is unable to make that determination. Ironically, though, Luther could have made his theological point without attempting to correlate fallen humanity's position with Satan's nature. The presence of original sin has removed the ability of humankind to choose the righteous path without the intervention of the Holy Spirit. Therefore, whether or not the image of God is conditional is moot; humanity cannot choose to live righteously before God. While this might seem to contradict Luther's own expositions of Romans 2, his position can be justified by recalling Augustine's dictum that obedience based in fear is not righteousness—obedience is only righteous when it is born of love, and loving obedience is a gift of God's grace. Luther, *Commentary on Romans*, 59–70; Chaney, "Martin Luther," 18–19.

69. Chaney, "Martin Luther," 20; Helm, "Calvin," 403–4; cf. Ortlund, "Image of Adam," 676–77.

70. Calvin, *Genesis*, 26; Cairns, *Image of God*, 128–29.

71. Zachman, "Jesus Christ," 47–48.

patristic emphasis upon righteous living, but still rejects the image of God in fallen man on the basis of human depravity.[72]

The more important consideration of the image of God in Calvin's theology is not centered on humanity in general, but upon Jesus' embodiment of the Father's image. While depraved man does not retain the image of God, the Perfect Son manifested it once more to the world by perfectly fulfilling the Law and the Prophets. The cross and resurrection, then are not simply an exchange of death for life, but rather the exchange of sin for the renewal of the *imago Dei*.[73] The image of God is not restored to the regenerate at the moment of salvation, but is assured at the eschatological resurrection when all evil is destroyed and all of God is open to the righteous believers. In the interim, the acceptance of the Christ's sacrifice produces obedience within the Christian (*Inst.* 2.16–2.17). Since this righteous activity occurs only through the Spirit of the Christ within the faithful, it is only by God's sovereign decision that goodness comes into the world. The image of God is a reward to be anticipated with the New Creation, and the inspiration of the Holy Spirit in the lives of Christians is the surety of it.[74]

After the Reformation, the Enlightenment did little to address the nature of the divine image directly. However as the supposed "return to Reason," the Enlightenment divided many leading intellectuals from the church. With the departure of these intellectuals, those who carried on the church traditions emphasized the Christian faith through practical expressions of daily life.[75] This latter movement led to the rise of Pietism: no longer content to accept orthodox dictum, people desired an experience of faith. The study of the Bible was considered in terms of personal edification for the proper conduct of a holy life.[76] In a very real sense, then, the rise of Pietism returned to the *imago Dei* preached by the church fathers. Pietism also reveals an unconscious conflict between the Reformed emphasis upon the depravity of humankind and the simpler approach of the post-Enlightenment church, since theoretically any human could live a pious life if they so choose. While it is overreaching to suggest that Calvinism was rejected, it is appropriate to recognize that the

---

72. Cairns, *Image of God*, 132–35.

73. Zachman, "Jesus Christ," 50.

74. Ibid., 59; Cairns, *Image of God*, 144.

75. The emphasis on faith-practice in daily life is a natural offshoot of the Reformation's efforts to remove theology from the limited realm of an oligarchy and present it to the people as a whole for examination and consideration. Unfortunately, it also inadvertently encouraged anew the compilation of proof-texts to support orthodox systems. On the other hand, it positively impacted the church by emphasizing the importance of individual commitments to the study of the Word of God.

76. Scobie, *Ways of Our God*, 14.

hamartiological liberality of the more elite philosophers had entered into the theology of the populace.[77] On the other hand, the more learned members of society rejected the tenets of Pietism in favor of an emerging emphasis on Deism, which viewed the image of God as essentially irrelevant. On the occasions when the divine image was addressed, it was considered achieved in the power of human reason. Kant's proposition that humankind has reached maturity and therefore without need of a divine image was typical.

The result of the rise of both the Pietists and the Deists in the Enlightenment therefore not only returned to the early church theology that emphasized righteous living as the key to the divine image (through Pietism), but also resumed the emphasis on reason as the pinnacle of humanity (through Deism). Enlightenment thinkers did not always utilize the terminology of the *imago Dei*, but the final developments of the period seem to assume the image of God without fully acknowledging it. Whether the lack of acknowledgment was due to piety or philosophy, the result was a lack of growth in the biblical theology of the era's treatment of the divine image.

Review of Modern and Recent Interpretations of the Image of God

When modernism—with its replacement of biblical theology proper with a history of religions approach—considered the image of God it essentially relocated the concept from the realm of confession and into the realm of academics. Intensive word studies on the four primary terms designating the divine image in the text began, as did a renewed conversation of the relationship of the "image" to the "likeness" of God. These linguistic efforts initially did little to add to the theological discussion. This changed, however, with the association of the image of God with the statues of ancient kings that were established to represent sovereignty over the borders of a nation or territory. This discovery led to an increased emphasis upon the connection between the *imago Dei* and the dominion stated in Gen 1:28 and greater discussion on what precisely that dominion might entail.[78]

Generally, interpretations of the image of God as an attribute of dominion fall into one of two categories: either the image bestowed upon humanity is simply a statement of God's ownership of Creation, or it is an authorization of sorts for humankind's own mastery of the planet. The prohibition against homicide in Gen 9:6 that recognizes God's unique authority over life supports the former interpretation.[79] However, while God's author-

---

77. Hochstrasser, *Natural Law Theories*, 8–9.
78. Grenz, "Jesus as the *Imago Dei*," 621.
79. Cameron, "Theological Anthropology," 58–59.

ity over life and death is complete, this definition of the image of God is too limited. It accords with prohibitions against murder, but is problematic when viewed from a New Testament perspective that emphasizes Jesus as the ultimate image of God. It would suggest that the Father "owned" Jesus, contradicting the testimony of the New Testament and the co-identification of the Christ with God that forms one of the foundations of Trinitarian understanding. Further, the use of the term "images" in the ancient Near East did not represent dominion in a nominal sense, but in a verbal one. The authority of the king over a given area dictated the implementation of laws and the execution of punishments.

The deficiencies of viewing the divine image as a simple stamp of ownership suggest that if the image of God is a representation of dominion, it is the bestowal upon humanity of the right to deal with the created realm in an authoritative manner.[80] Of course, this right is better viewed as a function of stewardship—the dominion of humankind should reflect the dominion of God.[81] This does assume, however, that humankind retains the *imago Dei*. If the image of God is lost, then any dominion inherent to the divine image is forfeit.

Since the presence or loss of the image of God is such a pervasive question for interpretation, contemporary theologians needed to address it. Unfortunately, since a consensus on what the image of God entails had remained elusive, it was impossible to establish if humanity retained it. Both the retention and the loss of the divine image seem to create certain paradoxes: if humanity has lost the image of God with the fall, then why is human action evaluated in terms of the image in Gen 9:6?[82] However, if the image of God is retained, then how can it be reconciled with the expressions, especially within Paul, of the sinfulness of humankind?

One method of dealing with the divine image is by utilizing a christological interpretation that expands upon Calvin's view that only Jesus had the true image of God. This approach accepts Calvin's proposal with the understanding that the Creative intention was that humankind become Christ-like. By combining Christology and anthropology, the *imago Dei* is retained, but only in the context of a relationship with Jesus.[83] The primal nature of humanity is left largely unaddressed. As a result, the christological interpretation of modern theologians generally fails to resolve any of the difficulties associated with the present study.

---

80. Laffey, "Priestly Creation Narrative," 28.
81. Berkouwer, *Man*, 396.
82. Cameron, "Theological Anthropology," 55.
83. Berkouwer, *Man*, 45; cf. Boer, *Ember*.

In *Church Dogmatics*, Barth forwarded the thesis that the *imago Dei* was a relational construct, primarily on the basis of humanity's creation as "male and female."[84] Unfortunately, this suggestion is incomplete. Animals too are male and female. And while relationships are critical to human beings, they are not unique to them. The image of God, on the other hand, is clearly given as a unique status and suggests a separation from and superiority to the animal kingdom. If, however, the relational aspects of the image of God are expressed as the ability to form and cultivate relationships *with the Creator* then there is a certain uniqueness involved. While God relates to all of his Creation, the interaction with humanity is distinct. It is significant that in the ancient Near East "images" of the gods were considered to represent not only a given god's appearance, but also a spiritual connection with that god. In the biblical context, this indicates that the essence of created man is an inherent connection with God.[85] The ability to connect with God has not been lost, but it has been crippled by sin.[86] With the coming of the Christ, the perfect fellowship of Jesus and God illustrates the true divine image. This synergetic presentation combining many of the tenets of previous theories is broad enough to accommodate various nuances.[87] It does not demand a loss of the image of God, but it does illustrate the corruption and subsequent redemption of it. As Christians are conformed to the Christ's image, they simultaneously conform to the *imago Dei*.[88] This approach seems to be an appropriate consolidation of the disparate interpretations of the image of God, except for its treatment of the dominion aspects of the image. Discussion of the dominion of Gen 1:28 is addressed almost incidentally, a simple outgrowth of the capacity for relationship. Such a consideration of dominion is not necessarily incorrect; however, it should not be considered as an afterthought or an incidental factor.

One feature of recent studies of the *imago Dei* is the realization that regardless of how one interprets the term, it necessarily impacts not only theological anthropology but also biblical interpretation as a whole.[89] Whenever the Bible refers to the image of God—either explicitly or implicitly—it does so from the context of worship.[90] The image of God is not present to explain

---

84. Barth, *Church Dogmatics* 3.1, 184; Niskanen, "Poetics of Adam," 418.

85. An observation often grounded in and attested by Gen 2:7, where the breath that provides life to humanity is the breath of God himself.

86. Berkouwer, *Man*, 88.

87. This method synthesizes (at a minimum) Calvin's christological approach, the church fathers' emphasis on righteous living, the moral concerns of the Philosophers, etc.

88. Cairns, *Image of God*, 170.

89. Cameron, "Theological Anthropology," 53.

90. Habel, *Literary Criticism*, 68.

humankind, but to exalt the Creator. If this is properly apprehended, then correlating the image of God as a relational aspect between God and man and as an element of dominion moves from presuppositional consideration to theological affirmation. As Bonhoeffer correctly noted, humankind's dominion is delegated and therefore demands a response of obedience to the God who grants it.[91] Similarly, Barth emphasizes this responsive character by recognizing that the divine image is not about what is *within* humanity, but rather about what is *of* God.[92] The relational context of the *imago Dei* prohibits limiting the divine image to an anthropological construct or to the creation narratives; it must be examined with consideration of the remaining biblical message and soteriology in particular, especially since outside of the creation account, every reference to the divine image refers to either sin or redemption.[93] The image of God is what affords humankind the offer of God's grace. This is represented in the christological interpretations of the image and Jesus's status as the perfect image of God; but it is also represented in the specific type of fellowship that is available to human beings in the presence of the Lord.[94] Understanding the divine image in this manner bridges the interpretive distance between Barth's understanding that the *imago Dei* unites man and woman in relationship and the theological purpose of the image.[95] While all manner of animals have relationships, only humans interact in a theological community.[96] This reading is given additional credence by the description of the community of faith as the body of Christ. Just as the image of God represents God's work in Creation so too does the body of Christ represent God's work in salvation.[97] Associating the image of God with both divine and human relationships answers the question of how the image of God can exist within sinful humankind. The divine image establishes the relational nature (and indeed, *need*) of humankind, but any relationship is by nature reciprocal. Even unregenerate humanity forms relationships with others, and all of humanity has a need for and the capability to cultivate a relationship with God through the grace of Christ. However, if there is not reciprocal response to the Christ's extension of

---

91. Bonhoeffer, *Creation and Fall*, 67.
92. Barth, *CD* III/I, 186.
93. Ross, *Recalling the Hope of Glory*, 81; Overstreet, "Man in the Image of God," 48.
94. Mostert, "Human Person."
95. Jewett, *Man as Male and Female*, 27.
96. Overstreet, "Man in the Image of God," 55.
97. "Thus, then, the will of the God of Israel as Redeemer is one with this will as Creator." Eichrodt, *Man in the Old Testament*, 32.

grace, then there can be no legitimate relationship between God and human. The fullness of the image lies dormant within each person.[98]

Finally, a particularly notable trend in recent theology has been the focus on the *utilization* rather than the *identification* of the image of God. This trend is predominant in liberation and practical theologies, where defining the *imago Dei* as reason, relationship, etc., is less important than emphasizing the natural result of the divine image: the equality of human beings. Since the divine image is imprinted on each person, whether male or female, Jew or Greek, it stands as the most important motivation for the equitable treatment of one's fellow person. It does not matter *what* the divine image is so much as *that* it exists. Liberation and practical theologians are not novel in this approach, as the early church had a rather robust emphasis upon social change; but it is notable that the use of this theological approach for political rather than strictly theological purposes seems to be on the rise.[99]

Summary Conclusions regarding Historical Interpretations of the Image of God

With such a varied base of interpretations, it is difficult to summarize the historical interpretations of the image of God. To a certain extent, the divine image remains undefined as no one approach has yet adequately addressed the full ramifications of the *imago Dei*. What is clear, though, is that it seems that a proper understanding of the image of God must include both an internal/divine relational component and an external/human relational

---

98. Towner, "Clones of God," 145; Brunner, *Man in Revolt*, 168; As a further extension of this understanding, it can be noted that if the relational aspects of the *imago Dei* are dormant, then so too are many of the aspects of dominion. Since humankind is not in right relationship with God, and since right relationship with God is the foundation for wisdom (cf. Prov 1:7), unregenerate human beings cannot properly and wisely exercise the dominion of their Created position. Rather than steward God's gift, sinful humanity seeks to assert dominion over this world independently of him. This independent assertion, according to Eichrodt, runs contrary to the fundamental nature of humankind. To be "true to his destiny" (or, if di Vito's formulation is preferred: "authentic") humankind cannot live as simply natural creatures. Eichrodt, *Man in the Old Testament*, 30; di Vito, "Old Testament Anthropology," 221.

99. Furfey, "Social Action," 108. There is also a strong biblical argument to bolster the practical use of the image of God from Leviticus. Perhaps the most well-known verse in the Bible for the treatment of others occurs originally in Lev 19:18b, under the guiding directive of Lev 19:2 ("Be Holy, for I the LORD your God am Holy") and in the center of the Holiness Code. The biblical ideal is not to teach people morality; the biblical ideal is to teach holiness, from which morality will inevitably flow. The image of God, as an aspect—perhaps even *the* aspect—of holiness, can expect a similar result (the implementation of moral behavior) when properly embraced.

reflection. Further, it must in some way be applied holistically rather than as a collection of individual facets.[100] A commonality must connect each aspect of the image. It is this simultaneous lack of definition and need for comprehensive application that demands a continued evaluation of what the image of God is and how it applies to the conduct of humanity.[101]

Since the image of God directly interacts with the nature of humankind, the nature of God, and the nature of the divine-human relationship, it is not inaccurate to suggest that in many ways the *imago Dei* plays *the* primary role in the Old Testament.[102] While the explicit terminology of צלם אלהים might be lacking, the nature of the divine image is conjoined to every interaction of God's grace.[103] Similarly, the New Testament testimony of the Christ's imitation of God calls for an affirmation and commitment to the embodiment of the Lord in the life of the Christian. As the Christ was—in addition to being fully God—fully perfect and obedient as a man, he demonstrates the example of what it is to be in the image of God in the New Testament.[104] As facilitators of the divine interaction and mediators of grace, priests do so in the Old Testament. But in either context—Old Testament or New Testament—the demonstration of activity is intended to illustrate the calling of all of humanity: whether following the Christ as high priest or emulating the Aaronic priesthood, humankind is expected to perform priestly activity.

PRESENTATION OF THESIS

The need to continually evaluate the proper understanding of the image of God serves as the impetus of the present examination. The examination of the terminology and the overall context of Genesis 1 as a priestly vision of temple-building suggest that the image of God should not primarily be considered

---

100. Van Wolde, *Stories of the Beginning*, 31.

101. Berkouwer, *Man*, 23; Walton, *Lost World*, 98.

102. Grenz, *Named God*, 361; Sherlock, *Doctrine of Humanity*, 17; Hall, *Imaging God*, 61. Interestingly enough, von Rad approached Creation from an opposite perspective and yet still arrived at essentially the same conclusion. Using the idea of concentric circles, he presents Creation as a large circle that spirals inward toward the redemptive relationship between YHWH and Israel. The present suggestion reverses that and suggests that the image of God reflects a proper relationship between God and humankind, and therefore the redemptive relationship spirals outward back to Creation. Ultimately, the end result is the same whether the divine image hints at later redemption or human beings are redeemed and therefore reclaim their calling as God's representatives. In either case, humanity is restored to God in a proper relationship. Cf. Rad, *Problem of the Hexateuch*, 139, 142.

103. Mathews, *Genesis 1—11:26*, 163–64; Middleton, *New Heaven*, 46.

104. Maloney, *Cosmic Christ*, 46–47; Brunner, *Man in Revolt*, 97.

as a form of royal iconography, but rather some form of cultic statement.¹⁰⁵ While this interpretation runs counter to the majority view, it better fits the actual biblical use of צלם, retains better compatibility with the understanding of דמות, and more accurately captures the priestly context of Genesis 1 and the human's role within the environment of the "cosmic temple" of Creation.

Since the image of God is best interpreted as a representation of cultic interest, the human dominion over Creation should be viewed as a form of ministry or curation.¹⁰⁶ In effect, the image of God primarily designates or demands that humankind at large serve as priests of YHWH within the Temple of Creation. The intrusion of sin into the created order in Genesis 3 is not so much a failure to retain royal authority, but rather a failure to maintain holy purity and the sanctity of the holy place.

This thesis answers all of the dominant questions surrounding the צלם אלהים. First, it accommodates the priestly, temple-building context of Genesis 1 better than a royal image reflecting the ideology of the court. Second, it provides a more reasonable connection between the image of God and the larger context of the Old Testament, particularly the prophetic condemnations of social injustice.¹⁰⁷ While royal imagery would certainly uphold social justice as a means of order, the nature of social injustice as a barrier to worship reflects priestly interests.¹⁰⁸ Finally, the interpretation of the divine image as a priestly commissioning better fits the immediate connection between biblical creation and worship/cultic response than a royal צלם.

Perceived difficulties to the priestly nature of the image of God by the presence of כבש and רדה are mitigated by the highly generalized nature of both terms. Similarly, the special election of Israel does not diminish a priestly interpretation of the צלם אלהים any more than it would a royal interpretation. Quite the opposite, the election of Israel is rooted in the role of guiding all the nations of the world so that *members of every nation* might enter God's Presence—a priestly interest.¹⁰⁹ The universal calling of humankind to serve as priests of YHWH is also fully compatible with the theology of the New Testament, whether using Peter's adoption of Israel's assignment as the identity of the church (1 Pet 2:9) or considering Paul's condemnation

---

105. Bray, "Significance of God's Image," 197.

106. Gentry and Wellum, *Kingdom*, 200. The two terms indicating human authority over Creation, כבש and רדה, can be used to indicate royal authority; however, both terms are relatively indistinct and do not warrant a specific application to royal interests. They are equally valid as terms of priestly or cultic authority. These uses will be further discussed in chapter 2 of the present study.

107. Bullock, *Introduction*, 25.

108. Ben Zvi, "Observations," 26.

109. Stuart, *Exodus*, 423.

of all humanity for a lack of perception of God (cf. Rom 1:21–23). The commissioning of Israel as a distinctly priestly people no more challenges an understanding of the image of God as a commission to priesthood than the assignment of the tabernacle/temple priesthood to Aaron challenges the role of the nation of Israel as a kingdom of priests. The situations are analogous. The failure of humankind to maintain properly their priestly commission necessitated the example of the priestly nation of Israel, which itself possessed the Levitical priesthood as a paradigm of holiness.[110]

WARRANT FOR RESEARCH OF THE צלם אלהים AS A PRIESTLY COMMISSION

The need to address the proper interpretation of the image of God is foundational since it addresses the basic nature of humankind.[111] Alternately, it is foundational since it addresses the essential relationship between humanity and God.[112] Since all of Creation in general and humankind in particular is called upon to worship the Creator, it is fitting to examine the nature of that worship and the role of humanity in conducting it. Further, if the צלם אלהים represents a universal assignment of priesthood, then it becomes possible to suggest that there is a definable central tenet to not only the Old Testament but also the Bible as a whole as the different aspects of priesthood are applied to, pursued by, or ignored by humankind. This concept of "Humanity's Priestly Role to YHWH" accommodates and enhances all three divisions of the Old Testament without compromising the nature of each of those divisions; and while it is irresponsible to demand this centralized concept on the basis of the interpretation of the צלם אלהים alone, the possibilities offered by this interpretation certainly warrant adequate study.

RESEARCH METHODOLOGY FOR INTERPRETING THE DIVINE IMAGE

Any study of this nature must take seriously the final canon of Scriptures. Whether the development of the present text is understood from a traditional viewpoint or as a reconstruction, ultimately the final form of the Bible must be considered for a *biblical* theology. Even if individual passages have been redacted or altered, those redactions reflect a composite and finalized view of

---

110. Leithart, "Attendants," 24.
111. Grunlan and Mayers, *Cultural Anthropology*, 268–69.
112. Bonhoeffer, *Creation and Fall*, 33–38; Barth, *CD* III/I, 183–85.

divine teaching.¹¹³ Further, any reconstruction of biblical passages is inherently dubious, since such reconstructions are by their very nature hypothetical. The extant text is therefore the only basis for valid theology.¹¹⁴ The present examination will therefore approach the canon as a unified entity. Any methodology that approaches the Scriptures in this manner—including but not limited to narrative criticism and literary theory—will be valid for this study.

However, while only the final form of the canon is valid for direct evidence, interaction with critical reconstructions will take place as necessary to examine how theories and theologies based on the reconstructed text might conform or diverge from a canonical theology.¹¹⁵ Further, even if a full reconstruction is rejected, the critical analyses of texts for priestly elements that supposedly comprise the P-source or that reflect priestly ideologies within the Scripture can be very valuable in emphasizing the prevalence of priestly materials and supporting the basic canonical reading.

Finally, some study of systematic or historical theologies demonstrates the compatibility of the present thesis with established theological doctrines of anthropology, soteriology, ecclesiology, et al. While it is not necessary to formulate the conclusions of this study with the terminology of systematic theology, the demonstration that the biblical theological conclusion presented is in accord with accepted orthodox understanding(s) of the nature of humankind is important.¹¹⁶

SUMMARIES OF CHAPTERS

The present chapter serves as a basic introduction to the specific concern(s) and thesis of this study. General background information establishes a context for the study, though care has been given to examine the actual biblical use of צלם and דמות and to grant that usage precedence over comparative studies, something not always historically done. Also, the introduction of the characteristics of priesthood provide a point of reference for proceeding observations. Finally, the basic methodology that will be used in the ensuing chapters is presented.

113. Childs, *Biblical Theology*, 104–5; Sailhamer, *Old Testament Theology*, 198; Rendtorff, *Canon and Theology*, 12; cf. Jacobson, "Structuralists," 109; Lohfink, *Das Siegeslied am Schilfmeer*, 35.

114. Scobie, *Ways of Our God*, 30.

115. Childs, *Biblical Theology*, 88, 101–2, 385.

116. Compatibility with orthodoxy is a theological and confessional concern, but also reflects academic legitimacy. A complete divergence from orthodox interpretations suggest a certain disregard for foundational studies that have been formed and upheld for centuries.

The second chapter of this work focuses on the exegetical and theological study of the image of God, with particular interest in Genesis 1. It establishes an interpretive method that utilizes Exod 19:6 as the focal point through which Genesis 1 might be understood. A detailed examination of Genesis 1 is presented, with particular interest in how the temple-building aspects of Creation intersect with cultic practice. An expanded exegesis and consideration of Gen 1:26–28 is emphasized, and the conclusion that the צלם אלהים in Genesis 1 is best understood as a calling of humankind into priesthood asserted.

Chapter 3 examines the theology expressed in additional biblical passages for compatibility with the thesis that the image of God is best understood as a priestly commissioning. Passages that present a creative event and a human response to that event are of primary interest. The examination begins with consideration of other mythic creation accounts within the Old Testament, followed by the analysis of cosmological, cultic, and social re-creation narratives. Prophetic eschatological visions that portray the ultimate fate of humanity are presented to demonstrate an ultimate priestly *telos* for humankind, while passages that suggest a priestly occupation for non-Levites in the contemporary society of Israel conclude the analysis.

The fourth chapter of this work summarizes, compares, and contrasts selected major Old Testament theologies with the proposed thesis. The selection of examined theologies is based on the focus on a dominant theme or central tenet within the Hebrew Scriptures of those works, and covers a broad period of Old Testament theological study beginning with Eichrodt's theory of covenant as the center of Scriptures and concluding with Brueggemann's theology of dispute.

Chapter 5—after summarizing the compatibility of the thesis with Old Testament theology—broadens the study beyond the Old Testament, and considers the viability of the thesis that the image of God commissions all of humanity to priesthood in light of the New Testament. Each of the major areas of the New Testament are considered and the consistency of the thesis with New Testament theology is demonstrated, before a general summary of biblical theology as a whole is stated.

Finally, the concluding chapter of this work establishes an outline for future studies. Exegetical implications are offered in light of the priestly anthropology proffered by this study. Further, theological considerations concerning both the consistent theme of the Old Testament and the teleological purpose of humanity are briefly introduced. Considerations applicable to the current practice of contemporary church activities then provide a conclusion to this work as a whole.

Chapter 2

Biblical Study on the Image of God

ESTABLISHING THE INTERPRETIVE PARADIGM OF GENESIS 1

A proper interpretation of the image of God in Gen 1:26–28 must necessarily account for and rely upon the overarching context of the Creation narrative of Gen 1:1—2:3.[1] For the divine image to indicate a priestly calling, the entire passage must suggest a proper context for understanding. There is little difficulty with this suggestion, as the "temple-building" aspects of Creation have been addressed repeatedly—both in ancient and contemporary studies.[2] Similarly, Genesis 1 has frequently been ascribed to priestly writers or suggested to reflect priestly concerns.[3] Therefore, a context respecting the viability of a priestly interpretation for the image of God is already well established.

---

1. Middleton, *Liberating Image*, 60. For the sake of simplicity, the simple use of "Genesis 1" will continue to intend the fullness of this passage, including the first three verses of the second chapter—Gen 1:1—2:3.

2. Philo, *De Spec. Leg.* 1.66; Fletcher-Louis, "God's Image," 82; Barker, *Gate of Heaven*, 66; Blenkinsopp, *Sage, Priest, Prophet*, 68; Walton, *Lost World*, 83; Middleton, *Liberating Image*, 81.

3. Firmage, "Genesis 1," 98; Speiser, *Genesis*, xxv, 8; Morgenstern, "Sources," 169. Generally speaking, proponents of the documentary hypothesis and less conservative scholars will ascribe Genesis 1 to the P source. However, even conservative scholars admit that the strong temple-building aspects of the passage—combined with the garden imagery of the temple—suggest that the Creation and the temple were theologically linked. This linkage more than justifies a priestly interpretation for the image of God and a properly cultic context for the passage as a whole. Morrow, "Creation as Temple-Building," 53.

The establishment of a priestly context for Gen 1:26–28 has not, however, precluded a general tendency to ascribe a royal interpretation to the divine image.[4] This interpretation does indeed have some legitimacy, both from the immediate context (the use of רדה and כבש) and from the larger context of Genesis 2, where the naming ritual of Gen 2:18ff. suggests a royal prerogative. This approach, however, is flawed in that while the naming ritual *could* represent kingly activity it is equally valid to suggest that the ritual reflected the priestly duty to separate things according to their created order. While the high term for priestly differentiation (בדל) is missing, the lack of the specific word does not invalidate the possibility. This is particularly true when the occurrences of בדל in Genesis 1 as acts of God are considered (vv. 4, 6, 7, and 14). Genesis 1 shows אלהים dividing the realms of light/dark, upper waters / lower waters, and celestial lights. It does *not* show God dividing between the mundane things of flora or fauna. The indication that animals and plants had a proper order is clearly present (למינהם), but the actual arrangement of the created things into that order is not. In other words, the divine order is clear, but the act of ordering is delayed.

When אדם is created, he is given the assignment to רדה and/or כבש the created order, but there is no narrative record of this assignment taking place. Since Genesis 1 is almost exclusively concerned with the divine acts of creation, this interpretation is reasonable. However, Genesis 2 then revisits Creation from a different perspective and reflects on both divine *and* human activity.[5] Where the cosmic perspective of Genesis 1 assigns a duty to humankind, Genesis 2 is the beginning of the human narrative fulfilling that duty.[6] In the course of this narrative, God first places אדם into a garden where the image is to "work" (עבד) and "keep" (שמר) it (Gen 2:15). While neither עבד nor שמר are exclusively cultic terms, they are used frequently to describe the activities of the priesthood in both their didactic and their custodial roles.[7] Further, while it could be argued that the activity of "keeping" the garden was appropriate for a king, it would have been both unexpected and inappropriate for a royal figure to "work" the garden.[8] Quite the opposite, one of the reasons a king might keep a garden—besides as a sign of opulence—was to

---

4. Brueggemann, *Genesis*, 32.

5. Deist, "Genesis 1–11," 5.

6. Middleton, *Liberating Image*, 290–91.

7. Morrow, "Creation as Temple-Building," 12; Beale, *Temple*, 67; Beale, "Eden," 7–8; cf. Gorman, *Ideology of Ritual*, 28–29; Hornung, *Conceptions of God*, 183; Schachter, "Garden of Eden," 75; Walton, "Historical Adam," 95.

8. Balentine, *Torah's Vision*, 88.

show association with the divine and suggest a sort of divine right or his own quasi-divine nature.⁹ The royal gardens were places of luxury not duty.

The garden as a place of duty suggests a service toward God rather than participation in godhood—or royalty, for that matter.¹⁰ With this context in mind, the naming ritual proper can be examined. Three critical aspects define the naming ritual. First, it is explicitly connected to Creation in general and to the incomplete (לא טוב) nature of Creation specifically.¹¹ Second, as creatures were formed and brought to Adam, they were clearly seen to be distinct from / "not fit for" Adam.¹² Finally, when Adam is finally blessed with his suitable עזר the passage immediately reflects (1) celebration at the finding of completion (Gen 2:23) and (2) a statement of the proper order of family life (Gen 2:24).¹³ The naming ritual of Genesis 2 is therefore not a royal act on the part of Adam, but rather a creative act on the part of God that is celebrated and a service activity on the part of humankind that accomplishes his designated task of providing order to Creation.¹⁴

9. Beale, *Temple*, 89; cf. Ortlund, "Image of Adam," 681–83.

10. T. Neofiti and Tg. Pseudo-Jonathon both expect Adam "to toil in the Law and to observe its commandments" as part of his residence in the garden, a task which Ben Sira states humankind was well equipped for since God "bestowed knowledge upon them, and allotted to them the law of life. He established with them an eternal covenant, and revealed to them his decrees" (Ben Sira 17.11–12). Also, while Genesis 2 does not describe Eden as a temple, the temple is described as Eden in Ezekiel 40–41. Similarly, Jub. 3:9 depicts a delay in אדם's entrance into Eden as a time of purification similar to what would be required to enter the temple, while *Genesis Rabbah* XXI.8 links the expulsion from Eden to the Jew's expulsion from the temple. Also, while it does not invoke temple imagery, Psalm 147 does connect the דבר of Creation with תורה in vv. 18–20 providing an early—though still not contemporaneous—witness to the connection between Creation and Law (cf. Ps 148:5–6).

Further, there is a distinctive difference in the type of service expected from אדם and that expected from humankind in other ANE creation myths. Both the Babylonian *Enuma Elish* and the Akkadian "When Anu had Created the Heavens" assign humankind the task of building a temple, but in both cases it is as simple slave labor, rather than as authoritative figures assigned to represent the gods. The status offered by the צלם אלהים is significantly greater than Israel's contemporaries' mythological anthropology. Berg, "Ben Sira," 150; Beale, *Temple*, 67, 90–91; Barker, *Gate of Heaven*, 69–70; Sailhamer, *Genesis Unbound*, 79; Middleton, *Liberating Image*, 66–67; Estes, "Creation Theology," 33.

11. It is important to remember that טוב does not reference a moral or ethical concept in the Creation accounts. The lack of "goodness" at Adam's solitude is hardly a moral or ethical wrong. However, on the basis of Gen 1:27, until both male and female were present, the creation of humankind (and, for that matter, the assignation of the image of God) was incomplete.

12. Mathews, *Genesis 1—11:26*, 213–15.

13. Ibid., 218–20.

14. Blenkinsopp, *Sage, Priest, Prophet*, 101–2; Middleton, *New Heaven*, 51; Middleton, *Liberating Image*, 89; cf. Rencken, *Israel's Concept*, 47. Walton does not interpret

Service response to divine activity is a particularly appropriate descriptive of priestly duty and suggests that the naming ritual and the "dominion" it represents is better interpreted as a cultic act than a royal one.[15] With this understanding in place, there is little reason to assume that a royal interpretation of the image of God in Gen 1:26–28 should be preferred.[16] If the royal aspects of Genesis 2 are deemed tenuous, then any royal aspects of Genesis 1 must be considered practically nonexistent. On the other hand, if Genesis 2's naming ritual *is* considered an act of discernment and order, then it adds credence toward interpreting the divine image as a priestly motif.

While the above discussion does not eliminate the possibility of a royal interpretation of Genesis 2, it does illustrate that it is completely viable to interpret the whole of Genesis 1—including vv. 26–28—apart from royal ideology. With this freedom, the aspects of Genesis 1 that best illustrate Creation as a *temple-building* exercise and the subsequent logical understanding of humankind as custodians of the temple and the image of God as a priestly aspect can be properly addressed.[17]

Review of Priestly Paradigms in the Interpretation of Genesis 1

The explicitly priestly interests of Genesis 1 are well agreed upon, as scholars from both liberal and conservative traditions have observed priestly

---

the naming ritual as an act of division/designation, but rather as a search for another like אדם who could "suitably fill the ordained role of humanity in sacred space." What is significant about this is that while his specific understanding of the naming ritual differs from that offered here, he nonetheless connects the entire ritual to the assignation of priestly duties to humankind in Gen 2:15. Walton, "Historical Adam," 103.

15. Beale, *Temple*, 68, 81. Brueggemann's interpretation of royal ideology actually opposes a royal interpretation of Adam quite directly. He notes that the ideology of the throne was designed to "evoke persons who become loyal conformists *without the capacity to judge, discern, critique, or risk*" (emphasis added). Since the divine image is universal and Adam is established as a paradigm for all of humankind, and the naming ritual of Genesis 2 is—under any interpretation—one of judgment, discernment, and critique, it stands quite separate from the royal interests of docility in its subjects. To the contrary, the presentation of Genesis 2 serves to demand a critical eye from all of humanity. Brueggemann, *Israel's Praise*, 113.

16. The term "preferred" should be noted here. While this study suggests that the royal interpretation of humankind has been overemphasized and (often) misapplied, this is not to suggest that there is not necessarily *any* royal connotations or ascriptions in Genesis 1–2. Both comparative extrabiblical studies and the biblical priesthood of Melchizedek demonstrate a pattern of connecting priesthood and kingship. The purpose of the present study is not to deny any possibility of royalty to Adam, but rather to emphasize the primacy of priesthood as the foundational calling of humankind. People may be royal in origin and character, but they are priestly in calling and function.

17. Cf. Beale, *Temple*, 91–96.

elements within the narrative.[18] The question is not, therefore, whether the Creation serves cultic purposes but rather how those purposes are served and whether the priestly elements of Creation demand a priestly motif from the image of God. With this in mind, the present discussion will not seek to review or establish all of the "temple-building" aspects of the text, but rather to reflect upon certain features of the narrative that impact and call for an explicitly priestly interpretation of the image of God. There are multiple approaches to this question, but three broad categories have been selected for the present examination: priestly symbolism in Genesis 1, priestly ideology in Genesis 1, and priestly terminology in Genesis 1.

Priestly Symbolism—The Heptadic Structure of Genesis 1

Passages dealing with non-economic numbers are generally assumed to reflect priestly interests. Some of those interests relate to the ideology and professional performance(s) of the priesthood; however, many of the numbers of the Old Testament seem to have been idealized. This idealization of numbers is not simply ideological, but reflective of numerology and serves a symbolic rather than performative role. Within the Creation narrative, the number seven is of particular importance. Seven's representation of completion or wholeness is commonly known, and is foundational to the overall pattern of Genesis 1.[19]

The general arrangement of Genesis 1 demonstrates multiple incidents of heptadic structure. While the most obvious heptad is the seven-day structure, other heptads are found in the introductory verse (7 words) and Gen 1:2 (7 x 2 = 14 words).[20] Similarly, key words and phrases occur in multiples of seven: God (7 x 5 = 35 times), both earth/land and heavens (7 x 3 = 21 times each), "and it was" (7 times), and "God saw that it was good" (7 times). While any of these occurrences might be dismissed individually, the

---

18. Speiser, *Genesis*, xxiv–xxv.

19. Cassuto, *Genesis*, 15; cf. Balentine, *Torah's Vision*, 60; Smith, *Priestly Vision*, 88; Bullinger, *Number in Scripture*, 158.

20. The seven word arrangement of the first verse could be considered particularly important, since it can be and perhaps is best read as an introduction or title of sorts for the entire chapter. Considering the deliberate construction of the chapter's seven days, it seems unlikely that a heptad in Gen 1:1 is coincidental. By deliberately titling the chapter with seven words, even greater emphasis is given to the number seven.

On the other hand, the debate over the role of Gen 1:1 and its connection with vv. 2–3 is ongoing, which urges caution in overemphasizing this observation. Ironically, if vv. 1–2 are connected, the numerology is even more interesting: rather than 7 + (7 x 2), the word pattern forms 7 x 3 and utilizes yet another number with connotations of completeness (the number three).

layering of these heptads in a passage with an overtly heptadic structure suggests a methodical presentation centered on the number seven and the completeness that it represents.[21]

Numerology of completion might indicate priestly symbolism, but it is not sufficient to demand a specifically cultic motif for the chapter as a whole. While the occurrences of the heptads might not warrant a temple-building interpretation for the chapter, the specific *usage* of the seven day structure is illustrative. If the number seven serves to draw attention to the idea of wholeness or completion, then the fact that it is completed in the Creation narrative by the Sabbath cannot be ignored.[22] While humankind serves as the greatest created thing on earth and completes the creation of the world, humanity's creation is nonetheless a *penultimate* rather than an *ultimate* act.[23] After the closing of the worldly creation (the affirmation of טוב מאד), the Sabbath is established as a divine thing that stands above the created order. It is a facet of Creation that provides a goal or purpose for humanity beyond mere existence.[24]

If the Sabbath serves as the goal of human existence, then it is sensible to suggest that the nature and duties of humankind, including the image of God, would provide the impetus or ability to pursue that goal.[25] Since

---

21. Morrow, "Creation as Temple-Building," 1–3; Cassuto, *Genesis*, 13–15; This is not to suggest that *only* the number seven is utilized in Genesis 1. The number ten (another number symbolic of wholeness) is found in the pronouncements of God, and the number three (a number of completion) is suggested in the repetition of "the seventh day" in Gen 2:2–3a and described in the Talmud in the division of the ten utterances into seven and three. Cassuto (and to a lesser extent Levenson) goes on to link similar word-concepts (such as Eden-East, Adam-Man, Helper-Rib) throughout the first three chapters of Genesis and suggests even more heptads. Cassuto's approach seems somewhat overzealous in its search for sevens; however, even without accepting all of Cassuto's pairings and extending the heptad structure over the entirety of Genesis 1–3 the general prevalence of numbers of completion in general and seven in particular is clear.

22. Morrow, "Creation as Temple-Building," 4.

23. Atwell, "Egyptian Source," 476; Dempster, *Dominion and Dynasty*, 56; Renckens, *Israel's Concept*, 104.

24. Blenkinsopp, *Sage, Priest, Prophet*, 105. Ironically, this argument about the Sabbath's role as the goal of humankind is made stronger by more liberal approaches to the text that assign Genesis 1 to the P document ca. 450 BC. The later Genesis 1 is, the more developed the Sabbath theology would have been when the final form of the text was redacted together. The full understanding of Sabbath theology as a call to abide in God affirms a teleological interpretation of Gen 2:1–3.

Unsurprisingly, the Sabbath commands serve as the center of instruction within the Ten Commandments. That the Creation moves toward Sabbath as the duty of humankind and the Decalogue centers on Sabbath as the commandment for Israel should hardly be considered accidental. Balentine, *Torah's Vision*, 127.

25. Renckens, *Israel's Concept*, 101.

Sabbath observance fell under the auspice of the priesthood, the pursuit of Sabbath can be seen as a specifically priestly task. The symbolism of the number seven culminating in the Sabbath therefore serves to not only emphasize the Sabbath but also identify a priestly role for humanity as the created things are subjugated for the Sabbath.[26]

Priestly Ideology—Division and Designation within Genesis 1

While the overall structure of Genesis 1 reflects a numerological concern, the specific methodology of the Creation reflects the priestly concern with the proper division and designation of things into their proper category.[27] For some time now scholars have recognized that Genesis 1 seems far more concerned with how God exhibited mastery over the substance of this realm than whether God created the substance *ex nihilo*.[28] That this exhibition of mastery seems to parallel the priestly occupation is not without significance.

The Creation account is very specific in its discussion of the divine mastery over creation. Holding an overtly polemical stance, Genesis 1 forbids consideration of the "cosmic battle" motif so prevalent in other ANE creation accounts.[29] Instead, the divine mastery over creation focuses more

---

26. This line of thought also serves to explain the punishment of Adam in Gen 3:17–19. Daniel Fleming's study of Ugaritic cognates demonstrated that the "sweat of [Adam's] face" in v. 19 was indicative of fear rather than labor. While Adam's punishment does reflect added labor (vv. 17b–18), the greater concern is the uncertainty that he would now have in the face of death. Recognizing that the Sabbath represents rest *in* God more than *from* work, the fear of death stands as an antithesis to the call toward Sabbath in Gen 2:1–3. Fleming, "By the Sweat of Your Brow," 93–100.

Similarly (though distinctly), Exod 20:8–11 can be more properly understood in light of Gen 2:1–3. The remembrance of the Sabbath day is directly connected with sanctification. Sanctification serves as the primary calling of the Israelites (cf. Lev 11:44–45; 19:2; et al.), and their sanctification is explicitly linked with their honoring of the Sabbath. The lack of work on the seventh day was an act of faith that God would provide and therefore a reversal of the Adamic fear of Gen 3:19. Cf. Mathews, *Genesis 1—11:26*, 180–82.

27. Renckens, *Israel's Concept*, 108.

28. Balentine, *Torah's Vision*, 83, 139; Brueggemann, *Genesis*, 29; Young, *Creator, Creation*, 36–37.

29. Cassuto, *Genesis*, 36–37, 39. This is not to suggest that the Hebrew Scriptures as a whole refuse to present the cosmic battle of creation. However, the acceptance or rejection of the battle imagery in other biblical passages is not particularly relevant toward a close analysis of Genesis 1. The purpose of the present study is not to debate the multiple creation narratives of the Old Testament, but rather to illustrate that in the present Creation account—which importantly is *the* foundational Creation found in the Scriptures—the imagery used deliberately subverts the cosmic battle mythology of pagan religions and establishes a specific tenor to the Israelite Creation narrative.

on *authority* than on *power*.³⁰ It is not the mighty force of God that bends the elements to his wishes, but the authoritative word of God that designates what the proper created order would look like.³¹

The specific expression of divine authority within Creation is through the supernatural performative utterances that demand a division between substances (as in days 1–3) or a designation among substances (as in days 4–6).³² Even the seventh day seems to reflect performative utterance, as the act of God's blessing (a verbal statement) is what produces the holiness of that day (cf. Gen 2:3a). God's activity in Genesis 1 is therefore almost exclusively designative.³³

Since humankind is created according to the divine image, and the divine image must in some way reflect either God's character, nature, or activity, and since the primary portrait of God in Genesis 1 is as a designator, it is reasonable to expect that the divine image ascribes to humankind a differentiating function. While it is ill-advised to suggest that the image of God is concerned solely with designation, the context of Genesis 1 makes it equally ill-advised to exclude a categorizing role from the divine image.³⁴

---

30. To be clear: this statement is not suggesting that Genesis 1 does not demonstrate the power of God at work. It does, however, maintain that the power of God is not considered apart from his pronouncements. The command of God is the vehicle through which God's power flows.

31. Brueggemann, *Genesis*, 26.

32. Sarna, *Genesis*, 7. Richard Neville has produced an excellent examination of whether or not it is proper to consider God's creative actions to be acts of division on the basis of his studies on מִין and its usage either adjectivally or adverbially. While his study is quite well done, it is predicated on the thesis that God's creation activity cannot be considered "priestly" since the final four days do not reflect division *per se*. That said, one can agree with Neville that days 4–7 lack divisive language while rejecting the idea that this lack indicates a lack of priestly differentiation.

The problem with Neville's argument is that he seems to accept differentiation as an exclusively separating activity. The reality is that many of the priestly duties of differentiation did not *divide* the acceptable from the unacceptable, but essentially *designated* things as proper or improper. Certainly the description of the unclean birds in Lev 11:14–16 seems to follow this pattern: any creature of a hawk-like designation (for example) is unclean. It is not necessary to divide the specific subcategories of raptors; the designation has established their unclean nature *in toto*. This is the dominant trait of priestly differentiation. Division is only present in the priestly activity insomuch as it serves to aid in preservation of designated distinctions. So while not all designations are divisive, all divisions are designators. Ultimately, Neville's argument serves to clarify *how* God's creative acts are priestly rather than separate God's activity *from* the priestly. Neville, "Differentiation."

33. Balentine, *Torah's Vision*, 139.

34. Renckens, *Israel's Concept*, 108. Further, the veracity of this observation is both supported by and supportive of the previous discussion surrounding Adam's naming ritual in Genesis 2.

Since the divine activity of Creation is well connected to the priestly duties of designation, and the image of God is contextually connected to the divine activity of Creation, the association of the divine image with priesthood is not only logical but also preferred. While this is insufficient to demand that the *imago Dei* be treated as an exclusively priestly designation, it does seem sufficient to demand that the divine image must reflect at least certain priestly obligations.[35]

Priestly Terminology—Verbal Expressions of Temple-Service

It is at best tenuous to build claims of interpretation on "priestly terminology" when examined discreetly. Individual words, even those which clearly denote cultic activity, should not serve as foundation stones for theology. However, with the heptadic structure of Genesis 1 reflecting priestly numerological interests and the descriptions of divine creative activity demonstrating a priestly connection, the frequent use of words typically understood as cultic within the chapter reasonably suggest a pronounced priestly interest.[36]

Many of the particular cultic terms and their impact toward interpretation have been previously addressed in this work, and do not need to be revisited. It is worthwhile therefore to examine certain elaborations and constructions that (1) have not been previously discussed or (2) have further ramifications not directly associated with the previous discussions.

While it is not a strictly priestly term, ברא is used in a particular manner by priestly writers in general (with a strict focus on cosmogony) and within Genesis 1 specifically. It is interesting to observe that of the six occurrences within Genesis 1, four of the uses serve as an *inclusio* of sorts.[37] Genesis 1:1 and 2:3 begin and end the Creation account, while the occurrence in Gen 1:21 introduces the first living creatures and begins the pericope that concludes with the creation of humankind in Gen 1:27. Furthermore, Gen 1:27 actually uses the term three times, emphasizing not only that the creation of humanity is the conclusion of the generative acts, but also drawing distinct attention to the formation in the image of God! This dual inclusion (Gen 1:1/2:3; Gen 1:21/1:27) and tripled expression (Gen 1:27) forms a distinct verbal structure that establishes the central point of the six days in the identity of humankind. The doubled expression of the צלם in Gen 1:27 ensures that the identity of humankind is cosmologically related to the divine image. Since צלם does seem to be a cultic term in the Hebrew Scrip-

---

35. Niskanen, "Poetics of Adam," 418; Barr, "Image of God," 12.
36. Balentine, *Torah's Vision*, 60.
37. Garr, "God's Creation," 84.

tures (as discussed in chapter 1), the relatively sparse use of ברא in Genesis 1 intertwines all of Creation with human expression of God.[38]

The connection between cosmogony and the human expression of God is further emphasized in Gen 1:14–16 with the description of the greater and lesser lights. With the exception of these three verses, the term מאור only appears in the Pentateuch in descriptions of the tabernacle's lampstands.[39] While this observation is common, it usually serves to suggest that the tabernacle (and temple) were inspired by and designed to reflect Creation.[40] However, in light of the overarching ideology of Genesis 1 and the connection of Creation to the human expression of (and service toward) God, it can be maintained that it is not the tabernacle/temple that was imitating Creation, but rather the Creation which imitated and prefigured the tabernacle/temple.[41] The Creation narrative itself therefore provides both the duty of priestly humankind and the place of service for priestly humankind—it is the original tabernacle/temple.[42] Outside of the Pentateuch, מאור

---

38. This connection also accounts for the curse upon Creation when humankind sinned. The biblical understanding of Creation links the physical world to moral truths and practice. "When anyone or anything, human or divine, rebelled against this fixed order, then the covenant was damaged and creation became distorted." Barker, *Gate of Heaven*, 59, 78.

39. Exod 26:6; 27:20; 35:8, 14, 28; 39:37; Lev 24:2; Num 4:9, 16. Also, 1QH 7:23–24, where the temple lampstand is itself directly described as a sevenfold light shining over Eden; a very likely allusion to Gen 1:14–19. Cf. Beale, *Temple*, 117.

40. Beale, *Temple*, 31; Goldingay, *Israel's Gospel*, 84.

41. This interpretation is even stronger if one subscribes to the documentary hypothesis, since it establishes the P material so late in Israel's history, well after the construction and design of the temple. While it could be argued that the original temple builders used natural imagery *to express* their worship, the deliberate construction of Genesis 1 subverts this intention and deliberately describes natural imagery *in terms of* worship. Whatever the intention of the original builders, the P writers of Genesis 1 have established a cosmogony that revolves around worship rather than a worship that relies upon cosmogony. Even this distinction may be unnecessary, as it is viable to imagine Creation and tabernacle/temple (and its attendant cultus) as mirror images of one another.

Fletcher-Louis is helpful in summarizing this point, noting that the idea of the priestly roles in the tabernacle/temple serving as a microcosm of Creation is already attested to biblically in Ezek 28:12–16 and extrabiblically in Sirach 49:16—50:1 (Hebrew text). Barker goes even further, suggesting that the temple itself served to mystically transposition the worshipers from the earthly realm to the supernatural place of God. Fletcher-Louis, "God's Image," 82, 91; Barker, *Gate of Heaven*, 61.

42. Cf. Knohl, *Sanctuary of Silence*, 155. The idea that the Creation is reflective of eternity is foundational to and affirmed by the discussion of Hebrews 9, where the ὑποδείγματα are representative of heavenly realities. While Hebrews 9 is—strictly speaking—referring to the tabernacle/temple and not to Creation as a whole, the general tenor of the epistle implies that *all* things of this Creation are intended to be replaced

is used by Ezekiel (affiliated with a priestly family) only once (Ezek 32:8) and found in the Psalms (used in temple worship) only twice (Pss 74:16; 90:8). The single non-cultic occurrence is in Prov 15:30, which appears to be a general usage. Psalm 74:16, however, directly speaks to God's role as Creator and Ps 90:8 and Ezek 32:8 reference the lights in punitive contexts that address the failure of righteousness or lack of honor toward YHWH. The non-cultic use of Prov 15:30 follows the declaration that God "hears the prayer of the righteous" and may not be as far from a priestly concern as initially presupposed. More importantly for the present context, though, is the association of the lights in Gen 1:14–16 with the establishment of signs, seasons, and days—most likely references to the religious observances of God's people rather than mere agrarian concerns and further evidences of Creation as cultus in this seminal text.[43]

Also important to a priestly understanding of Creation is the occurrences of מין in the generation of the animals. This term, serving to show designations, is found only in texts ascribed to priestly sources in the Hebrew Scriptures. Outside of the Creation narrative, the Pentateuch only uses מין in the flood narrative to designate the creatures brought onto the ark (Gen 6:20; 7:14) and in the lists of unclean creatures (Lev 11:14–29; Deut 14:13–18). The final occurrence of מין is Ezek 47:10 where it emphasizes the plethora of fish found in the river flowing from the Eschatological Temple. The uniqueness of this word both establishes the priestly context for Genesis 1 and prefigures (or reflects) the priestly concerns—such as the food laws—of later Israel.[44]

Finally, two words that are not inherently cultic should be addressed: קרא and ברך. While both of these terms have broad usage, the specific way that they are utilized in Genesis 1 cannot be excluded from an interpretation of nature of humankind and the image of God. קרא is used exclusively for designation in Genesis 1. Two of its three occurrences are in Gen 1:5 and Gen 1:8, where God names the day and night, and the earth and seas. It is not insignificant that Gen 1:4 and Gen 1:6–7 contain three of the five uses of בדל. This serves to ensure that קרא is taken as a formal designation rather than an arbitrary name. The next occurrences of קרא are found in the naming-ritual of Gen 2:18–23 where Adam is designating names to the creatures. This is made pertinent by the observation that while God names/

---

by a new opportunity to *worship* God in a proper context (Heb 12:27–29; 13:14–16).

43. Collins, *Genesis 1–4*, 47n29; also Rudolph, "Festivals," 23–40.

44. It may be worthwhile to note that while both flora and fauna are designated according to מין, humanity is not. There is no "kind" of human being. This could be traced to the role of humankind as designator rather than designated, or perhaps to the universal nature (or calling) of humankind.

designates cosmic features, he does *not* designate the animals; that task is left to Adam. While this observation is insufficient to demand a priestly interpretation to the divine image, the artistry of Genesis 1–2 suggests that this is not accidental and deliberately establishes a context for interpreting not only the image of God but also the commands of subdual and dominion.

A similar incident might be found in the use of ברך, which occurs only three times in Genesis 1: after the creation of the fish and fowl (Gen 1:22), after the creation of humankind (Gen 1:28), and after the "creation" of the Sabbath (Gen 2:3). Rather than designate these things, God blesses them. It may be considered important that the land animals—having yet to be given their proper names by Adam—did *not* receive a blessing from God. God seems to bless those things that are not under humankind's dominion and therefore reliant upon human action to receive a blessing. The next occurrence of ברך is in Gen 5:2, which is simply a reiteration of the blessing of Gen 1:28, while the next use after that is found in Gen 9:1 where God is blessing the "Next Adam" Noah with the same charge that the Original Adam received in Gen 1:28 (though with some modifications due to the lasting consequences of the flood).[45] The blessing of Gen 9:1 serves to connect Adam and Noah and suggest that their functions are the same.[46] With this connection in mind, it is notable that the following use of ברך—and the first use of the term by a human—is found in Gen 9:26 where Noah is praying *to God* rather than directly addressing his sons. The transmission of blessing is a patriarchal prerogative and does not demand an interpretation that the blessing of Noah is a priestly act; however, the content of Noah's blessing refers to Japheth's dwelling in the tents (tabernacles?) of Shem and a call to Canaan to be of service not toward Shem but toward YHWH. The content of the blessing seems therefore to incline toward a priestly context, even if Noah himself is not strictly designated a "priest."[47]

45. The phrase "Next Adam" is used in this context to illustrate Noah's role as the replacement progenitor of the human race following the "de-Creation" caused by the flood, without infringing on the usual use of "Second Adam" in New Testament analyses of Christ in Romans 5 and 1 Corinthians 15.

46. Seiss, *Holy Types*, 29; Habel, *Literary Criticism*, 68. This connection is made even stronger by noting the connection of Noah with the צלם אלהים in Gen 9:6.

47. Obviously, an argument could be made that the blessing—as a patriarchal prerogative—should not be read as a priestly matter at all. However, this seems short sighted. The amalgamated role of the patriarchs as *de facto* priest, judge, and prophet to their clans does not remove priestly elements from the context of the Scripture. The fact that a non-priest performed a given activity does not change the nature of the activity itself.

It could also be pointed out that Gen 9:28 records Noah living an additional 350 (7 x 50) years. There could be some significance to Noah living for a "perfect" number of Jubilees following the flood. If the anachronistic reading of the documentary

Summary of Thought regarding the Context of Genesis 1

A comprehensive treatment of the priestly elements is a study in itself and beyond the scope of the present work; however, the three elements of Genesis 1 that have been selected for this examination serve to illustrate the important interaction between the general context of Genesis 1 and the proper interpretation of the image of God.

While it is important to recognize the general temple-building aspects of the Creation account, the specific examples illustrated above serve particularly to focus those aspects on the priestly duties of humankind. The presence of priestly numerology is not simply a reflection of priestly patterning, but a conscious development of a theological theme toward the Sabbath and the appropriate response to the Sabbath.[48] The establishment of human beings and their call to reign over the created order leads immediately into the time of Sabbath, which both highlights the importance of Sabbath and helps focus the direction of human agency.[49]

Similarly, the failure to emphasize God's creative activity through designation naturally obscures a priestly function for humanity. On the other hand, recognition of the methodology of creation establishes a cultic context for the passage as a whole. Since the צלם indicates a representative aspect to humankind, it is reasonable—if not demanded—that the divine image carries with it an expectation of human distinction and differentiation.[50] This priestly duty therefore becomes an impetus for all of human activity.[51]

Finally, the manner in which the priestly language of Genesis 1 is used suggests not only a generally priestly context but also specifically priestly

---

hypothesis is preferred, the assignment of Gen 9:28 to the P source must logically influence the proper context for the blessing preceding it as a part of the intended redaction.

48. Balentine, *Torah's Vision*, 63–67. While he does not tie his conclusions specifically to priestly numerology, Steinmann's study of אחד suggests that the anarthrous construction of יום on both the sixth and seventh day serve to emphasize the special role of those days in general and the cumulative nature of the Sabbath in particular in a manner compatible with the present thesis. Steinmann, "אחד as an Ordinal Number," 583–84.

49. Habel, *Literary Criticism*, 66–71. There is no one Hebrew word that contains all of the nuances of "custody," but the overarching context of Genesis 1–2 certainly seems to suggest that the reign of humankind, including such "exalted" activities as the naming ritual and the habitation of the garden, are better seen as a sort of custody rather than sovereignty. Even adherents of a royal interpretation of the divine image generally accept that the biblical context relegates humanity to a dependent position as *judiciars* rather than independent sovereigns over the earth. Cf. Eichrodt, *Theology of the Old Testament*, 1:41.

50. Brunner, *Man in Revolt*, 50.

51. Blenkinsopp, *Sage, Priest, Prophet*, 67.

interests.⁵² While this could be dismissed as a simple reflection of priestly redaction, doing so ignores the oddity that the priestly interests involved all had to do more with the nature and duty of priesthood—particularly in the context of the temple or temple-based activity—than a more generalized concern for an inherent human authority. The result of these combined factors suggests that a royal interpretation of the divine image reflects a broader concern for the exaltation of God's people than the near context would allow, or at least broader than it would prefer. On the other hand, a priestly interpretation of the image of God conforms to the near context and further emphasizes its inherent focus on the ultimacy of God.⁵³

ESTABLISHING A THEOLOGICAL CRUX FOR THE IMAGE OF GOD: EXODUS 19

The immediate context of Genesis 1 certainly suggests that the image of God must be interpreted in a priestly manner. Since the divine image is a foundational aspect of a correct biblical anthropology, it is reasonable to expect that theological cues or at least echoes of this interpretive paradigm can be found in broader interpretations of the image of God. Additionally, since so much of the interpretation of the צלם has been influenced by assumptions of royal ideology, it seems reasonable to suggest that if the image of God is best derived from a cult-focused ideology that an alternate paradigm for interpretation should be introduced. However, the perennial problem surrounding the interpretation of the divine image has been the limited context of Genesis 1. This problem can be addressed by looking beyond the immediate context and even beyond the context of Genesis to the overarching story of the Pentateuch. If a central aspect for understanding the Pentateuch as a whole can be discerned, then it is reasonable to use that same central aspect in the understanding of Genesis 1.⁵⁴

Part of the problem in determining a centralized aspect to the understanding of the Pentateuch has been the incorrect application of source

---

52. Morrow, "Creation as Temple-Building," 12–13.

53. It can further be argued that Genesis 1–2 both stand not only apart from the idea of human reign/royalty, but also in antithesis against such interpretations! In addition to emphasizing the transcendent power of God (Gen 1) and the intimate authority of God (Gen 2, particularly Gen 2:8, 15–17, 19, 21), the opening chapters of Genesis reflect a direct condemnation of humankind's attempts at self-direction (Gen 3). Indeed, the entire primordial history of Genesis 1–11 presents the folly of human determination (cf. Gen 6:5–6 et al.) in contrast to the blessings of obedience (cf. 6:8 et al.)—obedience expressed most often in terms of worship and/or priestly activity.

54. Cassuto, *Genesis*, 1; Van Wolde, *Stories of the Beginning*, 4.

criticism.⁵⁵ Generally, advocates of source criticism have argued for a disconnected reading of the Pentateuch with each source considered quite differently. The problem with this advocacy is that it ignores the overall unity of the Pentateuch. Whatever the path of its composition, the extant Pentateuch presents a coherent and unified story. Therefore, each aspect of the Pentateuch may justifiably be examined according to that overarching story.⁵⁶

The question for interpretation then becomes, "what is the central aspect of the Pentateuch?" Ultimately, it seems there can be little argument against the reality that the Pentateuch serves as story of the formation of the people of God.⁵⁷ The Pentateuch serves in this way universally, as God creates all of humankind. It serves in this way specifically, as God calls Abraham to be the bearer of blessing for the world; and finally it serves in this way nationally as Israel is called to a unique role in the plan of God.⁵⁸ God's activities of both deliverance and punishment revolve around the motif of the people of God. Israel is delivered time and again because they are his people. Punishment is levied against both Israel and the nations for failure to act appropriately as God's people.⁵⁹ The shift of emphasis from the universal to the specific and national neither removes nor limits the prominence of

---

55. It should be noted that source criticism itself is not being rejected, but only the improper application of source criticism. There is much profit in studying the possible sources of the Pentateuch; however, this cannot be done to the exclusion of the present unity of the text.

It is entirely possible to analyze multiple sources while respecting the integrity of the Scriptures as they currently exist: Childs noted the fallacy of ignoring the overall context of the Scriptures while still holding to source critical principles. On the other hand, Goldingay's theological work illustrates that there is little need even to seek to reconstruct hypothetical sources to understand the narrative of the Scriptures and still maintain coherence and reasonability. The critical issue seems to be the intention of the scholar. For biblical theologians, the finalized form is the only actual Bible from which to form theology, and therefore the extant Scriptures should always be considered superior to possible sources. Source theology is not biblical theology, and is necessarily limited. Cf. Goldingay, *Israel's Gospel*, 40.

56. Jacobson, "Structuralists," 109; Dempster, *Dominion and Dynasty*, 32–33; Van Wolde, *Stories of the Beginning*, 1–4; Durham, *Exodus*, xxi.

57. Balentine, *Torah's Vision*, 63–66; Renckens, *Israel's Concept*, 12; Young, *Creator, Creation*, 36–37; Scobie, *Ways of Our God*, 469.

58. Renckens, *Israel's Concept*, 116; Habel, *Land Is Mine*, 121–22; Goldingay, *Israel's Life*, 125.

59. All of humanity is held to the standard of the people of God since all of humanity, as noted, ultimately exists to be a people of God. Israel was elected as God's People in a national (and as shall be noted, paradigmatic) sense, while all of humankind was created as a people bearing the image of God. Cf. Blenkinsopp, *Sage, Priest, Prophet*, 67; Middleton, *New Heaven*, 84–85; Goldingay, *Israel's Faith*, 517.

the people of God theme.[60] Quite the opposite, a close reading of the three establishments of the people of God indicates that the election of Abraham and of Israel *enhances* the theme and allows for the use of Exodus 19 as an interpretive paradigm for the entire Pentateuch.[61]

The Exemplary Role of Abraham

Since humanity as a whole was created in the image of God, the inherent calling toward holiness and a reflection of God is foundational.[62] That foundation is then given guidance by the election of Abraham.[63] Abraham's role as a conduit of blessing is often referenced, but it should be noted that the conduct of the blessing is couched in terms of imitation: it is by blessing that blessing is received (Gen 12:1–3). Abraham has long been recognized as an exemplar for Israel; however, there is no need to restrict his paradigm to Israel alone.[64] The implications of Genesis 12 are that any nation could receive the blessing of God if they properly honored the person (or later, the people) of God. This is implied in the covenant of circumcision (Gen 17:14), where a multiplicity of nations—not Israel alone—are promised to Abraham and the rite of circumcision is applicable to non-biological family (cf. vv. 12–13).[65] It is the presence in the tent of Abraham that indicates covenant membership.

Since this is the case, it is not inappropriate to designate Abraham as a covenant mediator.[66] His acceptance or intervention (as in the case of Sodom, Gen 18:22–33) of a people directly impacted their relationship with God. Even if Abraham acted passively, Genesis 12 already establishes that a people's treatment of Abraham would adjudicate their relationship with God, the source of blessing.

It is not only Abraham himself that must be treated correctly. The abductions of Sarah in Gen 12:10–20 and Gen 20:1–18 are explicit in showing that those affiliated with Abraham must be properly honored. It can also

---

60. Cf. Habel, *Literary Criticism*, 66; Blenkinsopp, "Abraham," 240–41; Schnabel, "Israel," 35–36.

61. Renckens, *Israel's Concept*, 12; cf. Waltke and Yu, *Old Testament Theology*, 538.

62. Cf. Goldingay, *Israel's Faith*, 22.

63. Beale, "Eden," 12. Technically, Abraham was still "Abram" during some of these examples; however, for sake of clarity and overall canonical understanding, only the name Abraham will be used in this discussion.

64. Middleton, *New Heaven*, 61; cf. Blenkinsopp, "Abraham," 240.

65. Wenham, *Story as Torah*, 37.

66. Moberly, *Old Testament*; Seiss, *Holy Types*, 121.

be argued, however, that Sarah is not simply an individual person, but also a representative of the tent of Abraham. In a sense, the abduction of Sarah is a violation of Abraham's private space. To violate Sarah is to invade the very location where the promise of God (the seed of Abraham) was to take place. In this sense, both the pharaoh and Abimelech levied insult against the man of God, violated the place of God, and threatened the promises of God. The punishments that they received were not simply martial; they were theological. The term used to describe the Egyptian afflictions in Gen 12:17, נגעים, typically carries a connotation of divine proscription and is prominently featured in Leviticus 13 in the descriptions of the skin diseases. The punishment against Abimelech is even more distinct: the closing of the womb is a direct statement of God's role as giver of life and is often assumed to be a divine punishment in the biblical context. In the case of both the pharaoh and Abimelech, their violations necessitated the honoring of Abraham for their afflictions to end. While the pharaoh's actions in Genesis 12 are not clearly described, the encounter with Abimelech is explicit in both Abimelech's confession and in his reparation toward Abraham.[67]

Even if Abraham's tent is not considered to be a holy place, the overall context of the entire Abrahamic narrative revolves around the call to and possession of the land itself. Unlike later Israel, Abraham was not directed to conquer the Canaanites, but at the same time the land was clearly and fully granted to Abraham as his and his family's possession and their possession alone (Gen 12:1; 13:14–18; 15:7; 17:8; et al.). This land-grant is implicitly limited, as ultimately the land belongs to YHWH, and Abraham serves as a representative and curator of the land. The holy place becomes Abraham's responsibility.[68]

---

67. While there is no overt honoring of Abraham in the text of Genesis 12, it should be noted that Abraham had already prospered greatly under the pharaoh (v. 16). When Abraham was sent off, it was with "all that he had" (v. 20b). This would have included the riches already accumulated, as there is no indication that the pharaoh reclaimed any of the livestock. Further, it could be argued that the act of returning Sarah to Abraham was itself a confession of sorts on the part of the pharaoh. The acquiescence of the god-king of Egypt to Abraham would not have been without implications.

68. Cf. Habel, *Land Is Mine*, 122–30. This assumption of responsibility may account at least partially for Abraham's intercessory activities on behalf of the Sodomites, as they are within the land and therefore under his watch care. God's revelation of Sodom's coming doom is explicitly tied to the need to maintain holiness within Abraham's family (Gen 18:17–19), but the immediate intercession after this revelation is suggestive.

It is also interesting that in what source critics do traditionally consider P narratives, the only elaborate discussions of Abraham as a personality are found in the establishment of the covenant of circumcision and in the negotiation for Sarah's burial plot in Genesis 23. Where the former narrative obviously touches on priestly interests, the latter is more subtle. While Abraham insists on purchase of the plot, the Hittites directly

Examining these features together reveals Abraham as a covenant mediator, the keeper of the place of God's Promise, and an intercessor between God and humankind.[69] Each of these roles is inherently priestly, establishing the patriarch as both a prophet (cf. Gen 20:7) and a priest. The example that Abraham was to establish, both for the world and for Israel, was a priestly example.[70] The importance of the Abrahamic saga is not only that it establishes the starting point for national Israel, but also that it reflects a demonstration of what the calling of God toward humankind is.[71] Further, if Abraham is exemplary for Israel—a recognized tenet—then it is important to acknowledge that the example he set was not a vague faithfulness, but rather a specific enactment of response, activity, and prerogatives that were distinctly priest-like.[72]

The Priestly Calling of Israel

If Abraham's example was specifically priestly, then it serves to inform the overall calling of Israel—which itself was established to serve as an example

---

acknowledge Abraham's special role before God (Gen 18:6a) and implicitly affirm his possession of the land (Gen 18:6b). While it would be too much to suggest this affirmation of Abraham's custody of the land was intentional by the Hittites, it is reasonable to suggest that its inclusion by the author was intentionally designed to bolster the legitimacy of Israel's claim to the land, particularly since the entire pericope serves to establish this point with Abraham's insistence on proper legal procedure.

69. Cf. Seiss, *Holy Types*, 32. The intercessory role of Abraham takes on an additional theological layer when considered from the perspective of Hebrews where Melchizedek is portrayed as a Christ-figure (Heb 7:11–28). If Melchizedek is understood this way (whether as a pre-incarnate Christ or simply as a type of the Christ), then it is not insignificant that Melchizedek interacts directly with Abraham with no recorded conversation with the Sodomite king despite the presence of all three men within the same pericope. Only priestly Abraham was honored with blessing and relationship.

A different but thematically related interaction is found in Abraham's intervention in Genesis 18, when YHWH manifests in human form (either directly or indirectly through an angelic intermediary). Abraham's activity includes the preparation of a meal (easily read as a sacrificial act) and petition for fellowship with Abraham within his place. The opening of the tents to the divine visitors establishes a holy place of sorts, and could be read as an act of temple-keeping. If so, then Genesis 18 reveals Abraham acting as intercessor, custodian, and mediator; again fulfilling the primary three activities of priesthood.

70. Middleton, *New Heaven*, 61.

71. Habel, *Literary Criticism*, 68; cf. Wenham, *Story as Torah*, 37, 107.

72. Firmage, "Genesis 1," 104; Habel, *Literary Criticism*, 66–72; Scobie, *Ways of Our God*, 472. This generalized statement is made more powerful by considering Blenkinsopp's correspondence between the dominion over the earth of Gen 1:28 and the subdual of the land in Numbers and Joshua. Israel's exemplary role "embodies in a more intense and concentrated form the hallowing bestowed on the earth in the act of creation." Blenkinsopp, *Sage, Priest, Prophet*, 111.

of and a priesthood for the world at large.[73] While Abraham is crucial for the foundation of Israel, it is national Israel that serves as the central descriptive of the people of God in the Pentateuch.[74] And within that central role, the primary emphasis of both the narrative and the non-narrative portions of the Torah serves to establish how humankind is to interact with God (consecration and intercession), fellow humans (mediation), the cult (instruction), and the land itself (custody).[75]

The polemical nature of the plagues of Egypt is well established, but rarely applied to its fullness in light of Israel's role for the world. The polemical narrative of the liberation from Egypt in Exodus 1–15 is first and foremost a theological discussion that directly relates to priestly interests. The narrative quickly moves to the reception of the law and the building of the tabernacle in the latter half of Exodus. The entire book of Leviticus explicates the law further, while Numbers continues that explication in its opening chapters. The narrative proper resumes with celebration of the Passover feast (Numbers 7–9). The remainder of Numbers chronicles the rejection of God's land through cowardice and the war between holiness and ungodliness among the Israelite people. Finally, Deuteronomy reiterates, reinterprets, and expands the law for the next generation.

Ultimately, the majority of the Torah is not concerned with narrative; but with regulations concerning the holy place, the holy people, and the role of Israel both regarding their need to be holy before YHWH and their authority over (and expected example for) the surrounding nations.[76] Further, the narratives within Exodus-Deuteronomy are directly and deliberately theological treatises rather than simply historical retellings.[77] These collective features establish that rather than have the law introduced in Exodus 19, the entirety of the Pentateuch is arranged and deliberately established to discuss the nature and role of Israel.[78] And since the content of that document is overwhelmingly concerned with priestly interests and items that fall

---

73. Balentine, *Torah's Vision*, 114; Durham, *Exodus*, 262–63; Middleton, *New Heaven*, 25, 63–64.

74. Middleton, *New Heaven*, 79–80.

75. Balentine, *Torah's Vision*, 114–23; Cross, *Canaanite Myth*, 295; cf. Blenkinsopp, *Sage, Priest, Prophet*, 1; Renckens, *Israel's Concept*, 31.

76. Firmage, "Genesis 1," 111; Balentine, *Torah's Vision*, 66; Livingston, *Pentateuch*, 227; Renckens, *Israel's Concept*, 15; Scobie, *Ways of Our God*, 472; Pleins, *Social Visions*, 71.

77. As Mowinckel succinctly observed, the P-writer's "work as a historian is in some degree only to provide the context of law." Mowinckel, *Erwägungen zur Pentateuch Quellenfrage*, 21–27; Cross, *Canaanite Myth*, 295.

78. Sailhamer, *Genesis Unbound*, 107; Habel, *Literary Criticism*, 65; cf. Cassuto, *Genesis*, 1; Durham, *Exodus*, xx.

under the priestly purview, it is reasonable to suggest that the priestly character of Israel is the dominant aspect of the people of God within the Torah.[79] If this is correct, then accepting Exod 19:6 as an—if not the—interpretive crux of the Pentateuch is not only reasonable but preferred.[80]

Israel's establishment as a nation was a creative act; this cannot be reasonably denied. A simple comparison of the two versions of the fourth commandment in Exod 20:8–11 and Deut 5:12–15 is enough to confirm the connection between the rest surrounding Creation and the rest emanating from deliverance.[81] What can be debated is the question of theological priority; or, asked another way, whether Israel's creation is a mimicry of the original Creation or whether Creation is a foreshadowing of Israel's creation.[82]

It might be better to remove the dichotomy of the previous question. There is no need to express the question as Israel or Creation. Since the primary concern for the people of God is the relationship with God, the examples of Creation and Israel do not present divergent options but rather convergent illustrations. Israel reflects Creation, but Creation prefigures Israel.[83] And as a result of this convergence, the calling for the people of God to be priestly in Israel should naturally flow into an understanding of the image of God in Creation.[84]

The primary concern with this convergent approach of interpretation is whether or not it forces anachronistic thought into the theology of Genesis. However, this concern is not as critical as it might initially seem. There are at least three recognized precedents for even an "anachronistic"

---

79. Cf. Eichrodt, *Theology of the Old Testament*, 1:99–101ff.; Middleton, *New Heaven*, 63–67; Goldingay, *Israel's Life*, 126; Childs, *Biblical Theology*, 112.

80. Balentine, *Torah's Vision*, 74; cf. Levenson, *Sinai and Zion*, 86; Durham, *Exodus*, xxiii.

81. Craigie, *Book of Deuteronomy*, 157; This is the simplest and most explicit connection between Israel's formation and Creation, but not the only one. Another well attested connection is found in the Song of the Sea (Exod 15) where the deliverance of Israel is reflective of Creation. Barker, *Gate of Heaven*, 66; Niehaus, *God at Sinai*, 182–85.

82. Fletcher-Louis, "God's Image," 85.

83. Beale, *Temple*, 31–32; Balentine, *Torah's Vision*, 71; Levenson, *Sinai and Zion*, 86; Goldingay, *Israel's Gospel*, 79; cf. Ross, *Recalling the Hope of Glory*, 82–85; Middleton, *New Heaven*, 44–45; Gentry and Wellum, *Kingdom*, 302–3; Niehaus, *God at Sinai*, 199.

84. Young, *Creator, Creation*, 33–34; Middleton, *Liberating Image*, 68. While using slightly different terms, Kutzko advocates this approach when describing Israel as the True Adam and suggesting that the nation itself serves as an "idol" for God. Balentine is even more deliberate in connecting the formation of Israel at Sinai with Creation, connecting the movement of the Spirit (Gen 1:3/Exod 31:3) and the completion and blessing of the holy place (Gen 2:2–3/Exod 39:43, 40:33). Fletcher-Louis, "God's Image," 85; Balentine, *Torah's Vision*, 67–68.

reading of the Creation account that allow the priestly tenor of Exod 19:6 to establish the pattern for interpretation of Genesis 1.

Historical Precedence: Light as Torah

The first example to provide precedence for using Exod 19:6 (and in fact, all of the Torah from Exodus 19 onward) as the interpretive lens for examining the Creation event is the rabbinic tradition of identifying the light of the first day with the Torah.[85] Simply put, rabbis noted that the fourth day saw the formation of the celestial bodies, so the light of the first day needed to reflect something else. Rabbis noted that apart from YHWH, nothing could exist, so the initial light had to represent a capacity for relationship between the Creator and the created realm—a relationship that is encapsulated within the Torah.[86] That the next two days represent cosmic events that are "above" human thought only further encourages this thinking. The first three days of Creation all address cosmology on a scale well beyond human comprehension. The fourth day—though scientifically as removed from human comprehension as the cosmology of the first three days—was relatable to humankind in two ways: first, an amorphous and untamed chaos as expressed in the initial verses of Genesis 1 can only be imagined while a sun and a moon were interacted with daily; second, the stated purpose of the celestial lights of the fourth day was to relate to human beings (cf. Gen 1:14b).[87]

85. Smith, *Priestly Vision*, 74, 83; cf. Cassuto, *Genesis*, 25–28; Jukes, *Types*, 27.

86. Greidanus, "Universal Dimension," 41–42; Balentine, *Torah's Vision*, 81, 123–24; cf. Smith, *Priestly Vision*, 15. Unsurprisingly, both רוח (Gen 1:2) and דבר have been described as essentially anthropomorphic terms designed to "emphasize the immanence of the transcendent God." While Genesis 1 does not use the latter term, the entire work of Creation was a spoken activity and the understanding of the role of תורה as a bridge between humanity and YHWH is well known, further affirming the possibility of this interpretation of light as a relational connection between humankind and God that—whether reflective of the תורה specifically or not—falls into the realm of priestly concern. Renckens, *Israel's Concept*, 96; cf. Sarna, *Genesis*, 7.

87. The interaction between the celestial lights and humanity also supports the proposition that Creation needs to be interpreted according to the received Torah. Leviticus 23 deliberately avoids the use of "feast" (הג) in the second verse, instead noting that these were "appointed times" (מועד) identical to the description of the lights of Gen 1:14. The implication of this is that the communion of God and his people represented by the feasts not only formed the center of Israel's identity, but also of Creation's order. Creation exists to facilitate worship.

This thought pattern is further expressed biblically in the opening verses of the Gospel of John, where Jesus is established as God's Word [Torah] (John 1:1–3), and the Light of the world (John 1:4–5); who incarnated in order to demonstrate how to relate to the Father (John 1:14–18). Ross, *Recalling the Hope of Glory*, 78, 82; cf. Van Wolde, *Stories of the Beginning*, 24 et al.

With this understanding, the relationship of created and Creator necessitated the establishment of the Torah.[88] Further if the rest of Genesis 1 is interpreted as a temple-building activity, then it is sensible for the Torah that instructs on the meaning, form, and purpose of the temple to be introduced prior to any temple construction.[89]

With the Torah as the foundational piece of Creation, humankind's natural role would be to preserve and administer the Torah.[90] It is easy to see this Torah administration as a part of the subdual and dominion of humanity.[91] Therefore, there is precedence for not only allowing the priestly call of Israel to illustrate the meaning of the image of God, but actually preferring it.[92]

---

88. Cf. Young, *Creator, Creation*, 35–37. While Brunner does not use the specific word תורה, he essentially affirms this interpretation by noting that "man is man by the fact that he is a creature who stands in a special relation to the Word of God." Apart from the divine word, there can be no functional humanity. Brunner, *Man in Revolt*, 71.

89. Cross notes, "The entire cultic paraphernalia and cultus was designed to express and overcome the problem of the holy, transcendent God visiting his pervasively sinful people." While this statement cannot be applied wholly to Creation (since it precedes the depravations caused by sin), the basic idea that the cult exists only to connect finite humanity to an infinite God is appropriate. Also, Sailhamer's contention that humankind's establishment in the garden was for worship and obedience to the Torah should be recognized and considered compatible with this suggestion as well. Cross, *Canaanite Myth*, 299; Sailhamer, *Genesis Unbound*, 79.

90. Balentine, *Torah's Vision*, 68; cf. Greidanus, "Universal Dimension," 43.

91. The idea that Torah is the fountainhead for dominion is further found in the rabbinic exposition of Prov 8:12–16. The Talmud directly connects the presence of wisdom with Torah; to have wisdom is to know Torah. It is only when this is done that a person is fit to rule (ch. 4; Mishna A—location 41418 [Kindle]). Though Prov 8:12–16 do not use רדה, the significant result of connecting reign with Torah remains.

Aside from rabbinical writings, the book of Deuteronomy connects the understanding of Torah with the right to rule in Deut 17:18–20, where the study of the Torah establishes the character of the king and the longevity of his kingdom (cf. v. 20b).

92. The natural retort to the rabbinic method would be to suggest that the rabbis utilized eisegesis to insert the Torah into the narrative before it is chronologically appropriate. This retort is somewhat mitigated by the observation that the cultural expectations of what was appropriate or "ought" to be done far preceded the written codifications of these "oughts." It can be argued that the giving of the Torah on Sinai was not significant because it gave new information—certainly many of the precepts of the Torah seem to be reflected in pre-Sinai narratives—but because it codified the existing understandings into a national document to form the nation of Israel from the gathering of (former) slaves.

Of course, if one accepts a source theory that relegates Genesis 1 to a later period, any supposed eisegesis is eliminated anyway. Ezekiel serves as a good example of this. Scholars who assign late dates to the P-source place it nearly contemporaneous with Ezekiel. This temporal closeness removes any surprise from Ezekiel's understanding of the image of God according to Exodus 25–40. But with that temporal proximity also comes support for the suggestion that the divine image in Genesis 1 is inherently linked to the priesthood.

Academic Precedence: The Revelatory Day Theory of Genesis 1

Another support for reading Genesis 1 through the lens of Sinai's Torah can be found in the revelatory day theory.[93] By suggesting that the seven days of Genesis 1 reflect seven different revelations to Moses, advocates of this approach essentially demand that the entire Creation account be read sympathetically—though not necessarily identically—to the Torah. If this is the case, then it not only becomes valid to examine the image of God in light of the thesis verse of Exod 19:6; it virtually becomes necessary.[94] This necessity is further supported by the recognition that the commandment that juxtaposes the Creation of the world with the creation of Israel, is the command regarding the Sabbath, over which the priests held a specific interest.[95]

The revelatory day theory also helps explain the overlay of temple-building and Creation in Genesis and of Creation imagery with the tabernacle in Exodus. Rather than specifically differentiate between temple instruction and Creation motifs, it is possible to look at both events simultaneously.[96] And if both events are simultaneously considered, then the

---

Finally, whether the story of the Creation was given to Moses in the 15th/13th century BC or recorded by priestly redactors in the 5th century BC, an understanding of God as the redeemer of humankind predates the record of the Creation. This predating opens any interpretation of the Creation narrative to a redemptive or covenantal understanding. Fletcher-Louis, "God's Image," 88; Renckens, *Israel's Concept*, 62.

93. For the present purposes, modern literary framework readings may be considered variations of the revelatory day theory. In each case, the primary purpose of establishing the seven days as constructs for understanding remains the same.

94. This is the general methodology of Balentine as well when he states that "in the liturgy of covenant-making, God concretizes the primordial commission by summoning Israel to a vocation of imaging God on earth as "a priestly kingdom and a holy nation" (v. 6). In other words, the Torah understand that *covenant-keeping*, from Israel's perspective, requires a solemn partnership commitment that places Israel in harmony with the liturgy of creation." Balentine, *Torah's Vision*, 123; cf. Middleton, *New Heaven*, 87–88.

95. Habel, *Literary Criticism*, 70–71; Collins, *Genesis 1–4*, 90; Barker, *Temple Theology*, 17. Since the revelatory day theory itself is simply being used to establish a precedent, the strengths and weaknesses of this theory are not the concern of the present work. However, one claimed weakness of this theory is directly applicable to the current discussion: the incompatibility of the revelatory day theory with Exod 20:11.

While this objection seems credible at first, it ignores the reality that the discussion of the Sabbath was making a *theological* point about the need to rest in YHWH rather than a *historical/chronological* statement about a literal (or nonliteral) Creation. The parallel passage in Deuteronomy 5 only strengthens this theological understanding, since the rest in vv. 12–15 is completely divorced from any discussion of the day of Creation.

Of course, this observation is not to defend completely the revelatory day theory; but it does illustrate that the theory is compatible with Exod 20:11 and the precedent and discussion of the present discussion is viable.

96. Barker, *Temple Theology*, 17–18. Young also essentially adopts this method

primary anthropological/sociological statement in each narrative—Gen 1:26–28 and Exod 19:5–6—should likewise be considered simultaneously and relatedly.[97] This consideration directly connects the image of God with the commission of Israel to priesthood.[98] This connection serves to not only inform the image of God as a priestly motif, but also to assign the divine image an active role. Just as Israel needed to act in order to serve as a priest-nation, humankind was formed with the image of God as a commission to fulfill rather than an inherent characteristic.[99] If this is the case, then the paradigmatic illustration of the Scriptures is continued.[100]

Biblical Precedence: The Coexistence of Multiple Creation Accounts as a Singular Expression

A further precedent that can be observed in reading Genesis 1 alongside Exod 19:6 is the hermeneutical pattern of treating the multiple accounts of Creation as sympathetic toward one another rather than as contradictory. While the Western tendency is to parse out the details of each creation account, the presentation of the Creation(s) in the Bible revolve around emphasizing different aspects of divine sovereignty/ordering, communion/

---

with his suggestion that Genesis 1 can only be properly interpreted in light of other creedal statements of the Hexateuch. Similarly, Walton's theory that the seven-days of Creation could have been enacted in liturgical services draws a parallel between the days of Creation and the cultic life of Israel. Young, *Creator, Creation*, 25; Walton, *Lost World*, 89–90.

97. Collins, *Genesis 1–4*, 90–94; Young, *Creator, Creation*, 27.

98. Habel, *Literary Criticism*, 70–71.

99. Mann, *Book of Torah*, 16; Middleton, *New Heaven*, 84–85; Grenz, *Named God*, 361. The mediatory-edifying role of the image of God is emphasized even more than this when Beale describes Gen 1:28 as the "first Great Commission." Similarly, while Fretheim notes that "there is no such thing for Israel as a nonincarnate God" as a statement of God's activity, it can equally well be considered an anthropological truth: by assigning the divine image to humanity, God has assigned humans the task of incarnating him from the beginning. Beale, *Temple*, 117; Fretheim, *Suffering of God*, 106; Goldingay, *Israel's Faith*, 28.

100. Van Wolde, *Stories of the Beginning*, 33. The high priest set the example for the priesthood (and possibly the Nazirites), who set an example for the Levites. The Levites were the paradigm tribe of the nation of Israel, which itself existed to set an example of priesthood for the world. And every human being is fundamentally expected to serve as a priest.

This general approach is then further affirmed by the incarnation, which served to provide a template for humanity (John 1:18) and the commission of the church into priesthood (1 Pet 2:4–10; Hebrews). Cf. Beale, *Temple*, 121; Middleton, *New Heaven*, 85; Blenkinsopp, *Sage, Priest, Prophet*, 108–9.

relationship between God and humanity, and the redemption/deliverance of humankind from chaos—including deliverance from sin, which as a violation of God's approved order is inherently chaotic. Each of these creative aspects work together to establish the overall theological emphasis of the Creation.[101] The biblical presentation is not intended to present multiple views of a synchronous event; the multiple creation stories intend on elaborating a sympathetic theology of the Creator God, and his continued interaction with his Creation.[102] In a very real sense, the mythic language of the Creation account must be read with the same emphasis on imagination as apocalyptic literatures.[103] Just as the apocalyptic material of Scripture necessarily uses imaginary language to present an eschatological portrait that exceeds human capacity of understanding, so too does Creation.[104] Since a full understanding of the formation of the present realm of reality from nonexistence cannot be apprehended by the human mind, it must be imagined.[105]

The imaginary portrait(s) of Creation in the Bible serve theological and polemical roles rather than historical and evidential ones.[106] This is not to suggest that Genesis 1 is not accurate in its presentation of the nature of God's Creation; the purpose is to emphasize that Genesis 1 is not primarily concerned with nature so much as it is concerned with a theological

---

101. Balentine, *Torah's Vision*, 75, 83; Gorman, *Ideology of Ritual*, 41; Barr, "Revelation," 8. Barr actually goes so far as to suggest that there is no real difference between the Creation, Flood, Exodus, and Exile narratives. While he overstates his case, his general point (that these events converge theologically and therefore must be considered synthetically to properly understand the theology of the Scriptures) is valid.

102. Young, *Creator, Creation*, 33.

103. Cf. Jacobson, "Structuralists," 104. It should be noted that the description of "imaginary" language should not be taken as pejorative or indicative of falsity or fiction. Imaginary language is used here to indicate the necessity to draw upon images and concepts that are comprehensible by the human mind to describe something beyond the scope of human experience and ability to adequately describe. Imaginary language is inherent to apocalyptic literature, creation accounts, and even theophanies (cf. Ezek 1); all of which go beyond the current realm of existence and therefore necessitate the formation of a mental image apart from known reality.

104. While he did not adopt this terminology, Calvin essentially came to this conclusion with his observation that God, who could have created all things instantly, chose to take six days to accomplish his work in order to accommodate human capacity of understanding. Calvin, *Genesis*, 19.

105. Even if Genesis 1 is rejected as an example of creation *ex nihilo*, this statement is valid. Whether forming the present reality from nonexistence or from a chaotic proto-matter, the Creation establishes a different paradigm from which all human thought is processed. The essential aspect of humankind's inability to understand the different reality that may or may not have existed prior to Genesis 1 remains the same.

106. Beale, *Temple*, 30.

statement of sovereign order.¹⁰⁷ This is why the temple-building aspects of Genesis 1 are so prominent. The scientific debates that modern readers insist upon would neither have been interesting nor necessary to the original audience that approached the Creation narratives with an *a priori* expectation of truth and interest in its relational aspects.¹⁰⁸

If this *a priori* understanding is recognized, then the next logical question must ask *how* the Creation establishes a relational context between humankind and God. In Gen 1:26–28, that connection is made via the image of God; in later texts, the connection is found in election, Torah, etc.¹⁰⁹ Ultimately, the connection between YHWH and his people is summarized in Exod 19:5–6. Reading the calling of Israel as a call to priesthood sympathetically with the creation of humankind in Gen 1:26–28 produces an image of God that reflects the priesthood of God's people.¹¹⁰

PRIMARY EXEGESIS OF GENESIS 1:26–28

Summary Observations on the Exegesis of Gen 1:1–25

While much has been written concerning Genesis 1 in general, and the temple-building aspects of Creation in particular; it is useful to reexamine the overall exegesis of both the chapter as a whole and the creation of humankind within that context to fully establish the priestly nature of the *imago Dei*.¹¹¹

Since so much has been written on Genesis 1, it is impossible to accommodate every paradigm or interpretive stance. Rather than debate every point, the present examination will present the writer's preferred interpretive approach along with justifications and appropriate critiques of alternate methods as necessary, and discuss much of the chapter in broad strokes. At specific junctures that are critical for interpretation, the discussion will be narrowed and elaborated as necessary.

---

107. Collins, *Genesis 1–4*, 260–61; Young, *Creator, Creation*, 34.

108. Walton, *Lost World*, 34.

109. Von Rad, *Problem of the Hexateuch*, 131, 142; Balentine, *Torah's Vision*, 123.

110. Cf. Greidanus, "Universal Dimension," 43–44. Barth's statement that "creation [is] the external basis of the covenant" is also applicable. While Barth does not claim the same priestly emphasis as presented here, the affirmation that Creation and covenant—and therefore Genesis 1 and Exodus 19—are connected is pertinent. Barth, *CD* III/I, 94.

111. Van Wolde, *Stories of the Beginning*, 4.

Genesis 1:1–2—A Purpose for Temple Building

In determining the outline of the chapter, Smith makes the important observation that the seven-day organizational feature was "a completely priestly innovation."[112] The uniqueness of this approach to Creation not only emphasizes the temple-building aspects of Genesis 1, but also provides a guide to properly interpreting Gen 1:1–2.[113] Since vv. 1–2 stand outside of the seven-day organization, they are best read as meta-structural statements that provide the larger and general context within which the seven days elaborate in a priestly manner.[114] Bonhoeffer's observation that Creation is best interpreted as a *qualitative* rather than *temporal* event is not unwarranted.[115] The establishment of God as Creator and the pre-Creation reign of chaos (as represented by the triply disturbing conditions of תהו, בהו, and תהום—the latter of which is often overlooked as a statement of chaos) establishes both the assumptions for the remainder of Genesis 1 and the need for a created temple: a place of order and light in the midst of chaos and dark.[116]

The emphasis on order and division/differentiation so prominent in not only the temple instructions but also the general codes of behavior issued to God's people in Leviticus and elsewhere ultimately serve as creative statements. They exemplify the nature of God as Creator and the purpose of

---

112. Smith, *Priestly Vision*, 87.

113. Cf. Walton, *Lost World*, 24–25.

114. Ibid., 44. Whether it is best to read Gen 1:1 as a title for the chapter as a whole or not is largely irrelevant: whether v. 1 is a title or simply a summary statement that provides context, the end result is identical in establishing the nature of God, the need for Creation, and the context for the remainder of the chapter.
  Similarly, there is neither need nor preference for gap theory interpretations or middle creation understandings of vv. 1–2. The purpose of these verses are entirely contextual for the overall creation theology of Scriptures and the establishment of an ordered Creation in place of chaos. There is nowhere any suggestion that the author of Genesis 1 intended to allow a place to insert a satanic fall or provide a platform for multi-staged creation(s); such ideas are not conducive to the purpose or the context.

115. Bonhoeffer, *Creation and Fall*, 32.

116. Reyburn and Fry, *Handbook*, 30; Cassuto, *Genesis*, 22–25. This reality intersects with Chaldean cosmogony in an interesting way. Chaldean myth presented the pre-created world as a place where "a holy house . . . had not been made," while Genesis 1 begins with the construction of a holy house, the Temple of Creation. Clifford, *Creation Accounts*, 143.
  This proposition stands contrary to Cassuto, who suggested that the language of Gen 1:1–2:3 is "tranquil, undisturbed by polemic or dispute." However, while Cassuto's point—that the story of Genesis 1 does not have the violence and chaotic warfare of other ANE creation accounts—is valid, his refinement of the narrative to the point that it ignores the connotations of בהו, תהו, and תהום and the cosmological assumptions of the ancient Israelite is unwarranted. Cf. Cassuto, *Genesis*, 7.

both the κόσμος and the human race in Genesis 1. Where there was chaos, there would be order and purpose.[117] The role of humanity in Creation was obviously dominion (v. 28), but the question of why dominion was needed and its purpose remains. If all of the created order was תב, then the dominion was not intended to *change* things; it served instead to *preserve* the order of Creation that stood in stark contrast to the chaos of preexistence.[118]

Genesis 1:3–5—Establishing the Relational Aspect of the Temple

An initial survey of the first day of Creation is simple: light was created and separated from the darkness, establishing time and the context of a daily creation motif. The use of the cardinal אחד is appropriate since prior to this day, there was no other day by which to order things.[119] Therefore, vv. 3–5 demonstrate day 1, while the successive days utilize the ordinal system that would be expected.

The deliberate presentation of day 1 as a solitary day, or at least as a day that was solitary prior to further creative acts, places extra emphasis on the importance of *what* was created. As the beginning of all existence, this day more than any other establishes the paradigm of order.[120] To simply insist on the light being a physical manifestation of light is insufficient. Bonhoeffer's observation about the qualitative nature of Creation certainly applies.[121] The movement between evening and morning in v. 5 obviously establishes a temporal setting for Creation, but is not necessarily contingent on the light

---

117. Van Wolde, *Stories of the Beginning*, 20.

118. Balentine, *Torah's Vision*, 68. This purposeful role for vv. 1–2 can be reinforced by an interpretation of בְּרֵאשִׁית. While some have used the anarthrous construction to claim that Genesis 1 does not support truly *ex nihilo* creation, this is actually a distraction from the purpose of the chapter. If בְּרֵאשִׁית is read not as "In a beginning" but instead "As a beginning" with a modal sense, then the establishment of order (Creation) is directly prescribed as a counter or solution to the existence of chaos. Even if the more traditional temporal interpretation is preferred, the anarthrous construction can still be defended—there is no article because there is no need to distinguish this Creation from any other, since nothing was yet in existence—and the overall context of the chapter continues to present a purposeful establishment of Creation.

In either case, it is interesting that the biblical narrative is "authentic" in its presentation of a cosmogony, as opposed to their polytheistic neighbors conflation where "cosmogony and theogony have become confused." This reality alone emphasizes the uniqueness of the biblical beginning statement. Renckens, *Israel's Concept*, 81; cf. Cassuto, *Genesis*, 30.

119. Nachmanides, *Ramban (Nachmanides)*, 32–33; Cassuto, *Genesis*, 30.

120. Cassuto, *Genesis*, 25; cf. *Bereshith Rabba* iii: 1.

121. Cf. Bonhoeffer, *Creation and Fall*, 32.

being a mere physical illumination.[122] Since this is the case, the examination of the light's nature and identity becomes an important concern.

As previously mentioned, there is a precedent for interpreting the light as Torah, the establishment of the Word by which all of Creation would be measured.[123] The fact that light was spoken into existence cannot be overlooked, and does support this interpretation to at least some degree. The Kabbalistic Zohar instead prefers to consider the light of day 1 to be an extension or emanation of God's being, and not *created* so much as *inserted* into this new realm.[124] Smith notes that the light is not described as created, but simply declared to be and it was. If the light of Gen 1:3 is related to the Glory of God (specifically in Exodus 40, in Smith's analysis) then it is a manifestation, not a creation.[125] Going further, Smith noted the replacement of the sun with God's glory in Isa 60:19 and the correlation of the presence of God with the eternal day in Zech 14:5b–9.[126] Bille and Sorensen's suggestions that light is indicative of communion could also be used to support this interpretation.[127] And the impossibility of seeing YHWH directly—well attested throughout the Scriptures—necessitates another means of perceiving him. With this understanding of the light, that perception is found in Creation.[128]

The oddity of ascribing the light to divine glory is in the evaluation of its "goodness" (v. 4b). An autobiographical statement from God on his own goodness seems out of place in the overall context assuming his role as Creator, a role which is inherently good in the biblical senses. However, if the light is not evaluated by its nature—divine eminence—but rather by its role as communion between Creator and Creation, then the declaration would not be merely descriptive so much as prescriptive to the readers: God's declaration is that a relationship with Creation is a good thing, and Creation apart from the Creator is not-good and incomplete.[129]

---

122. Walton, *Lost World*, 54–55; this is particularly true if the Revelatory Day theory of interpretation is favored, as the evening and morning of days 1–3 need not reflect *any* celestial movement and can be isolated as the evening and morning of God's speaking to Moses.

123. Cf. Mathews, *Genesis 1—11:26*, 146–47.

124. Similarly, *Genesis Rabbah* 3:4 connects the light of day 1 with the "effulgent splendor of the Divine Presence." Sarna, *Genesis*, 7.

125. Cassuto, *Genesis*, 26–27.

126. Smith, *Priestly Vision*, 77.

127. Bille and Sorenson, "Anthropology of Luminosity," 79.

128. It is impossible to say that this interpretation of light was behind Paul's discussion of natural revelation in Rom 1:20, but it certainly accords with Paul's statement and stands as the logical basis for natural revelation.

129. Mathews, *Genesis 1—11:26*, 147; cf. Walton, *Lost World*, 18. All of this discussion fully allows for an interpretation of the light as Torah. Torah, as God's Word, was

With relationship being foundational, it is only reasonable to assume that the remainder of Creation served to establish the context—the *place*—of relationship.[130] So while the first day is not a direct act of temple-building, it is contextually necessary for the remaining days. If there is no relationship, there is no need for a temple. Conversely, if Creation is not a temple, then how can there be a relationship with the divine?[131]

Genesis 1:6–8—Establishing the Space for the Temple

Having established the relational prologue for a temple through the light of day 1, God's next action is to divide the waters with the רקיע. The cosmological waters were penetrated by an expanse that served to part the waters and provide a place exempted from the entropy of chaos.[132] The repetition of רקיע in the pericopes of the fourth and fifth days establishes a connection between the tangible Creation that humankind inhabits with this cosmic barrier against chaos. It proclaims that the world was to be an ordered and maintained space exempted against any sort of celestial or cosmic disorder.

The phrase typically translated "let it separate" is notable in the Hebrew. Rather than utilize a jussive use of בדל (יבדיל), the text instead uses the combination of היה + participle (ויהי מבדיל). This distinction is significant since while most translators simply interpret the statement verbally ("let it separate"), the participle can instead be translated either substantively ("let it be a separation") or instrumentally ("let it cause separation"). This is important because of the connotations that can be ascribed to מבדיל. While the

---

not "created." In Jewish understanding, it is eternal. The entrance of the Torah as the first act of Creation not only honors the Word of God, but also establishes that all of Creation is to exist according to the precepts and truths of the Torah. Before anything else could occur, the means of relationship had to provide a *raison d'etre* for Creation.

If this interpretation is accepted, then the priestly context of Genesis 1 is enhanced even more than if the light is assumed to be divine glory; for divine glory was demonstrated in many places and to many people, but the Torah was guarded and entrusted to the Levites.

130. Balentine, *Torah's Vision*, 81. While Cassuto does not use the idea of place in his interpretation, he does note that both the Hebrew and Syriac associate the hovering (רחף) of the divine spirit over the waters with the imagery of a mother bird that cares for its young. This "paternal care of the Divine Spirit, which hovered over [the waters], assured its future evolution and life" and speaks directly toward the primacy of the relationship between God and Creation. Cassuto, *Genesis*, 25.

131. Cf. Van Wolde, *Stories of the Beginning*, 19, 23; Walton, *Lost World*, 96. The use of the word "temple" here indicates a holy place where human-divine concourse might take place. Whether the place is specifically and structurally a temple, or a tabernacle or high place is not the issue.

132. Walton, *Lost World*, 56.

participle is unique to this verse in the Old Testament, בדל is used repeatedly to indicate the separation of the Israelites unto YHWH. The election to holiness is enacted by God's "separating" the Israelites. More directly pertinent to temple-building, the holy place is divided from the most holy place in the temple/tabernacle by the veil that "separated" the two areas. Just as the holy drapes of the tabernacle served to distinguish boundaries and defend the holy places, so too does the רקיע create a boundary between the Creation and the chaos and defends the new place that was to be a holy temple for God.[133]

Understanding the רקיע in this manner does not negate the overall cosmological concepts of the earth as an island of sorts surrounded by primordial seas, nor does it ignore the Israelite understanding of the waters above as the source of necessary rains. Instead, this understanding adds a layer of theological understanding to the cosmology that not only respects the ANE understanding of the shape of the cosmos, but also serves to subject all of it to the will of God: even the primordial chaos was subject to the declarations of God, being placed in distinct locations and used as he desires either for growth (cf. Gen 2:5–6) or for judgment (cf. Gen 7:11).[134]

Genesis 1:9–13—Establishing the Structure of the Temple

Having established the space for the temple on the second day, God next begins to establish the structure of Creation. In an expansion from the previous days, there are two distinct phases of creative activity in the third day—each punctuated by the evaluation of goodness. First, the "dry ground" (יבשה) is

---

133. The idea of a "spread out thing" (one of the connotations of the root רקע) in relation to both tent-curtains and the created world, though using a different word than רקע, is also found in Job 38:4–7 and Isa 40:12, 21–22; further affirming an Israelite conception of the world as a tent providing security.

Other suggested corollaries between the tabernacle's separation of the holy and the common and Creation include: Gen 1:31/Exod 39:43; Gen 2:1/Exod 39:32; Gen 2:2/Exod 40:33; and Gen 2:3/Exod 39:43. Cassuto, *Genesis*, 9–10; Balentine, *Torah's Vision*, 139.

134. Cassuto, *Genesis*, 38; Eichrodt, *Theology of the Old Testament*, 1:93; Rendtorff, *Canonical Hebrew Bible*, 419; Walton, *Lost World*, 59. While the accepted cosmology of the ANE is almost certainly behind the division of the waters above and below, the observation that the רקיע separated the waters and provided a safe place within them is easily related to the exodus itself. As God relays the Torah—which certainly would have included the Creation account—within the narrative, he does so to a people who had just finished walking between two bodies of water. Accepting the formation of Israel at Sinai as a creative event, it is notable that just as the temple of Creation saw God separate the waters to provide a holy place so too did God separate the Red Sea to provide a people called to be holy safety as they journeyed to meet him.

manifested; second, the land produces vegetation of various sorts but always "according to its kind" (למינו).

The gathering of the waters into one place is certainly a further imposition of order upon primordial chaos. Whether this is suggestive of the formation of a celestial laver of some sort is debatable; however, the delimitation of the chaotic waters allows for the first appearance of יבשה. While not an exceptionally rare word, יבשה is used sparingly in the Old Testament (14 times) and always in either a creative or a soteriological context. The most important occurrences outside of Gen 1:9–10 are in Exod 14:16, 22, 29 where the word is deliberately used to describe the ground that Israel walked upon when led by YHWH through the ים־סוף. Further instances of יבשה reiterate and remind the audience of the exodus event (Exod 15:19; Ps 66:6; and Neh 9:11). Psalm 66:6 may conflate the crossing of the Red Sea with the crossing of the Jordan, which also is described as a dry-land crossing in Josh 4:22. The promise of restoration in Isa 44:3 does not reflect back to the exodus event *per se*, but rather anticipates the second exodus when the Remnant will be released from Babylon. The deliverance of the Israelites was—as already discussed—a precursor to the *creation* of the nation of Israel. The formation of the people of God is deliberately linked to the presence of the dry land found in the temple that is God's Creation.[135]

יבשה is also used three times in the book of Jonah, where it describes God's authority over the storm—a representation of chaos—in the language of Creation (Jonah 1:9, 13), and the vomiting of Jonah onto the dry land (Jonah 2:11) as an act of salvation. It is notable that the prayer preceding Jonah's expulsion is laden with temple imagery: the prophet who prayed for the temple (Jonah 2:4b, 7–9) was not vomited onto ארץ, but rather יבשה. The connection is distinct and suggests that the dry ground motif of Creation was linked not only to cosmic authority but also temple worship. In

---

135. There is one additional occurrence of יבשה besides the Jonah references: Exod 4:9, where YHWH tells Moses to pour water from the Nile onto "dry ground" as a demonstration of God's power. While this initially seems to refer to the actions in Exod 7:14–19; the text does not portray this occurring. Instead Moses strikes the river with his staff to initiate the plague.

While it is possible that Exod 4:9 and Exod 7:14–19 are referring to the same incident, an alternative exists. God does not directly mention the first nine plagues in Exodus 4, except to refer to "all the miracles" preceding the death of the Pharaoh's firstborn (vv. 21–23). Understanding this, it is possible to read Exod 4:9 as a conflation of all the plagues, beginning with the waters of the Nile (the first plague) and ending with an outpouring of blood (the final plague). That the outpouring of blood occurs on dry ground connects the death of the Egyptians with the deliverance of the Israelites and embodies both the justice and the grace of YHWH. Read in this manner, Exod 4:9 does not refer to the first plague anymore than—and arguably considerably less than—it refers to the crossing of the Red Sea on dry ground.

this manner, every instance of יבשה outside of Gen 1:9–10 overtly demands the presence of God or connects to the place of God. Since this is the case, the argument that the dry ground of the third day is a temple motif not only remains sustainable, but also becomes preferable.[136]

The second phase of the third day then builds upon the foundation of יבשה to erect the flora that provides structure to Creation.[137] The critical aspect of vv. 11–13 is found in the phrase "according to their own kind" (למינהו). This phase, as previously noted, is used exclusively in priestly contexts and directly relates to the differentiation and discernment entrusted to the priests in their evaluations of holiness.[138] The conflation of creation narratives and salvation narratives establishes the role of the priests: they were to ensure things were holy by ensuring that they were good and in the proper place.[139] The third day of Creation, then, establishes the place of God/temple with the יבשה, but also orders Creation according to kinds and provides the context for the duties of the people of God/priests.

Genesis 1:14–19—Establishing the Schedule of the Temple

The fourth day of Creation is perhaps the most overtly priestly passage to this point. The formation of the celestial bodies as physical lights for the world is—theologically speaking—mostly irrelevant. The important aspect of this passage is not *that* the cosmic lights were formed, since light was already present from day 1, but rather *why* they were formed.

The text is explicit in assigning the celestial lights the calendaring of "signs and for seasons, and for days and for years (Gen 1:14 ESV)." Collectively, these clearly refer to the establishment of holy days and share the same phraseology for seasons (or literally, "appointed times") as Lev 23:2 and Lev 23:44.[140] The discussion of the Israelite feasts and festivals in Leviticus 23 is immediately followed in Lev 24:1–4 with a discussion of the

---

136. While he does not relate it directly to the יבשה, Clifford does suggest that the Creation narrative as a whole subtly but distinctively introduces the land and seed themes of the Old Testament. Since the land serves as a cypher of sorts for communion with God, it can claim a certain inherently soteriological role not dissimilar than what is here proposed. Clifford, *Creation Accounts*, 139.

137. Walton, *Lost World*, 57.

138. Cf. Mathews, *Genesis 1—11:26*, 153.

139. This conflation of Creation and Salvation also gravitates against the perception that Creation is a secondary concern of the Scriptures (contra Dempster). Salvation and Creation theologies both serve the same purpose of instilling a holy status into humankind. Cf. Dempster, *Dominion and Dynasty*, 58.

140. Smith, *Priestly Vision*, 98.

lights of the tabernacle. The connection between the appointed times (מוֹעֵד) and the lights (מָאוֹר) in both passages can hardly be considered accidental. This pairing becomes even more significant when considered in light of the priestly duty to "arrange" (עָרַךְ) the lights, setting them in order before YHWH. While priestly arrangement is not identical to the divine designation/division of Genesis 1, it is equivalent in the sense of establishing an ordered pattern for the proper conduct of worship.[141]

Since the formation of Israel and the tabernacle simultaneously represented a new creative act and established exemplars for worship to the rest of the created world, the juxtaposition of the lights and the appointed times is not only reasonable but also expected.[142] Since the biblical creation accounts should be read sympathetically, the formation of the place of worship and the times of worship in Genesis 1 and in the Exodus-Leviticus passages should inform one another.[143] There is a great deal of legitimacy to asking whether the lights of Leviticus 24 represent the celestial bodies of Genesis 1, or if the lights of Creation represent the lamps of the tabernacle. While it can be said that the lights of the tabernacle were arranged according to the calendar, it may also be asserted that, theologically speaking, the stars were created with the express purpose of pointing people to the feasts to come.[144] In truth, the best approach is not to determine priority but to appreciate the synthesis of the two passages as dual creations of the place of worship—whether the Israelite tabernacle or the Temple of Creation itself.[145]

Genesis 1:15–19 might seem rather mundane compared to the theologically pregnant v. 14; however, the overall context of the Creation narrative opposes a merely mundane interpretation. First, the fact that the cosmic luminaries served to "give light" upon the earth should not lead one to ignore the previous connection between the light of day 1 and the Torah or the Presence of God. The sun, moon, and stars therefore serve as instruments for the knowledge of YHWH.[146] Care should be taken at

141. Beale, *Temple*, 34.

142. Ibid.

143. This was fully recognized in antiquity and formed part of early Jewish writings: Josephus Ant. 3:145, War 5:217; Philo Rer. Div. Her. 221–25, 227; Vit. Mos. 2:102–5, Quaest. Exod. 2:73–81; et al. Beale, *Temple*, 46.

144. Barker, *Gate of Heaven*, 58–59; Gorman, *Ideology of Ritual*, 39.

145. Beale, *Temple*, 62. Similarly, Solomon's temple—decorated with flowers and trees—is designed as a garden sanctuary, which easily allows parallels to be drawn between the temple and Gen 1:11–13 and/or Gen 2:8–9. But whether those parallels base the aesthetic of the temple on Creation or the aesthetics of Creation on the temple depend entirely on whether one is looking at Creation as a chronological activity or a cultic one. Barker, *Gate of Heaven*, 57; cf. Morrow, "Creation as Temple Building," 6.

146. Cf. Cassuto, *Genesis*, 46.

this point; this is not suggesting a form of nature worship or inordinate natural theology. Instead, it reflects on the previous connection between the luminaries and the appointed times. As guides for the religious calendar, the sun and other celestial bodies become pointers to the feasts and festivals of the Torah, where the Presence of God was experienced. This position is strengthened by the work of the sun and moon in dividing (בדל) between the light and darkness—a work clearly patterned after God's creative activity in Gen 1:4, 6–7. In other words, YHWH established light and divided it from the darkness. The celestial bodies, as managers of the ritual calendar, reflect when and how the light is shed on the earth to divide between the holy and the unholy. This theomorphic activity of the cosmic luminaries clearly connects not only with the idea of temple, but also with the idea of the priestly activity that further mimics God's work.[147]

Genesis 1:20–23—Creation of Living Things and the Security of the Temple

The fifth and sixth days of Creation share a common theme of populating the realms previously established in the second and third days, respectively. In this, they serve to provide both orderliness (through their symmetry) and purposefulness (through the introduction of living creatures). The connection between life and order is further enhanced by the inclusion of the למינו formula, where all life properly follows its own kind. While the theological statements of life and order are both the primary and the obvious emphasis of these two days, the specific pattern of the fifth day adds an element lacking from the other days of Creation. Rather than the normal creative speech statements ("Let there be X" / And there was X), Gen 1:21 elaborates the creative speech and emphasizes the creative action of God.[148]

The elaboration of the creative speech is found in v. 21a, where the response to the statement of creating fish and fowl is elaborated to include not only fish and fowl but also "the great sea creatures" (התנינם הגדלים). Just as importantly YHWH did not simply "make" (עשה) the sea creatures, but "created" (ברא) them. These distinctive inclusions serve to elevate the creation of day 5 beyond the normal sphere of fish and fowl in two critical

---

147. Smith, *Priestly Vision*, 97–98. The connection between the luminaries and אדם can also be strengthened by noting that though different words are used (משל and רדה), only the luminaries and humankind are assigned authoritative roles within Creation. Further, in its celebration of YHWH's majesty, Psalm 8 distinctly notes the authority of both the luminaries (implicit in their ordination) and humanity (explicit in their rule). Van Wolde, *Stories of the Beginning*, 18.

148. Vogels, "And God Created," 349–50.

ways. First, the creation of mundane objects seems to favor עשה; it is generally accepted that ברא involves some form of special or supernatural agency that is reserved for God alone.[149] In the context of Genesis 1, ברא is used only in Gen 1:1, 27; Gen 2:3; and in the present verse. Both Gen 1:1 and Gen 2:3 are discussing the overall Creation event and therefore should be understood as expecting a particularly supernatural emphasis. Gen 1:27 reflects on the creation of humankind, who bearing the divine image are both inherently mundane and equally inherently spiritual creatures.[150] The distribution of ברא therefore suggests that the creatures of day 5 serve a supernatural or cosmic purpose in some way.[151]

The key to understanding this purpose may reside in the specific and deliberate inclusion of the תנינם. Variously translated in the English, the normative reading of תנינם is as a supernatural creature most often associated with primordial chaos (cf. Isa 27:1; 51:9; Jer 51:34; Ezek 29:3; 32:2 [metaphorically]; Ps 74:13). Even in passages where the תינן is translated "serpent" either a supernatural demeanor or background to the expression is prevalent, as shown in Exod 7:9-10, 12 (cf. Deut 32:33 and Job 7:12) where the serpent is in contradistinction to YHWH, and Pss 91:13 and 148:7 where it is subjugated by God or his messianic king. With this pattern of usage, the best reading of תנין expects an inherently supernatural connotation.[152] If this expectation is combined with the contemporary cultural tendency to associate the untamed seas of the world with primordial chaos, the great sea monsters touch—in the eyes of the original audience at least—both the mundane and the supernatural worlds.[153]

Considering the polemical nature of Genesis 1, the statement of day 5 serves to not only populate the mundane world with living creatures in an

---

149. Garr, "God's Creation," 86–87; Morgenstern, "Sources," 201.

150. This dual nature of humanity will be discussed further in a proceeding section; however, even a brief consideration of Gen 1:26–27 and Gen 2:7 suggest an intimacy between God and human beings that warrants a creation (ברא) in Genesis 1 rather than a mere formation (עשה). Even in Gen 2:7 where Adam is shaped (יצר) there is a sense of intimacy between God and humanity that is not inherent to עשה.

151. A comparison between the Hebrew ברא and the Akkadian *banu* (which may be the Akkadian cognate) further supports the idea that ברא is indicative of something that transcends normality. It is this idea of transcending normality that encompasses the Old Testament idea of the supernatural. Since God is involved with his Creation, it is "natural" for him to work within it. However, while the signs, wonders, and other miracles of YHWH can be—with this in mind—deemed "natural" they are not normal experiences, and therefore are best categorized as supernatural despite the intimacy between God and his world. Cassuto, *Genesis*, 69.

152. Vogels, "God Created the *Tanninim*," 357.

153. Ibid., 358.

orderly system; but also clearly establish God as the creator and master over the supernatural creatures of chaos.[154] This establishment of divine creation serves the polemical purposes of contrasting the sovereignty of YHWH against the pagan creation accounts and providing assurance to the Hebrew audience that though chaotic beings exist in the world, they are under the dominion and limitation of God.[155] While not an overt statement, this declaration establishes the legitimacy and security of the temple as a place of worship: the chaos-beasts are creatures of the water; the temple is over the water and protected by the מבדיל.[156] Creation is not a part of chaos; it is a Sanctuary that even the dragons can enter into only as God allows.[157]

Genesis 1:24–25—Creation of Living Things and the Proper Temple Order

As discussed under Gen 1:20–23, the population of living creatures serves to provide both symmetry and purposefulness to Creation. As with the fifth day, the various animals are created "according to their kind" (למינהו). This establishment of order is perhaps even more important for the sixth day than the fifth, simply because human beings—the ones who would

---

154. Walton, *Lost World*, 65–66; Smith, *Priestly Vision*, 60. The text may hint further at these dual realms in the blessing of v. 22. The water creatures are to fill the waters, but the birds do not multiply in the air and instead multiply on the earth. There is a distinction between waters and earth rather than between the waters and the air, perhaps utilizing the same cosmological concepts as day 3 in addition to the division of chaos in day 2.

155. Mathews, *Genesis 1—11:26*, 156–57; Cassuto, *Genesis*, 50–51; Vogels, "God Created the *Tanninim*," 360.

156. The mythic language of Genesis 1 is a further affirmation of this reading. The only significant problem that presents in this interpretation is the summary statement that the creation of day 5—which obviously included the תנינם—was "good." However, this concern is unwarranted. Whatever later connotations may have been applied to the תנינם, the point of Genesis is simply to assert that the תנינם were created in accordance with divine will.

A proper interpretation of the creation of the תנינם should reflect an understanding that the טב of Genesis 1 is not a moral statement, but a perfective one. The ultimate sovereignty of God is reflective of the divine purpose and plan. As long as the תנינם serve a divine purpose, then the goodness of day 5 is not imperiled (Maimonides, *Guide for the Perplexed* 3:13). Any arguments of theodicy provoked by later references to a cosmic battle with the תנינם are extraneous to Genesis 1's purpose and unlikely to concern a people who accepted the both the righteousness of God and the reality of evil from a starting position of trust; cf. Renckens, *Israel's Concept*, 17; Dempster, *Dominion and Dynasty*, 42.

157. Interestingly, if the תנינם are associated with the נחש of Genesis 3, then the sin of the garden served to undo the effects of day 5 by failing to protect the sanctuary (Eden) from evil invasion. Beale, *Temple*, 87.

appreciate and understand the orderliness of Creation—are land animals themselves and the majority of their interactions with other creatures take place on land.

The repetition of the למינו-formula in both sections is distinctive, and lends understanding to the dietary laws.[158] Setting aside the unnecessary suggestion that the dietary laws were intended for healthful reasons and the illogical suggestion that the division between clean and unclean animals in Leviticus 11 was arbitrary, the most natural reading of the text of Leviticus is to consider unclean animals as those which violate the principles of life and order—principles established at Creation.[159]

The connection between Leviticus 11 and Gen 1:20–25 connects the priesthood to a proper understanding of Creation itself, essentially placing Creation into the purview of priestly authority.[160] Just as it can be asked whether the tabernacle lights were the type or the archetype of the lights in Gen 1:14, the question can be raised whether Creation was established to illustrate the cleanliness laws, or whether the dietary laws were presented to teach the true nature of Creation. In either case, however, the emphasis remains on expositing the nature of YHWH as a God of Life and Order.[161]

---

158. Mathews, *Genesis 1—11:26*, 157.

159. Neville, "Differentiation," 213. The suggestion that the dietary code of Leviticus was intended for nutritional or healthful reasons is unnecessary in light of the contextual connections between the laws and holiness and the linguistic connections between the laws and Creation. Further, Leviticus 11 should be read in light of Lev 10:10–11 where the priests are commanded to (a) distinguish/divide between the clean and the unclean and (b) teach all the statutes of YHWH.

The distinction between classifications in Lev 10:10 is marked by בדל, the determinative activity of God in Creation (Gen 1:4, 6–7, 14, 18). But just as importantly is the connection with v. 11 where the priests are commanded to teach the statutes of God. This command to teach can reasonably be argued as a reiteration or a result of the priestly discernment: by dividing properly between the clean and the unclean, the priests teach the statutes (and for that matter, the orderly and living nature) of God.

Gesenius actually argues that Lev 10:10 is likely a later redaction to the text. If this is true, it only serves to add credibility to the argument that the priestly task to divide is sympathetic with his task to teach. If v. 10 is a later redaction, then it was inserted into the text parallel to ולהורת demonstrating a connection in the minds of the redactor between the discerning and the teaching tasks. As a result, the divisions of the unclean and clean are themselves a teaching element to lead people to an understanding of who the Lord is. The cleanliness laws are therefore teaching tools for a greater understanding of God's nature. Gorman, *Ideology of Ritual*, 44; Goldingay, *Israel's Life*, 611, 617; Gesenius, *Hebrew Grammar*, 351.

160. Smith, *Priestly Vision*, 91–92.

161. Firmage, "Genesis 1," 109–10.

Detailed Exegetical Analysis of Gen 1:26–28

The preceding examination of the days of Creation has served to establish the temple-building and/or priestly concerns of Genesis 1. This emphasis on temple and sacral concerns cannot be ignored when interpreting the pinnacle of Creation, human beings, and the nature of those beings as the image(s) of God. Even before any examination of vv. 26–28 is begun, there is already a certain expectation that humankind will serve a temple role. Ultimately, the question is not *whether* humanity has a temple role, but rather of *what* that temple role might consist.[162]

Gen 1:26: The Designation of Humankind

וַיֹּאמֶר אֱלֹהִים נַעֲשֶׂה אָדָם בְּצַלְמֵנוּ כִּדְמוּתֵנוּ וְיִרְדּוּ בִדְגַת הַיָּם וּבְעוֹף הַשָּׁמַיִם וּבַבְּהֵמָה וּבְכָל־הָאָרֶץ וּבְכָל־הָרֶמֶשׂ הָרֹמֵשׂ עַל־הָאָרֶץ:

Beginning with ויאמר אלהים, v. 26 begins in complete conformity with vv. 3, 6, 9, 11, 14, 20, and 24. This conformity, however, is immediately subverted by the replacement of the impersonal jussive that has followed each of the previous introductory formulae with a cohortative verb. Rather than the impersonal declarations that expect a response from Creation, the formation of humanity begins with a deliberation indicating a divine involvement. While the sovereign command of God is behind each of the previous creative acts, there is a level of marked intimacy in the present phrase.[163]

While the specific verb of creation (עשה) is unremarkable, the deliberation itself warrants considerable thought. The priestly nature of Genesis 1 and its deliberately polemical features weigh against the critical suggestions that the plural in v. 26 is simply a vestige of polytheistic thought; it is incongruous to presume such an obvious error would occur in such focused polemic.[164] Similarly, the suggestions that God is somehow collaborating with Creation itself requires an anthropomorphism that is deliberately avoided elsewhere in Genesis 1, where there is a careful distinction between living creatures and the nonliving structures of the world (cf. v. 16 and the deliberate avoidance of שמש and ירח/לבנה).[165] Elimination of these two interpretations leaves only the suggestions that God is self-deliberating

---

162. Blenkinsopp, *Sage, Priest, Prophet*, 67–68.

163. Firmage, "Genesis 1," 101; Van Wolde, *Stories of the Beginning*, 24–25; cf. Renckens, *Israel's Concept*, 96–97.

164. Ryle, *Book of Genesis*, 18; Fletcher-Louis, "God's Image," 83; Renckens, *Israel's Concept*, 94; cf. Speiser, *Genesis*, 8.

165. Livingston, *Pentateuch*, 140; Walton, *Lost World*, 65.

or addressing the heavenly court. Again, the polemical nature of Genesis 1—combined with the monotheistic tenor and absence of any mention of the divine court—suggests that God was not deliberating with other supernatural beings.[166] This leaves only a divine self-deliberation as a contextually consistent interpretation.[167]

The self-deliberation of God may be interpreted as either an inner dialogue or simply an expression of the divine mind utilizing a plural of majesty. The idea of an inner dialogue is unlikely the primary concern. There are four passages in the Old Testament utilizing a plural in the context of divine deliberation: Gen 1:26; 3:22; 11:7; and Isa 6:8.[168] Notably, each of the four occurrences involve a degree of intimacy between God and humankind: in the divine-touched nature of humanity (whether as a positive (Gen 1:26) or

---

166. Fletcher-Louis, "God's Image," 83. Suggestions that monotheism was a late addition to Hebrew theology, and that they were primarily henotheistic still fail to bolster this position. Whether Israel was more properly henotheistic or monotheistic does not change the clear emphasis on the solitary activity of YHWH in Creation. Even when other elements are brought in to "assist" in the formation of the world (such as the earth being responsible for producing plants [v. 11] and animals [v. 24]), the creative activity is both fully under the sole authority of God's command and lacking any suggestion of heavenly assistants.

Further, scholars who claim a late monotheism are often advocates of the documentary hypothesis as well. This is a self-defeating position, since the P-document underlying Genesis 1 was itself a late addition to the Scriptures. It would be unusual for the same priests who advocated monotheism to concurrently suggest that the heavenly host aided God in Creation.

Some scholars, such as Middleton, continue to prefer the context of a divine court and see this as not a deliberation *per se* between God and the heavenly host, but rather an explication before the host of what God's intention as sole creator is. Interestingly, one of the examples Middleton choses to support his assertion is the transition of responsibility for the garden from Adam to the cherub in Gen 3:24 (cf. Gen 2:15) and the intertextual examples of the heavenly host in Isaiah 6 and similar passages. However, while Middleton could be correct, it is notable that the transfer of Eden from Adam to the cherub retains concern for the custody of the holy place. Similarly, comparison of humankind with the angels (or more properly seraphim) in Isaiah 6 only reinforce a cultic understanding of the *imago Dei*, since Isaiah 6 is a clearly cultic context and the seraphim serve as some form of temple attendants insuring the holiness of those present (cf. Isa 6:6–7). Finally, the angels proper (מלאכים) have been linked in cognate studies to idealized and non-autonomous messenger figures that serve to bring divine instruction and edify the faithful in the will of God. That all three of these duties (custody of the holy place, intercession and purification of the unclean, and edification in the divine will) are linked to priestly tasks cannot be lightly ignored. Middleton, *Liberating Image*, 59–60; Handy, "Dissenting Deities," 24–29.

167. Reyburn and Fry, *Handbook*, 50.

168. It should be observed that it is only in Gen 1:26 that the divine deliberation precedes a creative act. This is a unique deliberation that serves to emphasize even more the special importance of humankind. Cassuto, *Genesis*, 55.

a negative (3:22) feature), the need for God to interact with the humans attempting to besiege heaven by force (Gen 11:7), and the willingness of God to interact with humankind in a soteriological manner (Isa 6:8). In each of these passages, there is presentation of divine sovereignty. This connection between sovereignty and the deliberation of God suggests that the plural of majesty is the most natural reading of the text. This is not to suggest that there is no room for self-deliberation in the context, but rather to recognize that the emphasis of the self-deliberation is not on the inner dialogue of the divine but on the careful pronouncement of God.[169] When the deliberative God speaks, it is with purposeful and authoritative action that directly impacts humankind in general and human activity specifically in at least three of the four occasions. In Gen 3:22, the deliberative speech of God results in the ejection of humankind from the garden "lest he reach out his hand and take also of the tree of life and eat"—prohibiting human activity. Similarly, Gen 11:7 precedes God's confusion of the rebels of Babel—prohibiting human activity. Isaiah 6:8 presents an opposite result where God's deliberation results in Isaiah's surrender to his prophetic role—initiating human activity. Considering this distribution, it is reasonable to suggest that the divine deliberation of Gen 1:26 also sets the stage for the initiation of human activity. God is not holding a debate within himself, but sovereignly establishing the role of humankind.[170]

The deliberative intimacy of the formation of the human creature also serves to distinguish the creation of humanity from the other created beings. This distinction effectively designates or "divides" humankind from other living creatures, continuing the depiction of God's creative work as one of separation or division. The separation of humankind is also accomplished by a transition away from the למינו formula: human beings are not, in Genesis 1, formed "after their kind" but rather in the image and likeness

---

169. Cf. Brunner, *Man in Revolt*, 98. Similarly, while Gen 1:26 does not inhibit a Trinitarian understanding of God or the community found within the divine *hypostaseis*, it does not require a Trinitarian interpretation. The ability to see the Trinity in this text by post-resurrection Christians is a function of progressive revelation and not an interpretation that an ancient Israelite would likely have recognized. Contra Murphy, "Trinity," 176–77.

170. Cassuto, *Genesis*, 55–56; cf. Firmage, "Genesis 1," 101; Murphy, "Trinity," 174.

of God.¹⁷¹ This marks a critical shift in the text and presents an expectation upon humankind that is absent from the rest of Creation.¹⁷²

נַעֲשֶׂה אָדָם בְּצַלְמֵנוּ כִּדְמוּתֵנוּ

The rest of Creation, both nonliving and living, was formed with a role specific to its nature. The heavens (skies) and the dry ground's role in Creation was inherent to its very existence. Flora and fauna were expected to follow a set role, determined according to its kind, lest they violate the proper order and enter into uncleanliness. Humankind, on the other hand, is neither created for nor assigned a future role expecting them to act independently or according to their own manner.¹⁷³ Instead, humanity was assigned the role of emulating God directly.¹⁷⁴

The previous discussion of צלם and דמות have already established that the biblical connotation of these terms prefers a cultic aspect. More specifically, the preceding examination of Genesis 1 reveals God not only building the temple of Creation through the priestly activity of division, but also arranging the various pieces of Creation in an orderly and distinctively cultic manner. Combining both the general connotation and the specific context of Genesis 1, the best interpretation of the image of God is revealed.

---

171. Mathews, *Genesis 1—11:26*, 153; Van Wolde, *Stories of the Beginning*, 24. The emphasis on Adam's creation in the image of God is so distinct that the alteration of this formula in Gen 5:3 where Seth is formed in the image and likeness of Adam has generated considerable discussion. If the image of God is considered conditional rather than effectual, then the suggestion that Gen 5:3 argues for the loss of the divine image is possible. However, it is possible to read the transmission of the image of Adam to Seth in a positive way: Adam received the image of God, so the statement that Seth was "like Adam" in both דמות and צלם actually confirms that the generations following Adam did indeed share in the image of God. It provides a continuity with Adam, which then provides a continuity with the image of God. The use of the image of God in Gen 1:26 forms a disjunction between Adam and the rest of the living creatures; the use of the image of Adam in Gen 5:3 serves the opposite role of providing a conjunction and continuity between all of humanity and the original recipient of the *imago Dei*. This interpretation establishes the continuity that still exists even in the postdiluvian reestablishment of humankind (cf. Gen 9:6) and in the calling of Israel as God's representative nation.

172. Brunner, *Man in Revolt*, 82; Van Wolde, *Stories of the Beginning*, 29–30.

173. Berkouwer, *Man*, 23; Gogarten, "Das Problem," 493. Even the naming ceremony of Gen 2:18–25 avoids למינו when describing the relationship of Eve to Adam. She is not "after his kind" but suitable to him (כנגדו). The passage is careful to both distinguish Eve from Adam and affiliate her with him, but in no case is that a suggestion that they were to live according to their own pattern. The subsequent temptation of nascent humanity ties directly to this dependency: the Serpent's trap relies on humanity gaining the same self-determinative role that God has (Gen 3:5).

174. Eichrodt, *Theology of the Old Testament*, 2:127; Fletcher-Louis, "God's Image," 83–84; Sherlock, *Doctrine of Humanity*, 31.

While God is sovereign in his work, the imagery of the chapter is not overtly royal—the authority of God is presented more as a function of his nature as Creator and his *priestly* work of designation and ordering.[175] Since a priest is an authoritative figure, there is neither need nor benefit to assume that the sovereignty of God in Genesis 1 demands a royal interpretation of the divine image. On the other hand, the temple setting and cultic activity of God in Genesis 1 virtually demand a priestly role from the image of God. To this point in Scriptures, God is the priest over his Creation; with the creation of humankind, that priestly role is shared or delegated to the creature as an act of worship to the Creator.[176]

It might be noted as well that God is never called a priest. The understanding of God as priest is not based on a pronounced title, but on the activity that he performed.[177] Similarly, the image of God should not be looked at as a title or condition, but rather as a calling or performance assignment.[178] If humankind is to represent God, they will only do so through their activity.[179] The image of God is expressed through activity; it cannot therefore be lost, but only ignored.[180] This accounts for the continued presence of the image of God in humanity; the call to obediently curate the Creation remains, whether or not people respond to it.[181]

---

175. Goldingay, *Israel's Gospel*, 94; Neville, "Differentiation," 210–11.

176. Fletcher-Louis, "God's Image," 84; cf. Boer, *Ember*, 5. The greatest difficulty in describing God as a priest is the mediatory role of the priesthood. However, it is quite possible that the intercessory role of the priesthood has been misunderstood. Cody and Leithart have argued persuasively that he primary role of the priesthood was not intercessory but custodial. Alternately, Nelson has argued that the primary priestly duty was divinatory—a suggestion supported not only by the oracular use of the Urim and Thummim, but also by the priestly role of discerning between the clean and unclean. Either suggestion makes mediation or intercession a secondary activity of the priests.

An examination of the text of Genesis 1 reveals a well-ordered world; a world *before* it was disrupted by sin. With the coming of sin into the world, Creation was marred and humanity's relationship with God jeopardized. Any continued custody of Creation would necessitate a means of correcting the disharmony of sin, while a disrupted relationship between God and humankind would depend on the instruction and guidance provided by the priestly divinatory role. In either case, while the mediatory role is critically important it is not an independent role. It serves to reconnect humanity with God in a way that was originally present and therefore best seen as a function of custody or edification rather than a distinct role in itself.

177. Smith, *Priestly Vision*, 67; Goldingay, *Israel's Gospel*, 94.

178. Fletcher-Louis, "God's Image," 85; Mouroux, *Meaning of Man*, 28; Middleton, *Liberating Image*, 27, 35.

179. Hall, *Imaging God*, 61; Van Wolde, *Stories of the Beginning*, 30.

180. Sherlock, *Doctrine of Humanity*, 43; Van Wolde, *Stories of the Beginning*, 26–27.

181. Fletcher-Louis' analysis of this is apt: "The priestly image-of-God-in-humanity theology says that idolatry is ruled out of court because to locate divine presence and

וְיִרְדּוּ בִדְגַת הַיָּם וּבְעוֹף הַשָּׁמַיִם וּבַבְּהֵמָה וּבְכָל־הָאָרֶץ וּבְכָל־הָרֶמֶשׂ הָרֹמֵשׂ עַל־הָאָרֶץ׃

The declaration of humankind's creation in the divine image is directly followed by a distinct clause assigning humanity dominion over other creatures. This clause, along with the command to subdue Creation in Gen 1:28, is the primary source of the royal interpretations of the divine image. However, while רדה can designate royal sovereignty its usage in the Hebrew Bible does not prefer it. A royal figure is only related to רדה directly in six of its twenty-three occurrences[182] and indirectly in only four occurrences.[183] Outside of these ten occurrences (of which two are debatable) and the two uses in Gen 1:26, 28; רדה generally refers to a simple position of advantage or superiority from which the exercise of dominion flows. Of the remaining eleven occurrences, Ezek 34:4's reference to "shepherds" would certainly include royal figures, but cannot be assumed to exclude other leaders of the nation including the wayward priests that would have been of particular interest to Ezekiel.[184] The treading of the winepress in Joel 4:13 is a result of a divine judgment where YHWH roars from Zion (v. 16), which can legitimately be interpreted as a royal picture; however, the connection between Zion and the temple mount (Ps 78:68–69 et al.) and the responsive nature of this judgment against sin cannot be ignored. Further, the primary importance of Zion is found in the communion there between God and humankind, particularly in the eschatological hope of Israel.[185] Communion with the divine is not a royal prerogative (in Israel, at least), but a priestly one. Similarly, God's dominion over the fire that entered Jeremiah's bones in Lam 1:13 is surrounded by indictments of cultic failure rather than royal imagery (cf. Lam 1:4, 8–9a, 17, 22, et al.). The house of Israel, not the house of Judah/David, exercises dominion in Isa 14:2, and the "upright" in Ps 49:15 is indicative of those who are righteous rather than those who are royal. The five remaining occurrences of רדה all present dominion as a collective activ-

---

action in another part of creation or in that which we create is to absolve ourselves of *our own responsibility to bear divine presence and action*" (emphasis added). The bearing of divine presence is inherently cultic, and even ancient neighbors of Israel that celebrated a god-king directly tied the god-king to the cult as well as the court. Fletcher-Louis, "God's Image," 85.

182. Num 24:19; 1 Kgs 5:4; Isa 14:6; 41:2 (assuming that YHWH is being presented as a royal figure—though the context of v. 4 suggest that the authority and dominion that God is invoking is based not on royal prerogative but his role as Creator); Pss 72:8; 110:2.

183. 1 Kg. 5:30 [2 Chr 8:10]; 9:23; Ezek 29:15 (though this is a reference to the kingdom(s) as a whole, and does not refer to an individual royal figure in any way).

184. Goldingay, *Israel's Life*, 723.

185. Ross, *Recalling the Hope of Glory*, 82–83.

ity of a nation rather than specifically royal. The enemies of Israel exercise dominion in Lev 26:17 and Neh 9:28, while the Israelite people themselves are forbidden dominion over one another in Lev 25:43, 46, 53.[186]

Ultimately, the biblical usage of רדה is used in both overtly royal and decidedly common contexts. It can indicate oppression, as with the reign of the pagans over Israel; but it can also simply be a factual statement, as with the dominion of Solomon's administrators. With this recognition, there is no reason to impose a specifically royal connotation on Gen 1:26 when a generalized ascription of advantageous position resulting in an authoritative status is both more consistent with the general use of רדה and more in keeping with the priestly tenor of Genesis 1.[187]

The objects of human dominion are comprehensive; including not only the animals of sea, air, and land, but also the land itself. Contrary to Sailhamer's suggestion that the "land" of Creation is isolated to the promised land, the intention of Gen 1:26 is to emphasize the expansiveness of human responsibility throughout each of the spheres of Creation.[188] The inclusion of the structure of Creation (the land) alongside the animals further suggests that the dominion of humanity exists for custodial reasons, as the inanimate land is not subject to the rule of human kings.

Overall, Gen 1:26 serves as a direct statement of divine intention for human beings. The assignation of the image of God upon humankind is a statement of intentionality that is focused more on the task of humanity than any specific condition.[189] It is by living as the image of God that humankind fulfills their ordered purpose in Creation.[190] The statement of dominion that follows the image of God is a mode or a result of the divine image: it is by serving as the image of God that humans have custody of Creation and by properly maintaining the Creation humankind reveals God's own nature.[191]

---

186. It is worth noting that the use of רדה in the priestly materials of Leviticus and the prophecies of those from priestly backgrounds (Jeremiah and Ezekiel) distinctly avoid a royal designation of רדה, favoring instead statements of restraint to the common person in Leviticus and observations of judgment for cultic violations in the two prophetic books.

187. Not coincidentally, when not acting in a religious capacity Israelite priests often served as magistrates. This expression of their authority coincides with the general ascription of authority found in Gen 1:26–28. Blenkinsopp, *Sage, Priest, Prophet*, 2.

188. Sailhamer, *Genesis Unbound*, 54–57.

189. Sherlock, *Doctrine of Humanity*, 32; Firmage, "Genesis 1," 102–3.

190. Davies, *Anthropology and Theology*, 202; Van Wolde, *Stories of the Beginning*, 26–29; cf. Jewett, *Man as Male and Female*, 21.

191. Mouroux, *Meaning of Man*, 28; Blenkinsopp, *Sage, Priest, Prophet*, 81; Davies, *Anthropology and Theology*, 145; Van Wolde, *Stories of the Beginning*, 26; Smith, *Priestly Vision*, 70.

Gen 1:27: The Creation of Humankind

וַיִּבְרָא אֱלֹהִים ׀ אֶת־הָאָדָם בְּצַלְמוֹ

בְּצֶלֶם אֱלֹהִים בָּרָא אֹתוֹ

זָכָר וּנְקֵבָה בָּרָא אֹתָם:

Structurally, v. 27 is an interruption to the text; its poetry is distinct from both v. 26 and v. 28 and its absence would not directly affect the flow of thought from v. 26 to v. 28. In fact it seems like the interpolation and the distinction of its poetry draw special attention to the uniqueness of this particular verse in Genesis 1. It is insufficient to observe that Gen 1:27 is simply poetic; the subject matter and the overall context of Genesis 1 ensure that it is read as a mytho-poetic statement. Further, Cassuto asserts that the tetrameter of the verse reflects epic poetry designed to elevate the grandeur of the verse.[192] It is not simply serving to invoke the passions of the readers as poetry does, but rather directly connecting those passions to the divine source.[193]

The poetic construction is a basic tristich, with the first two lines forming a chiasmus and the third serving as a synthetic statement. Both line A and B utilize the creative verb ברא, emphasizing both intimacy and purposefulness;[194] while the chiasmus places the emphasis of human existence upon their image-bearing capacity. It is notable that both the emphasis (צלם) and the action (ברא) of these lines contain connotations of divine purpose.[195]

Where lines A and B serve to emphasize the assignment of duty to humankind, the synthetic line C ensures that all of humanity received this role.[196]

---

192. Cassuto, *Genesis*, 11.

193. Cf. Collins, *Genesis 1–4*, 78–79.

194. Throughout the Old Testament, the use of ברא is isolated to mythic contexts. Whether divine judgment, theophany, or reference to Creation/re-Creation; ברא consistently connects the supernatural realm with the mundane realm in an intentional way.

Morgenstern, influenced by Schwally, inadvertently argues for just this position, since he considers even ברא to be a more mundane expression of the Creation than *creatio per dictum*. However, while Morgenstern is quick to argue that the presence of both the intimate ברא and the transcendental divine fiat indicate a conflation of earlier sources, this argument ignores the essential unity of Genesis 1. In a chapter that is emphasizing the glory of the Creator, the fact that God interacts with his Creation-Temple in an intimate way does not impede his majestic nature but in fact amplifies it: the God who is so great to create by statement alone is also the God who is so good to interact with his Creation in a more personal way. Morgenstern, "Sources," 171–75.

195. Cf. Cassuto, *Genesis*, 57. The absence of דמות in v. 27 serves as further evidence that any distinction between צלם and דמות is largely artificial. The terms are similar enough in v. 26 that the summary emphasis of v. 27 does not need to repeat both words: by emphasizing the divine image, the likeness is assumed.

196. Niskanen, "Poetics of Adam," 428.

The structure of line C duplicates line B with the exception of the replacement of בצלם with זכר ונקבה, and the change of plurality in the direct object. This duplication lends support to the idea that the image of God is a relational aspect, as its parallel listing of genders certainly hearkens to community.[197] But while the image of God must include some elements of relationship, there is no reason in the present context to limit the divine image to a simple communalism. Verse 27 is better read with an emphasis toward inclusion, expanding the purposeful creation of humankind from the individual Adam to the entire race.[198] To a certain extent, זכר ונקבה can be read not only for the inclusion of women, but also as a merism stating that every human being is created by God and assigned the purpose of representing him in this Creation.[199] Against arguments that v. 27 is a late interpolation, the creation of both male and female serves to prepare humanity for the reception of blessing in v. 28—being fruitful and multiplying demands both man and woman.[200]

The simplicity of Gen 1:27 in both construction and content belies its importance. As a poetic summation, the verse does not add a great deal of new information to the passage, but instead serves as an emphatic culmination of the Creation: ultimately Genesis 1 was written to humans to inform them of both who God is and who they were to be.[201] The deliberate use of ברא provides both intimacy with God and a supernatural purpose to humanity, while the image of God itself serves as the role of humankind and reflects on what God has already done in Creation.[202] It is informational in theology and applicational in anthropology.[203]

197. Jewett, *Man as Male and Female*, 27.

198. Renckens, *Israel's Concept*, 109; Frevel, "Gottesbildlichkeit und Menschenwürde," 273; Schroer and Staubli, "Bodily and Embodied," 16.

199. Van Wolde, *Stories of the Beginning*, 27–29; Niskanen, "Poetics of Adam," 428; cf. Sherlock, *Doctrine of Humanity*, 87.

200. Mathews, *Genesis 1—11:26*, 173–74. It is notable that the categorical terms of איש and אשה are absent, while the sexual terms of זכר and נקבה are preferred. The latter set of terms are suggestive of the activities of life rather than gender roles. Further, since the image of God is a calling to act as God acts it is also pertinent to observe that while some of the divine acts of Creation were isolated to men (such as the distinguishing of proper order by the priests), other acts are decidedly feminine (the creation of life cannot take place within men; it is the blessing of women to be the life-givers). Therefore, it becomes necessary for both male and female to exist if humankind is to truly represent who God is as his image-bearers. This is particularly noteworthy since the image of God has been alternately ascribed to both the authoritative and the procreative aspects of humankind. Cf. Niskanen, "Poetics of Adam," 432–33.

201. Sherlock, *Doctrine of Humanity*, 31–32; Walton, *Lost World*, 67; cf. Frost, *In His Image*, 41.

202. Cf. Middleton, *New Heaven*, 41–43.

203. Davies, *Anthropology and Theology*, 145–51; Brunner, *Man in Revolt*, 28, 50; cf.

Gen 1:28: The Direction of Humankind

וַיְבָ֣רֶךְ אֹתָם֮ אֱלֹהִים֒ וַיֹּ֨אמֶר לָהֶ֜ם אֱלֹהִ֗ים פְּר֥וּ וּרְב֛וּ וּמִלְא֥וּ אֶת־הָאָ֖רֶץ וְכִבְשֻׁ֑הָ וּרְד֞וּ בִּדְגַ֤ת הַיָּם֙ וּבְע֣וֹף הַשָּׁמַ֔יִם וּבְכָל־חַיָּ֖ה הָֽרֹמֶ֥שֶׂת עַל־הָאָֽרֶץ:

Having declared his intentions for human life and created them accordingly, God next speaks directly to humanity. The verse neatly divides between two divine actions: the blessing of God and the speech of God. The critical factor for interpreting this verse is in understanding how these two actions relate to one another. Read simply, the two clauses coordinate sequentially: God blessed, then he spoke. However, just as the dominion over Creation in v. 26 was a descriptive elaboration of the image of God and the creation of the sexes in v. 27 revealed an expanded role for the image of God; so the divine speech of v. 28b is best read as an explanation of the blessing of v. 28a.

וַיְבָ֣רֶךְ אֹתָם֮ אֱלֹהִים֒

Before adequately addressing the connection between v. 28a and v. 28b, it is necessary first to consider the connection between v. 28 as a whole and vv. 26–27. Whether v. 28 is connected with v. 27 as its immediate predecessor or with v. 26 (treating v. 27 as a later interpolation), it is directly related to humanity's creation in the image of God. It is important nonetheless to determine if the relationship is to the image of God or to the creative act.

God had previously and would again bless parts of Creation that did not bear the divine image (v. 22; Gen 2:3); recognizing this, it seems best to attribute the blessing of God to the creative act itself rather than to the image of God.[204] It is with this understanding that the syntax of v. 28a must be understood. The clause could be attributive, describing the creative act itself as the blessing; resultant, a consequence of having been created; or consequent, the natural continuation of the creative act. The attributive use would be unusual, particularly in light of the subsequent explanatory dialogue. It is possible to suggest that the blessing is a result of Creation; however, then there must be an accounting for the elements of Creation that are not directly blessed in the text, including land animals. Therefore, the best interpretation of this text is to recognize the blessing as a continuation of the creative activity of God.

There is another connection between the blessing and God's creative work in Genesis 1. The blessing of created things occurs in vv. 22, 28, and

---

Beale, *Temple*, 47; Collins, *Genesis 1–4*, 132.

204. This is not to suggest that the assignment of the image of God was not a blessing upon humankind, but rather to properly understand that possession of the image of God—either as condition or as calling—is contingent upon being created.

Gen 2:3; each of those verses describe something that was not simply made in the normal sense (עשה), but created with a supernatural connection (ברא). It would be incorrect to say that blessing is contingent on ברא in Genesis 1, but there is a distinct connection between the two terms. The mythic formation of living creatures expects a blessing that the more mundane aspects of Creation lack.[205] The particular role of the blessing in Gen 1:28 is to declare to humankind, and thereby perhaps to all of Creation, the special role of humanity in representing God and to confirm the actualization of the deliberations of v. 26.[206] This actualization is further emphasized by the word order of the clause: rather than follow the normal *verb-subject-object* pattern, v. 28a utilizes a *verb-object-subject* pattern that draws attention to the object as the recipient of the blessing. While the implications of Hebrew word order should not be overemphasized, neither should they be ignored. The alteration of word order fits the overall emphasis of this passage in transitioning from the cosmic activity of God alone to the relational activity between God and humankind.[207]

וַיֹּאמֶר לָהֶם אֱלֹהִים פְּרוּ וּרְבוּ וּמִלְאוּ אֶת־הָאָרֶץ

The initial statement of the blessing upon mankind is an almost verbatim duplication of the blessing of v. 22, with the exception of the replacement of seas with land. Like the previous clause, the word order serves to emphasize the human recipients of this blessing. Where v. 22 stated there was a blessing and elaborated it (ויברך אתם אלהים לאמר), the construction of v. 28 treats the two actions separately. This break in pattern is not greatly significant, but it does serve to slow the reading down and provide an additional emphasis on the humans involved.

Since the fertility of humankind is a duplication of the blessing in v. 22, it is incorrect to overly emphasize the multiplication of humanity as an aspect or performance of the image of God. Even so, it is pertinent that those

---

205. This observation is made in the micro-context of the verses in question. Genesis 1:1 and 2:3 both indicate that all of Creation is a result of ברא, and therefore connect the entire Creation-Temple to God. Even so, the special uses of ברא within the theological bookends of Gen 1:1 and 2:3 should be noted and their contributions to the smaller contexts appreciated.

Another aspect of the blessings and their relationship to ברא might be seen in their Piel construction. The Piel of ברך assumes a factitive or a resultative syntax. The factitive Piel is often treated too similar to the causative Hiphil. But while the Hiphil emphasizes the cause of an activity, the Piel emphasizes the activity that was caused. The assumed "intensification" of a verb by the Piel is not entirely accurate: the action is not intensified so much as emphasized. In the case of Genesis 1, the Piel ברך emphasizes the end state of the created things: they are formed and brought about to an end state of being blessed.

206. Van Wolde, *Stories of the Beginning*, 24; cf. Beale, *Temple*, 117.

207. Balentine, *Torah's Vision*, 86–87; Fretheim, "Reclamation of Creation," 363.

creatures that were specifically created (ברא) in the divine image are the ones that received the specific command to "be fruitful and multiply."[208] The other objects of Creation were simply assumed to do so according to their kind. The intentionality of the spread of human beings is notable.[209]

וְכִבְשֻׁהָ וּרְדוּ בִּדְגַת הַיָּם וּבְעוֹף הַשָּׁמַיִם וּבְכָל־חַיָּה הָרֹמֶשֶׂת עַל־הָאָרֶץ׃

In a stark contrast to its initial duplication of v. 22, Gen 1:28's next clause expands the blessing of humankind well beyond the blessing of the sea creatures. While v. 22's blessing of the sea creatures was disjoined from the blessing to the fowl, v. 28 enjoins humanity's call to be fruitful and multiply to the calling to subdue (כבש) and reign over (רדה) the living things of Creation.

The correct understanding of רדה as a general statement of power or authority derived from superior position rather than a distinctly royal term has already been addressed, but the addition of כבש to the description of human dominion needs to be addressed. The general sense of כבש is one of forcible subdual, without any specific connotation of royalty but also somewhat unusual for a cultic context.[210] An examination of the actual Hebrew usage of this term reveals a distinct pattern that is germane to its interpretive context.

There are no spiritually neutral occurrences of כבש; the "trampling" subdual of the term is either directly related to sinful activity or connected to acts of righteousness. The term occurs fourteen times in the Old Testament, with six negative occurrences. Each of these occurrences involves the forced oppression of a fellow person, either through slavery (Jer 34:11, 16; Neh 5:5 [twice]; and 2 Chr 28:10) or (the appearance of) rape (Esther 7:8); events which are well outside of Gen 1:28's command to subdue the *non-human* creatures of Creation. Negative occurrences of כבש present a dehumanizing action that treats other human beings like animals in direct violation of their

---

208. Van Wolde, *Stories of the Beginning*, 28–29.

209. The mythic language of Gen 1:20–22 contrasts with the mythic language of v. 28. In the former passage, the fish are to fill the "waters" of the sea, not simply the sea itself. The inclusion of the waters, representative of chaos, is distinct. The birds are then separated from the fish of the waters by a disjunctive *waw* and told to multiply, but without the specification of fruitfulness.

On the other hand, humans—like the inhabitants of the primordial waters—are to both be fruitful and multiply. But where the emphasis on the divine creation of the תנינם in vv. 20–23 serves to limit the reign of the sea-dragons, the assignation of the human in the image of God subverts this limitation and unleashes the reign of the person. The sea-dragons were to fill the waters, but they could not dominate them. Human beings, as revealed in the next phrase, multiplied with the mandate to dominate Creation—including the seas (though notably not the waters of chaos, which were outside of the Creation-Temple).

210. Smith, *Priestly Vision*, 101; McKeown, *Genesis*, 27.

co-possession of the צלם אלהים.[211] On the other hand, the positive occurrences of כבש occur most often when discussing the subdual of the promised land (Num 32:22, 29; Josh 18:1; and 1 Chr 22:18) or the eschatological deliverance of Israel from sin and oppression by YHWH himself (Mic 7:19; Zech 9:15). The remaining occurrence (besides Gen 1:28) in 2 Sam 8:11 refers to David's plundering of his enemies, which is immediately and directly connected with David's dedication of that plunder to the Lord. This analysis reveals that within the Hebrew Scriptures themselves כבש serves exclusively theological purposes: condemning a false anthropology, or affirming the dominion of the Place of God (the promised land), service to God (as in David's dedications), or the direct activity of God to address sin and oppression. So while it would be incorrect to claim that כבש is a priestly term *per se*, it is completely valid to observe that within the Scriptures themselves the term is used exclusively in contexts that relate to priestly concerns of holy place and holy people rather than any specifically royal ideology.

In Gen 1:28, both the ideas of a holy place and holy people conducting service to God are manifested.[212] The Temple of Creation is to be properly managed as a part of the service of צלם/אדם.[213] The forceful connotation of כבש can simply be a recognition that nature will not bend to human will easily. Alternately, it can reflect the fact that humankind was assigned a duty to work (עבד), and work should be performed with some degree of exertion. The work of Adam was to manage the garden and, presumably, its resident fauna (Gen 2:5-19); the work of the priests was to curate the tabernacle or temple (cf. Num 3:7-10, 38, et al.).[214] The idea that the "subdual" of Creation—in whatever form that might have taken—took effort on the part of humankind is insufficient to ignore the overall temple context of not only Genesis 1 in general but also the blessing upon humanity in Gen 1:26-28 in particular.[215]

---

211. Cf. Sherlock, *Doctrine of Humanity*, 37.

212. Firmage, "Genesis 1," 109-10.

213. Mathews, *Genesis 1—11:26*, 175; Beale, *Temple*, 96, 113; Walton, *Lost World*, 148. The connection of the צלם with holy people in a holy place is biblically implied by Ezek 28:12-16 and extrabiblically explicated in Sir 49:16—50:1 where the high priest was likened to a second Adam. If the likening of Adam's role as an "idol" of YHWH cosmically to the high priest's role as an "idol"of YHWH microcosmically is valid, then there is little reason to differentiate the general role of Adam toward Creation from the role of the high priest within the cult. Fletcher-Louis, "God's Image," 99; Seiss, *Holy Types*, 29; cf. Goldingay, *Israel's Faith*, 517.

214. Cf. Mouroux, *Meaning of Man*, 34.

215. The specification that human כבש applied to the animals could also be linked to sacrificial activities, further connecting this passage to a priestly milieu. However, this specification should not be pressed too strongly, as the listed animals include not only the creatures of earth and sky, but also the fish of the sea that are not listed as

Summary Observations of Gen 1:29—2:3

While the creation of humanity is the pinnacle of Creation, it is not the end of the narrative. The narrative continues, but where the previous section (Gen 1:3–25) served to inform the context for the creation of humankind this closing section serves to describe the activity of the created being.

Genesis 1:29-31—Provision of Sustenance for the Temple Inhabitants

The divine statement of provision is immediately connected to the blessing of humanity in v. 28. The blessing of v. 28 averred humankind's right of authority, but the continued speech of vv. 29–31 assign the responsibility of authority.

The responsibility of authority is not immediately seen in v. 29, which serves as a simple statement of sustenance for human beings. The declaration to the created humans of what they were to eat, however, is directly connected with the assignment of food for the other living creatures of both earth and sky. The fact that God has provided nourishment for human beings forms a foundation for the nourishing of animals. Since humankind had the dominion over both the animals and the earth itself (ארץ), the plants were under human authority as much the creatures. By declaring that the flora existed to feed both humans and animals, God effectively assigned human beings the task of caring for the animals.[216] This assigned care again reaffirms that the dominion of humanity was not necessarily oppressive but rather simply a function of superior position.[217] It further serves to broaden the reign of humankind over Creation beyond royal or militant ideology.

The provision of food for the animals is still a direct act of God. This simultaneously elevates the provision beyond human authority and assigns the provision to human activity. It is beyond humanity in that it is an act

---

acceptable sacrifices in Leviticus.

On the other hand, it is quite interesting that human dominion is over the fish of the sea, but not explicitly the creatures of the "waters of the sea" as in v. 22. While Ps 8:8b could be used to argue against this point, it is notable that Psalm 8 characterizes the ים with the defined (orderly?) term ארח rather than the more indistinct (chaotic?) מים utilized in Genesis 1. Since the presence of the תנינים in Psalm 8 is only implied in v. 8b rather than directly stated, the suggestion that the תנינם are at least somewhat apart from the rest of Creation remains viable, and that the reference to them in v. 22 is a polemical encouragement about how God himself is sovereign over them.

216. Mathews, *Genesis 1—11:26*, 175; Deist, "Genesis 1–11," 5.
217. Cf. Laffey, "Priestly Creation Narrative," 31.

of divine will declared and then made so (v. 30b), but it is an assignment to humanity in that humankind—as the image of God—was to adopt this same activity as a part of their own responsibility.²¹⁸ The connection of the provision for humankind and for the rest of the creatures reflects a hierarchical transfer of power: God provides for humanity, and humanity—using what God has provided—keeps watch care over the rest of the living things.²¹⁹

The concluding verse of the chapter shows again the divine discernment of God as he evaluates and establishes Creation as good. Overall, the provisions of vv. 29–31 do not demand a priestly theology, but they do suggest a transfer—or perhaps better, an assignment—of power from God to humanity.²²⁰ The language of this transfer is nurturing rather than militant, suggesting that this assignment is not based on royal ideology. Since the overall context of Genesis 1 is priestly, this passage is best read as custodial: humans are to care for the inhabitants of the Creation-Temple.²²¹

Genesis 2:1–3—Establishing Sabbath and the Sanctification of the Temple

The concluding epilogue of Genesis 1 focuses on the completion of God's creative work and the sanctification of the day. As an epilogue, Gen 2:1–3 function similarly to the prologue of Gen 1:1 and summarizes and confirms the divine origin of Creation in general and the person of YHWH as Creator specifically.²²²

---

218. Van Wolde, *Stories of the Beginning*, 26.

219. In certain respects this arrangement is similar to Genesis 2, where God forms the garden, and then assigns its curation (along with appropriate prohibitions) to Adam (Gen 2:15–17) immediately before establishing Adam's dominion over the animals (vv. 18–19). Throughout Genesis 1–2 the dominion or authority of humankind is paralleled with an assignment of service and the responsibility of care.

220. Firmage, "Genesis 1," 102; cf. Laffey, "Priestly Creation Narrative," 27.

221. Knohl, *Sanctuary of Silence*, 155; cf. Blenkinsopp, *Sage, Priest, Prophet*, 79; Firmage, "Genesis 1," 110. In the context of a Creation-Temple, the assigned animal-husbandry could also be interpreted as the care for potential sacrifices, a notion that further enhances a cultic flavor of this transference of power to humankind. Cf. Middleton, *Liberating Image*, 149.

222. Atwell, "Egyptian Source," 476. Though the divine name of YHWH is not used in Genesis 1, which exclusively prefers אלהים, the overall biblical context confirms that the God who Created is יהוה himself. Genesis 2 affirms the connection immediately. Even if these two Creation narratives did originate in different sources, the extant text connects them intimately and the monotheistic Yahwism of any priestly redactor cannot be ignored: the Creation as presented can only be the work of YHWH.

The verbal pattern of Gen 2:1–3 is distinct, as the verbs reflecting interaction between God and Creation are exclusively Piel/Pual. The divine actions of rest (שבת) and descriptions of God's now chronologically past work (עשה) use the Qal stem, but the active or current completion (כלה), blessing (ברך), and sanctification (קדש) are all in the Piel/Pual stem. The factitive intensification of these verbs emphasizes the final state of Creation as much as the תוב מאד of Gen 1:31. God's work in Creation was fully completed. However, while the completion of God's work is emphasized, that completion took place on a day when God did *not* engage in any creative work. Indeed, the text suggests that Creation is only complete when God ceases his creative activity. The rest of God is integral to the completion of Creation.[223]

It is axiomatic that the rest of God in Gen 2:3 is foundational for later Sabbath laws. However, the overt connection between Gen 2:3 and the Sabbath laws has diminished careful consideration of what *was* to be done on the Sabbath or—in an illustrative manner—on a seventh day.[224] The Sabbath was a day of rest from the work of humankind, but it was also a day of religious observance and often the culminating day of a festival or feast. More pertinently, priestly discernment and proclamation is frequently tied to the seventh day: it is when declarations of cleanliness were made (cf. Lev 13:5–6, 27–28, 34, et al.). In other words, while the seventh day was when God rested from Creation, it was also the day when priests engaged in their work. It is critical to note that the cessation of work on the Sabbath is always stated as a ceasing of human and animal labor and a time to focus on—or rest *in*—God.[225] For the priest, whose entire vocation was a representation of God, the seventh day was a day of activity. In other words, on the day

---

223. Balentine, *Torah's Vision*, 92; Cassuto, *Genesis*, 61.

224. Considerations of the priestly activity that took place on *a* seventh day do not necessitate that the seventh day was the Sabbath. However, the pattern of six days plus a seventh is extant in the priestly duties. Since priests were obligated to work—even on the Sabbath—the seven-day pattern becomes even more important than whether or not they performed a given activity on the Sabbath day *per se*.

225. Mathews, *Genesis 1–11:26*, 179; Stuart, *Exodus*, 460. This also accords with Walton's notion of divine reign—to rest is to trust YHWH as Creator and King, and that trust should naturally elicit service. Also, while the language of "resting in God" is not present, the idea of separating from the work of the world to abide in the presence of God can be obtained from the *lamed* preposition in Exod 20:10 (שבת ליהוה) and the contrast between mundane work and holiness. Similarly, while Ps 46:10a uses רפה to indicate stillness, it does so after the cessation (משבית) of human warfare (v. 9, cf. v. 6a) and as a prelude to the worship of Ps 46:10b. Finally, the search for manna in Exod 16:27–30 may be characterized by work rather than worship, but the problem of the people's work stems from their lack of faith in divine provision rather than the physical activity itself (cf. Heb 4:7–16). Cf. Walton, *Lost World*, 74–76.

when God rested, the priest made demonstrations of divine will and designations of divine order.²²⁶

Combining this paradigm with the creation of humankind in the image of God results in a sense that God's rest on the seventh day of Creation was—like the assignment of provision for the animals in Gen 1:30–31—a transfer of responsibility.²²⁷ God had arranged all of Creation and established it as both good and complete. God's rest on the seventh day, however, leaves Creation without one to declare what is good.²²⁸ That is, it would leave Creation without this direction had not humankind been created in the divine image. As representatives of God, humanity became the voice of what is good.²²⁹ This activity of discernment was a direct function of the צלם אלהים and a function which is normatively associated with the priesthood, further confirming a priestly nature to the image of God.²³⁰

The connection between priestly activity and the seventh day of Creation can be rejected as anachronistic, but doing so only strengthens the suggestion that the seventh day represents a transition from divine work to human work. Freed from any presuppositions of later Sabbath laws, Gen 2:1–3 actually only designates the seventh day as a day of rest for *God*.²³¹ There is no command or even expectation within the text for the rest of Creation to rest.²³² The emphasis on the human assumption of the divine

---

226. King, *Realignment*, 60. While he is discussing the tabernacle, Garr makes the observation that "God's chosen agent finishes the tabernacle project." Garr uses this argument to show that the concise work of the initial Creation had ended, but that certain work was ongoing; however, it also serves to reveal an occurrence of transferred activity in a context that is as applicable to Creation as it is to the re-Creation represented by the tabernacle. Garr, "God's Creation," 89; cf. Cassuto, *Genesis*, 68.

227. Middleton, *Liberating Image*, 89; Van Wolde, *Stories of the Beginning*, 27; cf. Collins, *Genesis 1–4*, 49n43.

228. This understanding seems contra Walton, who suggests that the Sabbath from Creation was never intended as a cessation of activity but rather as an assumption of normative activity rather than the unique creative activity of Genesis 1. However, the present view and Walton's are not incompatible. Where Walton suggests the Sabbath reflects the *deity* taking up normal activity, the present interpretation suggests the responsibility of the *divine image* (humankind) to take up their own (normative) designated activity. Both are expected, even if only implicitly. God rests by assuming normative activity; humankind serves by maintaining proper custody of the temple. Cf. Walton, *Lost World*, 71–74.

229. Middleton, *Liberating Image*, 212; Laffey, "Priestly Creation Narrative," 27; cf. Balentine, *Torah's Vision*, 86–88; Eichrodt, *Man in the Old Testament*, 30; Cassuto, *Genesis*, 68; Brueggemann, *Israel's Praise*, 12.

230. Cf. Blenkinsopp, *Sage, Priest, Prophet*, 81.

231. Middleton, *Liberating Image*, 212.

232. Firmage, "Genesis 1," 110. Brueggemann notes, however, that later Sabbath laws are directly tied to allowing the land to rest (Lev 25:6; 26:34; et al.). Applying these

image beginning at Gen 1:27 naturally fills the role of answering what happens when the Creator rests: when the Creator rests then the Creation must work. As the divine representatives over Creation, it falls upon humankind to ensure that the work is orderly and good.[233] Since the Creation is itself a temple, then the one supervising the works of Creation is best seen not as a king but as a priest.[234] This final observation is particularly interesting if the Sabbath of Gen 2:1–3 is understood not as God resting *from work*, but rather resting *in the temple*. This understanding parallels the Sabbath of Creation with the inhabitation of the tabernacle (Exod 40:34) and affirmation of the temple (1 Kgs 8:10–11), and is suggestive of intimacy between God and his Creation in general and his image-bearers in particular—a critical aspect of the priestly work.[235]

---

later statutes to Genesis 1 is not as problematic as it may initially seem. If the laws of the Sabbath are more concerned with allowing the land to rest than the people upon it, then it can be remembered that in an agrarian society, the land is worked for provision. If the Sabbath is observed by resting in God with faith that he will provide, then it would be necessary to avoid working the land and implicitly seeking provision from the labors of the worker rather than the kindness of YHWH. Cf. Brueggemann, "Kerygma," 411.

233. Middleton, *Liberating Image*, 212; Balentine, *Torah's Vision*, 93–94; Laffey, "Priestly Creation Narrative," 27; Van Wolde, *Stories of the Beginning*, 26; Brueggemann, *Israel's Praise*, 12.

234. Habel, *Literary Criticism*, 70–71. It is also worth notice that God is never clearly identified as a king *per se* in Genesis 1. While there can be no doubt that he is the authoritative figure over Creation, this authority is never explicitly a royal authority. The fact that other Scriptures are explicit in assigning kingship to YHWH (particularly the Psalms) does not demand that such an ascription take place in Genesis 1. And while Middleton is quick to point out that royal metaphor need not be explicit to be present, it can be suggested with equal certitude that royal metaphor is not necessary to represent divine authority. On the other hand, the temple environment of the Creation is well suited to a priestly understanding of humankind that would not only logically continue the work of the Creator, but also interact with God on the basis of his deity rather than his royalty. Middleton, *Liberating Image*, 71, 90.

235. Mathews, *Genesis 1—11:26*, 177–78; Balentine, *Torah's Vision*, 81, 86–87; Renckens, *Israel's Concept*, 92. This understanding also serves to guard against a misapplication of the fourth commandment. The forbiddance of common מלאכה was not to prescribe a forced idleness, but rather to serve as a reminder of the human purpose in Creation. The sanctification of the Sabbath has an inherent idea not only of separation but also of discernment—the recognition of what should be separated and how (in a matter not greatly dissimilar from Adam's work in the naming ceremony of Genesis 2). This interpretation is affirmed by Jesus' response to the Pharisees in Matthew 12, where though the disciples were picking grain in a "common" field, the Christ's rebuttal emphasized the honoring of God in the tabernacle (vv. 3b–4) and temple (v. 5) and demonstrated as a principle for living in Paul's argument about the sanctity of each day (Rom 14:5–9).

The idea of human service within the Creation-Temple as God inhabits it also forms an interesting connection with the Mesopotamian creation ideology and cultic

Ultimately, whether or not the later seventh-day duties of the priesthood are invoked, the Sabbath of Creation establishes not only the opportunity but also the responsibility of caring for the Creation-Temple to humanity.[236]

A PROPER UNDERSTANDING OF THE IMAGE OF GOD AND CREATION IN A PRIESTLY CONTEXT

The preceding discussions establish both a basic interpretive context for the image of God and a specific application of both the meaning and activity behind the image of God. Regarding the former, the temple-building aspects of Creation are firmly established. Specifics of the interpretations of each element may vary, but the context reflects both priestly literary and ideological motifs.

Further, an examination of the overall context of the Creation reveals that the temple-building God forms his work as a priestly figure. He designates/divides (בדל) and categorizes things within their proper order (למינהם).[237] Further, he ensures that the Creation-Temple is afforded a proper curtain against primordial chaos (מבדיל) and ordains the temple schedule with the lights (מאורת) of the heavens. The polemical nature of Genesis 1 avoids the battle mythology that royal ideology favors and instead focuses divine sovereignty into the speech of God: authoritative speech that is equally at home in a cultic as a royal setting. Overall, the presentation of Genesis 1 uses terminology that is either neutral in regards to ideology or favorable toward priestly ideology. The insertion of royal ideology into Genesis 1 by modern interpreters tends to place excessive weight on Akkadian and Egyptian cognate studies without regard to either the immediate biblical context or the reality that both Akkadians and Egyptians conflated their kings with priests and/or deities and therefore fail to divide between

---

understanding that establishes Marduk as king and the priesthood in the role(s) of "temple administrators and various cultic officials or priests." While Middleton connects this portrait only with the cultic holdings (temples, shrines, etc.), if all of Creation is determined to be a temple—as Genesis 1 presents it—then there is no need for a royal understanding of the צלם אלהים since YHWH serves as king and humankind as the attendants working to provide substance for the Creation, but also to serve God himself. Middleton, *Liberating Image*, 168, cf. 157.

236. Atwell, "Egyptian Source," 477; Walton, *Lost World*, 145; cf. Brueggemann, *Israel's Praise*, 12.

237. Gorman, *Ideology of Ritual*, 40; cf. Goldingay, *Israel's Life*, 611–12.

royal and cultic ideologies in the manner that biblical writers would have.[238] On the other hand, the biblical use is consistently related to cultic contexts.[239]

As these observations are applied specifically to Gen 1:26–28 and focus on the biblical occurrences of צלם, it becomes clear that a royal interpretation of the image of God is unlikely. On the other hand, suggestions that the image of God is simply the relational or communal nature of humankind make the opposite error of focusing too much on the dialogical consideration of v. 26a to the exclusion of the rest of Genesis 1, where God's primary presentation is not as one who deliberates but rather as one who designates—the function of a priest. If the image of God is reflective of who God is, then the logical interpretation of the צלם would reflect God's priestly activity as it is expressed in Genesis 1.[240] With this understanding, the most natural understanding of the image of God is as an assignment of priestly duties to humanity. Further, the assignment of Creation to human authority effectively represents a transition of (priestly) responsibility from God to the human representative.[241] Since God had established the Creation-Temple, the assumption of responsibility by humankind serves to establish humanity as curators of the temple: priests.

The right understanding of the image of God does not preclude any royal ascriptions or other ideological infusions in other anthropological texts, but it does—in light of the foundational importance of Genesis 1 for theological anthropology—establish the expectation that any biblical understanding of humanity will manifest the assigned priestly occupation(s) of curation and discernment in some distinctive, and arguably primary, way.[242]

---

238. Miller, "In the 'Image,'" 296; Niskanen, "Poetics of Adam," 420; Bird, "Male and Female," 140; Middleton, *Liberating Image*, 36; Further, the god-images of Assyria and Egypt have typically been found in temples or other worship places and seem to intend the kings' quasi-divine nature rather than simply their royal status. It is likely for this same reason that Egyptian priests are also occasionally referred to as divine images. The representation of deity occurs in kings by divine birth, but it is imaged in priests by divine activity/intermediation. Beale, *Temple*, 83, 89; Livingston, *Pentateuch*, 141; Middleton, *Liberating Image*, 110–11; Middleton, *New Heaven*, 44.

239. Even Bird, a proponent of the royal man interpretation, acknowledges that the dominion expressed in Genesis 1 "is not exclusively, or even predominantly, royal language." Bird, "Male and Female," 154.

240. Cf. Kessler, *Old Testament Theology*, 128.

241. Cf. Walton, *Lost World*, 145.

242. Said another way, the ascription of priesthood serves to make a person *more* human. Davies, *Anthropology and Theology*, 151; cf. Collins, *Genesis 1–4*, 132; Smith, *Priestly Vision*, 12.

Chapter 3

Examination of Biblical Compatibility of the צלם אלהים as a Priestly Calling

EXAMINATION OF SELECTED PASSAGES FROM A PRIEST PARADIGM

Since Genesis 1 is the quintessential Creation passage of the Old Testament and Gen 1:26–28 the foundation for biblical anthropology, any understanding of the צלם אלהים as a commissioning of humanity as priests or a calling to priestly activity should be discernible in other creative and occupational passages of the Bible.[1]

It is not necessary to examine every Creation passage in the Hebrew Scriptures for compatibility, so long as an adequate representation of passages is studied. Samples of mythic Creative accounts should be first considered, though Creative accounts that do not involve the human role in Creation and focus exclusively on divine activity need not be examined.[2] Second, consideration will be given to terrestrial events that are cast as Creative or re-Creative events (such as the flood and the formation of Israel). A tertiary study will include eschatological passages that present the establishment of the new heaven and earth in terms of Creation.

1. Middleton, *Liberating Image*, 64; cf. Smith, *Priestly Vision*, 177. The immediate examination will be restricted to Old Testament passages; New Testament passages will be examined in the fifth chapter of this publication in the discussion of biblical theology.

2. Psalm 29 serves as a good example of this sort of writing. While the song is replete with Creation language and theology, the actual interchange between the divine and the human is limited to a call to praise (shared with the בני אלים, v. 1) and a hope of blessing (v. 11) without any sort of detail concerning the relationship between humanity and God.

An overview of occupational passages need only focus on the direct topic at hand rather than the breadth of human experience.[3] As such, the primary concern will be to examine passages that reflect some measure of universal scope to the priesthood and/or movement toward an anthropology that assumes a priestly teleological result. These passages will provide insight by their suggestions of compliance with or subversion of priestly activity and duty.

ALTERNATE CREATION PASSAGES AND THEIR CONNECTION TO PRIESTHOOD

When examining Creation passages, the dual nature of each creation narrative must be considered. The synchronous nature of the narratives suggests that since Genesis 1 is embedded in priestly theology and culminates in a priestly calling, then a priestly aspect should be present between the various other passages.[4] The diachronic nature of the Scriptures, however, allows for different emphases to be expressed; therefore, any priestly elements could be discreet rather than predominant.[5]

Selected Mythic Creation Passages

While the Old Testament is filled with mythic references, passages that directly connect both the Creation event and the relationship between God and humankind are relatively few. Certainly, God's creative role is found in numerous readings, but many of these occurrences—including most of the sapiential occurrences—utilize God's creative aspect as an invocation of authority or control of the world rather than as a direct foundation for

---

3. Cf. Van Wolde, *Stories of the Beginning*, 1.

4. Sailhamer, *Old Testament Theology*, 191–92.

5. Smith, *Priestly Vision*, 157–60; Sailhamer, *Old Testament Theology*, 185–88; cf. von Rad, *Problem of the Hexateuch*, 93. While von Rad makes his observation in regards to the land, the general intention of his statement is applicable to much of the Old Testament's theology, particularly in light of both the synchronic nature of its writings and the known appropriation of older imagery by the prophets to indicate a new divine work. Girdlestone, *Grammar of Prophecy*, 66; Kaiser, *Back Toward the Future*, 53; Barr, "Revelation through History," 6–8.

relationship between human beings and God.⁶ Nonetheless, there are three passages that seem to fulfill these criteria: Genesis 2, Psalm 8, and Job 42.⁷

Priestly Purpose in the Garden of God (Genesis 2)

Many of the priestly features of Genesis 2 have already been discussed, and so will only be briefly reiterated here. However, there remain a number of features of Genesis 2 that deserve further elaboration. It is appropriate to begin this elaboration with the poetic introduction of v. 4.

The introductory תולדת formula establishes a priestly context for the reading of the entire passage. Previous work from Francis Andersen, continued by Matthew Thomas and bolstered by earlier analyses of John Skinner, have established that the תולדת is best read as either a superscription or a dual-functioning conclusion/introduction.⁸ With this in mind, the presence of the תולדת in v. 4 establishes a priestly context and interest over Genesis 2. This is an important recognition, as it immediately rejects the assumption that Genesis 2 reflects royal ideology and that the naming ceremony was a royal activity. By framing the "second Creation story" within a תולדת, the structure immediately submits any interpretation of Genesis 2 to a priestly ideology.⁹ Further, if the hinging effect of v. 4 exists to ensure

---

6. It can be argued—rightly—that soteriology is a function of Creation. The fact that salvation results in a New Creation affirms this position. However, since soteriology is a distinct and well-attested subcategory it seems reasonable at this point to hold this discussion examining only texts dealing with Creation proper. Soteriology will be further considered in chapter 4, while the establishment of Israel and the rebirth of the world after the flood will be further discussed in the next subsection.

7. The exclusion of Psalm 148 from the example selection may be conspicuous; however, it is not arbitrary. While the psalm is replete with Creation imagery, there is little direct interaction with the divine outside of the generalized calling to praise him. The emphasis on royal praise of YHWH (v. 11) is offset by the merism of v. 12 where both the young and old are similarly commanded to praise God. There is a sense that the calling of vv. 11–12 is a general one to every strata of society. Since the Psalms favor a cultic context, there seems little reason to call for priests to praise God, since they would theoretically have been the ones leading the song in the first place.

What is of particular interest is the promise of strength to the Godly ones in v. 14. The particular term used (חסיד) has a general sense of piety and covenant devotion, but it is also used in Deut 33:8; Pss 50:5; 79:1–2; 132:9, 16; and 2 Chr 6:41 in contexts that specifically expect the presence and practice of a priest.

8. Andersen, *Hebrew Verbless Clause*, 40; Thomas, *These Are the Generations*, 15; Skinner, *Critical and Exegetical Commentary*, 41.

9. While it can be claimed that royal ideology and priestly ideology do not have to be distinct, these claims mostly invoke the priestly/divine kings of Mesopotamia and Egypt. The problem with this is twofold: first, it ignores the biblical distinction between the offices of king and priests and assigns more weight to comparative studies than

that Genesis 2 is read synchronically with Genesis 1 as C. John Collins suggests, then the cultic patterning of Genesis 1 should naturally influence the understanding of Genesis 2.[10]

The second observation to make regarding Genesis 2 is the location of humanity in the garden. Gardens are often associated with kings in the ancient Near East, and it may initially seem reasonable to assign royal imagery to אדם on this basis. However, the cultivation of gardens by royalty was not because gardens were seen simply as the prerogative of kings (though the expense of maintaining a garden certainly mitigated any non-royal gardens), but rather because gardens were primarily associated with the gods themselves. Gardens were places of deity, and the royal cultivation of a garden served to associate the king with the gods and establish a statement of divine right or favor.[11] The placement of Adam within a garden was not, therefore, an ascription of royalty to humanity but rather an association of humankind with God. It was an assignment to a holy place.[12] And unlike ANE kings who looked to their gardens as places of leisure, the garden was the place of work for אדם. The cultivation of the garden, with its juxtaposition of human work and divine proximity, should therefore serve as a priestly motif rather than a royal one.[13]

If the cultivation of the garden was priestly, then the activities within the garden—including the naming ceremony of vv. 18–20—are better read as priestly activities rather than royal ones.[14] The specific vocabulary of the naming ceremony has already been discussed; combining the vocabulary of the naming ceremony itself with the overall context of תולדת and garden confirms a cultic rather than a royal expression in Genesis 2. Aside from a forced compatibility with comparative religions that ignores the polemical nature of biblical creation narratives, there is little reason to suggest that Genesis 2 is primarily interested in a "royal man."[15] On the other hand, the

---

the extant text. Second, it ignores the polemical aspects of Genesis 1–2 that rejected the anthropology and theology of the Mesopotamians and Egyptians. If anything, the creation of humankind in the image of God serves to subvert rather than rely upon external anthropologies. Cf. Bird, "Male and Female," 144; Brueggemann, *Israel's Praise*, 27, 29.

10. Collins, *Genesis 1–4*, 101, 109, 121; Smith, *Priestly Vision*, 157.

11. Middleton, *New Heaven*, 44; Beale, *Temple*, 83.

12. Barker, *Gate of Heaven*, 61; Seiss, *Holy Types*, 30; Balentine, *Torah's Vision*, 88–89; Walton, "Historical Adam," 95, 102–3; Gentry and Wellum, *Kingdom*, 211.

13. Beale, *Temple*, 81, 84; Gorman, *Ideology of Ritual*, 28–29; Hornung, *Conceptions of God*, 183.

14. Beale, *Temple*, 68.

15. This is not to suggest that there is no possibility of royal character within Genesis 1–2. The contrast between the biblical valuation of even the "common" human

context of Genesis 2, especially when intersected with Genesis 1, establishes the priestly activity (the naming ceremony/acts of distinction) and locus (the garden) of humankind.[16]

Priestly Dominion over the Earth (Psalm 8)

While there are a number of questions—both structural and interpretive—regarding Psalm 8, certain key elements related to the thesis of this work are well attested. First, the chiastic structure of the psalm is established, and emphasizes the interaction between God and humankind in vv. 4–5.[17] Second, while the exact structure of Psalm 8 may be disputed the general pattern of recognizing the transcendence of God over Creation in the first half of the chiasm and the responsive dominion of humanity (and the rest of the created order) in the second half is well attested. Finally, the imagery of Psalm 8 very clearly reflects the imagery of Genesis 1.[18] Considering the role of this psalm and the nature of Genesis 1, it seems as if Psalm 8 is a worshipful response to the theological statements of Genesis 1.[19] Where Genesis 1 establishes the theological context of humanity, Psalm 8 expects a reflective celebration of God from humanity.[20]

---

and the relative lack of concern for humanity at large found in the royal ideologies of other ANE nations is well noted, and a royal ascription to humankind serves this point well. The primary question at hand is whether or not such a royal understanding of humanity is of first importance, or if it is secondary. Since the broader concern of the Scriptures is consistently to present YHWH himself as the only True King, and the distinct concern of Genesis 1–2 is to present YHWH as the Creator, it seems reasonable to suggest that the interaction between the creature and the Creator, between the human and the divine is more important than any royal implications of the passage and that a priestly understanding of humankind's nature and role supersedes the polemical understanding of a universally royal characteristic.

16. Beale, *Temple*, 83–85; Eichrodt, *Man in the Old Testament*, 30. Humphreys inadvertently establishes this point also with his observations that the God of Genesis 1 is completely "other" while in Genesis 2 God's relationship with Adam establishes a connection not previously found in the narrative. While his interpretation (particularly of the complete otherness of God in Gen 1) can be challenged, his observation that the interaction between God and humankind in Genesis 2 presents humanity actively engaged in divine activity is notable. Humphreys, *Character of God*, 42–43.

17. Kraut, "Birds and Babes," 11; Smith, *Priestly Vision*, 29–30.

18. Collins, *Genesis 1–4*, 84; Bratcher and Reyburn, *Translator's Handbook*, 77; Childs, *Biblical Theology*, 113; Cairns, *Image of God*, 27.

19. Gentry and Wellum, *Kingdom*, 184; cf. Brueggemann, *Genesis*, 28; Craigie, *Psalms 1–50*, 106.

20. Kraut, "Birds and Babes," 16; Collins, *Genesis 1–4*, 84–85. Incidentally, if source theories are accepted and the priority of Psalm 8 and Genesis 1 reverses, the general relationship between the two passages remains intact. If Psalm 8 has the priority, then

The initial verses of Psalm 8 are certainly power-oriented, and the presence of צוררים, אויב, and מתנקם all seem to suggest a militant context that might indicate royal ideology.[21] Further, the superscriptive לדוד would allow for royal interests. However, while vv. 1b–3 are clearly concerned with divine power, the mention of enemies lacks any mention of the cosmic battle that mythopoetic Creation narratives of the ANE so often describe. Aside from the terminology for the enemies themselves, the only "militant" word found is the strength or bulwark of God: עז.[22] Further, the enemies are clearly subservient to God. Rather than contend with him, the enemies are subdued not by force, but by proclamation: God's strength is "appointed" (יסד) against the enemies. This appointment is very similar to the *creatio per dictum* of Genesis 1. The word יסד itself is most frequently found in construction or the establishment of law codes. It describes civil authority or sovereignty rather than forcible subjugation. The strength of God is established before his enemies not by cosmic battle, but by the declarations of Creation.[23] With this in mind, the simple presence of enemies is not enough to establish a militant context for Psalm 8.[24]

The second half of the psalm elaborates indirectly upon God's power by examining the dominion of humankind that arises from humanity's existence מעט מאלהים. The human descriptive does initially seem to invoke certain royal images: the crowning (עטר) of humankind and the placement of Creation under human feet—a possible reference to the footstool of a king. However

---

the Creation was celebrated in worship, which then birthed the formal narrative of Genesis 1. The movement from worship song to doctrinal statement does nothing to sever the connection between a worship context (as in Ps 8) and the priestly imperative of Genesis 1. Eichrodt, *Man in the Old Testament*, 30.

21. Cf. Habel, *Land Is Mine*, 16.

22. Notably, the composers of the LXX—whether because of an interpretive decision or because they were using a different vorlage—state in v. 2 [LXX: v. 3] that it is not God's strength that is established, but rather his "praise" (αἶνος). Not only does this translation thereby lessen the militant aspects of the psalm, but also it refocuses the setting on a temple environment.

23. Middleton, *Liberating Image*, 66; cf. Dahood, *Psalms I*, 50–51. A comparison with Ps 147:18–19 and its connection of God's authority over creation and God's declarations to Israel also illustrates the connection between the authoritative (or appointed) word of YHWH and not only Creation but also the priestly role of humankind.

24. The connection of יסד with civil authority does not necessarily demand a secular context either. Remembering that the תורה was both the cultic foundation and the civil authority of Israel affirms the connection between civil and religious authority, a connection attested to by the equality of the priest and the judge (Deut 17:9, 12) and magnified further by the subordination of the king to Levitical oversight (Deut 17:18). Cf. Leuchter, "Levite in Your Gates," 421–22; Sprinkle, *Book of the Covenant*, 37, 161; Goldingay, *Israel's Life*, 712.

while עטר is indeed a term for crown or crowning, it is a generalized term that most often represents a bestowing of favor rather than a coronation of royalty (which would prefer נזר).²⁵ Similarly, the exercise of dominion utilizes a generalized verb for rule, משל. This is the same word used in Gen 1:16 to describe the "rule" of the sun and moon over day and night.²⁶ Other early occurrences of משל continue to suggest an idea of oversight or management, but not necessarily of forceful or even royal reign (cf. Gen 3:16; 4:7; 24:2; et al.).²⁷

Of course, a lack of royal ideology in Psalm 8 does not necessitate a priestly ideology. It should be noted, however, that the reign of humankind is specifically tied to both the nearly divine nature of humanity (v. 5a) and the observation that human dominion is over the works of God's Hands (v. 6a). These connections reiterate the limitation of human reign as curation rather than any independent rule. The curation is essentially a function of being "a little lower" than the divine.²⁸

The exact translation of מעט מאלהים has been debated extensively, particularly in light of the LXX adoption of παρ᾽ ἀγγέλους. While the LXX should not be arbitrarily dismissed, the translation of אלהים as ἄγγελοι seems to reflect later tendencies to distance the transcendent God from mundane humanity and preserve YHWH's holiness. Typically when divine beings other than God are intended, the direct article is affixed or the genitive

---

25. The root עטר occurs only seven times in the Hebrew Bible. Of those occurrences, one is clearly describing a physical encircling (1 Sam 23:26) while three are obvious statement of the bestowal of favor rather than any sort of royal position (Pss 5:13; 65:12; and 103:4). Similarly, the crowns of Tyre in Isa 23:8 seem indicative of favor being bestowed upon the "merchant princes" rather than any true coronation to royalty. The use of עטר in Song 3:11 refers to a "wedding crown/circlet." With this distribution, it is reasonable to suggest that if a royal connotation was intended in Ps 8:5 a different term would have been used. This suggestion is made even more distinct since all four of the psalms using עטר are "of David" establishing the same milieu for each of them and suggesting the same connotation(s) of favor rather than royalty.

26. Considering Gen 1:14b, it can be strongly asserted that the rule of the sun and moon was distinctly *liturgical*, which—in light of the strong dependency of Psalm 8 on Genesis 1—is suggestive that the rule of humankind in Ps 8:6 is similarly a cultic authority.

27. A particularly interesting occurrence of משל is found in Zech 6:13, where it is used to describe the reign of the Branch from a throne in the temple of God. The interpretation of Zech 6:11-14 is complex, particularly considering the relationship(s) between the throne of the Branch and the throne of the priest (v. 13b); however, it is sufficient to note that the *royal* authority of the Branch is delimited by the observance of the will of God (v. 15) and his reign becomes one of management and preservation rather than dominance and initiation. This subservience of royalty to the will of God is foundational to the orthodox understanding of the king of Israel, who obtained the authority to reign only after he had first received the approval of the priesthood (Deut 17:18-19). Cf. Goldingay, *Israel's Life*, 714.

28. Craigie, *Psalms 1-50*, 108.

בני אלהים is preferred. Further, the close association between Psalm 8 and Genesis 1 reinforces a reading that human beings were made a little lower than God himself.[29] The closeness between God and humanity suggest an intimate proximity, and connect with the צלם אלהים.[30] This is important as divine proximity—an idea associated with the holy place—is the foundation for the curative dominion of humankind.[31]

Finally, it is worthwhile to recognize that humanity's status מעט מאלהים is produced by the remembrance (זכר) and concern (פקד) of YHWH. Both of these words are quite common and general; nevertheless, it might be prudent to consider the association between זכר and the covenant and the frequent association of פקד with a supervisor's inspection of a subordinate. The covenant was, theoretically at least, to be enforced by the priests, while the subordination of a person in the holy place to a supervisor could reflect priestly hierarchy and piety. Further, neither the concept of covenant nor the establishment of a hierarchy can be divorced from the idea of election: the existence of a covenant with Israel was the proof of their chosen status as God's people.[32] Similarly, within Israel the Levites as a tribe and the Aaronic line in particular held a special status on the basis of their relational status. While it would be irresponsible to build too much upon these associations, their presence does affirm the possibility of a priestly emphasis in Psalm 8.[33]

If a priestly emphasis is detected in Psalm 8, then it bolsters the proper understanding of the image of God as a priestly motif in Genesis 1.[34] But even if no emphasis is detected in Psalm 8, an examination of the psalm reveals that it does not impede or detract from a priestly understanding of Genesis 1. Considering the close connection between the two passages, the positivity/neutrality of Psalm 8 is important.

---

29. Of course, if Gen 1:26 is interpreted as a holy council then the ἄγγελος translation can be supported; however, the singular creative work in Gen 1:27 remains an impediment to the holy council interpretation in Gen 1:26 and—consequently—the ἄγγελος translation of the LXX. Cf. Kraut, "Birds and Babes," 23–24.

30. Keil and Delitzsch, *Commentary*, 5:94; Craigie, *Psalms 1–50*, 1983, 108.

31. Firmage, "Genesis 1," 109–10.

32. Trimm, "Did YHWH Condemn," 521; similarly, the biblical idea of God's remembrance is directly tied to the promises of God. It is because God has promised that he remembers. Therefore, both the covenant and the remembrance of God are founded in the same act of relationship: the issuance of divine promise.

33. This possibility is further adduced by the observation that "cult ... is granted as a means through which God's creative power is mediated." The authoritative content of Psalm 8 is predicated upon Creation theology. If the cult (priesthood) is the correct mediatory body for Creative power, the ascription of human dominion most naturally connects with the sacramental rather than the royal. Brueggemann, *Israel's Praise*, 10.

34. Weiser, *Psalms*, 144–46.

Priestly Response to Creation's Glory (Job 42)

Before analyzing Job 42, it should be noted that Job 38–41—where Job is held accountable by God the Creator—does not directly relate the role of humankind to the Creation. The creative imagery of Job 38–41 is intended to demonstrate the transcendence of God; it does not describe any context of relationship with human beings. In many ways Job 38–41 actually serves to subvert the idea of relationship, or at least to ward against excessive familiarity in making demands of the divine.[35]

On the other hand, the dictates to Eliphaz in Job 42:7–9 do suggest a cultic interest (at least in the prose prologue to the poetic discourse). Having established God as Creator in Job 38–41, the prose reveals both Job's righteous response (Job 42:1–6), and the admonition of those who have not been righteous (Job 42:7–9).[36] Interestingly enough, the admonition of the three "wise" friends establishes a priestly role for Job: it is when they sacrifice that Job will pray and God will relent of punishment.[37] So while the creative imagery of chs. 38–41 does not invoke relationship, the correct response to the truths of Creation is submission by the righteous and intercession for the unrighteous. Further, the righteous response of Job consists predominantly of reiterations or quotations of what God himself had said (cf. Job 40:3 and 42:1; 38:2 and 42:3; 38:3, 40:7 and 42:4).[38] This reiteration of divine speech is certainly reflective of the role of a priest, especially in light of Job 42:8 and its sacrifice of *seven* bulls and *seven* rams. Therefore, while Job 42 does not demand a priestly connotation of biblical anthropology, it is consistent with it in a mythic context.[39]

Selected Theological Re-Creation Passages

The idea of limiting Creation Theology to the formation of the world is an artificial, post-biblical interpretive construct. The fact that God is the Creator informs not only the establishment of the Torah, but also the prophetic invectives calling for repentance and the sapiential material guiding daily

---

35. Hartley, *Job*, 534; Bullock, "Wisdom," 9.
36. Hartley, *Job*, 537–38.
37. Alden, *Job*, 412.
38. Ibid., 407–8.
39. Hartley suggests that Job's activity is purely patriarchal and not priestly; however, Job is not acting to intercede for his family or clan. The external focus of this intercession, the priestly numerology, and the designation of Job as the עבד of YHWH suggest that this is much more than mere patriarchal privilege. Cf. Hartley, *Job*, 539.

life.⁴⁰ Further, the foundational events of the Old Testament are presented as distinct creative acts. By establishing a "new thing" God formed a new creation. The formation of new creations within the Scriptures, while distinct, still allude to and reflect the same foundational aspects of God's character that the normative creation passages express.⁴¹ If a pattern can be found in the re-Creations of the Hebrew Bible, it is reasonable to expect that same pattern to be present within the original Creation passages in general and the quintessential Creation passage of Genesis 1 in particular.⁴² By examining the re-Creations of Scripture, a more detailed interpretive context for Genesis 1 can be confirmed.

The connections between Abraham and the formation of the Israelite nation and the Creation of Genesis 1 have previously been addressed and will not be further discussed, though they should be recalled and considered appropriately. Events both prior to and after the Sinai covenant attest to the relationship between God and humankind at specific points of what could be considered re-Creation events.⁴³ The flood narrative of Genesis 6–9, the establishment of the tabernacle and temple in Exodus 25–40 and 1 Kings 6–8, and the reconstruction of the nation as related in Ezra-Nehemiah and 2 Chr 36:22–23 serve as examples of cosmological, cultic, and societal re-Creative events.

Cosmological Re-Creation and Priestly Response (Genesis 6–9)

The punitive and salvific aspects of the flood are well attested; however, it is a mistake to consider either aspect apart from the bold creative motifs of the flood and its reversal of Creation.⁴⁴ The declaration of destruction in Gen 6:7 declares that God will destroy (מחה) that which he has created (ברא). The latter term has already been clearly shown to represent a mythic exchange between the divine and the human, establishing an interpretive context that transcends the mundane. When this is paired with מחה—indicating an obliteration of something so that it no longer exists—a fuller

---

40. Ross, *Recalling the Hope of Glory*, 82–82; Young, *Creator, Creation*, 33–37; Berkouwer, *Man*, 23.

41. Brueggemann, *Israel's Praise*, 27. Gorman says it well: "The world view of the Priestly writers has as its framework three distinct orders of creation—the cosmological, the societal, and the cultic. . . . What must be seen, however, is that these various orders are not independent of one another but are intricately connected." Gorman, *Ideology of Ritual*, 44.

42. Gronbaek, "Baal's Battle," 38–39; Smith, *Priestly Vision*, 136–37.

43. Garr, "God's Creation," 88.

44. Wenham, *Story as Torah*, 23; Mathews, *Genesis 1—11:26*, 344–45.

understanding of the cosmic-scale destruction of the flood is possible.⁴⁵ Considering the close ties of the flood to the original Creation, this larger understanding warrants considerable elaboration.

Despite the inevitable variations over specifics, the chiastic structure of the flood narrative has long been recognized and its climax around Gen 7:17–8:5 accepted. While the pattern of the flood has been accepted, the interpretations of that pattern remain disputed and have often failed to consider the role of the flood in the context of Creation Theology.⁴⁶ This failure is a mistake, since when the language of the flood is examined, the dual nature of the flood as an end to the old world and the formation (creation) of a new world becomes explicit.⁴⁷ The following chiastic structure is proposed to address this failure:

A₁. God's Declaration of Destruction (Gen 6:11–22)

    B₁. Noah's Differentiation of Animals (Gen 7:1–10)

        C₁. The Beginning of the Flood (Gen 7:11–16)

            D₁. The Decimation of Creation (Gen 7:17–24)

            D₂. The Remembrance of Creation (Gen 8:1–12)

        C₂. The End of the Flood (Gen 8:13–19)

    B₂. Noah's Sacrifice to YHWH (Gen 8:20–22)

A₂. God's Declaration of Blessing (Gen 9:1–7)

It is important to recognize that the chiastic peak of God's remembrance is not isolated on Noah, or even the human race, but rather includes all of the living creatures on the ark, the various inhabitants of Creation.⁴⁸ With this in mind, Noah's activities serve as curations of nature that are

---

45. Vos, *Eschatology*, 81; Garr, "God's Creation," 85.

46. The statement that the pattern of the flood has been accepted is made broadly, in reference to the accepted presence of chiasmus within the narrative rather than to any universally accepted boundaries of the chiasmus. This is to be expected, since the structure of the chiasmus is largely dependent upon the interpretation of the themes of the flood and the importance of structural balance between the elements.

While structural balance certainly has its place and importance, the mythic elements of the flood narrative lend themselves to a thematic interest rather than a structural one. With this in mind, the presented chiasmus contains obvious structural imbalances. Considering the fact that only approximately a third of the "flood narrative" actually deals with the floodwaters themselves (Gen 7:11—8:12) and the remaining two-thirds are concerned with the preparations and responses of God and Noah, a certain amount of thematic favor might be expected.

47. Wenham, *Story as Torah*, 23; Garr, "God's Creation," 87; Busenitz, "Introduction to the Biblical Covenants;" 183; cf. Mathews, *Genesis 1—11:26*, 350–51.

48. Vos, *Eschatology*, 81.

well in keeping with the charge to אדם.[49] This general observation is then bolstered by the specific instructions to build the ark itself. God gives detailed instructions on the construction of the ark. Elsewhere in the Bible, specific divine instruction on how to build structures is found only in cultic contexts: the tabernacle, the temple, and—if considered to be free-standing structures—altars. Even the divine instruction on building implements is restricted to overtly cultic objects (the ark of the covenant, the furnishings of the tabernacle/temple, et al.) or soteriological symbols such as the bronze serpent of Num 21:4–9. With this in mind, the detailed issuance of the ark's blueprint to Noah is significant. It designates the ark as a holy place—a form of a temple.[50]

The designation of the ark as a temple is enhanced further by formation of the covenant in v. 18. Noah's entrance into the ark is contingent on his covenant relationship with God, just as entrance into the Jerusalem temple would be contingent on a right standing with God in accordance with the Sinai covenant and, for that matter, entrance into Eden relied upon the relationship אדם had with the Creator.[51] Of course, the right standing with God to enter the inner temple is reserved for priests. While the temple entry requirements do not seem to apply immediately to Noah, the narrative almost immediately begins to present Noah in increasingly priestly ways. While there is no significant statement of intercession in Genesis 6, Noah does serve either as a mediator between God and the Creation in his husbandry of the animals or as a curator of Creation in his work to preserve the animals. In either case, the priestly title is absent, but Noah's performance is beginning to reflect priestly motifs.

The priestly aspects of Noah's work are brought to the fore in Gen 7:1–10. The general charge in Gen 6:19–20 to bring two of each animal onto the ark is an act of curation, but the specific elaboration of Gen 7:1–10 to ensure seven pairs of the clean animals reflects the (eventual) need for sacrificial intercession. Further, the "taking" of the animals is an active work on the part of Noah (vv. 2–3); it was a deliberate differentiation between clean and unclean. This differentiation is distinctively priestly and mimics/prefigures the evaluation of animals in Leviticus.[52] It may also be significant

---

49. Wenham, *Story as Torah*, 34.

50. Cf. McKeown, *Genesis*, 55. At the same time, the ark serves as a microcosm of Creation, since the filling of the ark with both flora and fauna in Gen 6:19–21 serves to populate the structure in a manner not dissimilar from days 3, 5–6 of Creation. However, since Creation itself was a temple, the ark's nature as a microcosm strengthens rather than weakens the temple similarities.

51. Beale, "Eden," 14; cf. McKeown, *Genesis*, 56.

52. Mathews, *Genesis 1—11:26*, 374; Hamilton, *Genesis*, 287.

that while Noah found favor with God and walked righteously, there is no similar statement for his family as a whole. And yet, the family as a whole was allowed to enter the ark. This may be similar to the access that priestly families had to holy meals (cf. Lev 21:16–22:16, et al.). Alternately, the activity of Noah—as a priest-figure—served to mediate his family's presence in the holy place.[53]

The actual mechanics of the flood clearly represent a reversal of Creation. Where day 2 of Creation saw the separation of the waters above and below and the formation of a space for the temple, the flood begins with the removal of that separation as waters burst upon the earth both from above *and* from below. Where Creation restrained the primordial chaos, the flood unleashes it upon the earth and removes the sacred space of the Creation-Temple.[54] It is at this point that the enclosing of the living things—both human and otherwise—within the ark becomes particularly interesting. The unleashing of the waters brings the world back to a chaotic state and removes the space available for the Creation-Temple. But the ark, constructed as a floating object, rises above the primordial waters. The ark as a temple structure ensures that the temple of God remains a place of sanctuary and protection, despite the coming "triumph" of chaos.[55]

Though the terms are not used, the mythic defeat of the earth by the waters of chaos essentially returns Creation to the state of תהו ובהו that existed prior to God's work in Genesis 1. Genesis 7:17–24 therefore end with a nigh complete reversal of Creation. Two significant things remain: first, there is no removal of the light of day 1. Second, Noah and those in the temporary temple of the ark remained. If the light is interpreted in terms of divine connection with Creation, then the survival of Noah becomes contingent on a priestly nature; and, in fact, it is the survival of Noah and the animals in the ark that sets the stage to transition from God's work in un-Creating to God's work in re-Creating.[56] After the prevalence of chaos and the un-Creation of the flood, Gen 8:1 invokes the remembrance of God, which most likely is a reference to Gen 6:18–21.[57] The existence of this covenant and the promise of life predicates a reversal from un-Creation to re-Creation.

Significantly, the re-Creation demonstrates many of the same elements that the Creation itself did.[58] There is a clear parallel between the movement

---

53. Mathews, *Genesis 1—11:26*, 368, 370; McKeown, *Genesis*, 56.
54. Mann, *Book of Torah*, 23; Hamilton, *Genesis*, 292–93.
55. Cf. Barker, *Gate of Heaven*, 72; Hamilton, *Genesis*, 295.
56. Mathews, *Genesis 1—11:26*, 351.
57. Ibid., 382.
58. Gentry and Wellum, *Kingdom*, 162; Waltke and Fredricks, *Genesis*, 128.

of the spirit in Gen 1:2 (ורוח אלהים על־פני המים) and the wind of Gen 8:1b (ויעבר אלהים רוח על־הארץ). The change from "waters" to "earth" establishes the continuity with the original Creation, since the re-Creation would not be an original formation from primordial waters but a purified structure brought through primordial waters.[59] At the same time, the emphasis of continuity should not overlook that the chaos-waters of the flood are restrained in a manner not dissimilar to the waters of day 2, with both the waters below (מעינת תהום) and the waters above (ארבת השמים) specifically addressed in Gen 8:2a.[60]

The re-Creation of Genesis 8 differs from the original Creation of Genesis 1 in that God does not specifically produce "dry ground" (either יבשה or חרבה); the narrative simply states that the mountain tops became visible. Because the formation of the earth on day 3 of Creation was the formation of the structure of the temple, it is interesting that in place of the emergence of dry ground there is the settling of the ark upon the mountain. The ark's role as a temple has already been noted; the grounding of the ark on a high place, where temples were typically built, is not accidental.[61] The ark itself is the proverbial dry ground. In this respect, both days 2 and 3 of Creation have been duplicated.[62]

While the flood began by undoing the beginning of Creation and reversing day 2, the flood ends with the reemergence of the land creatures repopulating the earth even as they did at the end of Creation (day 6). The exact terminology differs, but the animals' departure from the ark למשפחתיהם parallels their formation and procreation למינהו and suggests that the world—now purged of the abundance of human sin—is once more in the right order.[63] The תב מאד of Creation has been reestablished. It should be noted that the animals did not simply leave the ark: it was Noah's duty to lead them out of the ark with the express purpose of guiding the animals to multiply (Gen 8:17). Noah's dominion over the animals expressed itself in

---

59. Hamilton, *Genesis*, 300.

60. Gentry and Wellum, *Kingdom*, 162. The use of תהום in both Gen 1:2 and Gen 8:2a should not be overlooked. Both creative activities begin with God's Spirit/Wind directly supervening over the Abyss.

61. Beale, "Eden," 14; cf. Matthews, *Genesis 1—11:26*, 389.

62. The (possible) relationship between the יבשה on day 3 and Exodus 14 and their roles in Creation/Salvation theologies reveal and clarify this duplication. It is also interesting to consider that the ark settled on the mountain on the first day of the first month (Gen 8:13)—the same day that the tabernacle was erected in Exod 40:2—further emphasizing the perspective of the ark as a temple that bridges Creation and the later Israelite cult. Balentine, *Torah's Vision*, 141.

63. Neville, "Differentiation," 217.

the multiplication and preservation of life. In this way, Noah's role parallels the command to humankind in Gen 1:28–30.[64]

Having been brought through cataclysm and re-Creation, Noah's first activity after leaving the ark is to erect an altar—the first explicit occurrence of an altar in the Scriptures—and perform a sacrifice.[65] The divine response to this sacrifice is a promise of the continuance of the "new" Creation.[66] Sacrificial activity was, of course, the prerogative of family patriarchs in the pre-Levitical period of Israel. However, the deliberate association with ceremonially clean animals (טהור) and the responsive promise of God suggests that there is more to Noah's sacrifice than simple patriarchal activity.[67] Both the chiastic structure of the narrative and the use of טהור form a correspondence between the sacrificial work of Noah and his previous priestly work of differentiation.[68] Further, the sacrifice seems excessive as "some of *every* clean animal and some of *every* clean bird" (Gen 8:20 ESV, emphasis added) was offered. If this were simply a familial act of thanksgiving, the large number of sacrifices is startling.[69] On the other hand, the dedication of a holy place typically expects a greater number of sacrifices (cf. Lev 9:1–5; 1 Kgs 8:62–64; Ezra 6:16–18). Possibly Noah was ceremonially re-dedicating the earth to YHWH as his temple, but regardless the specific nature of the sacrifice suggests that Noah is acting as a priest rather than simply a patriarch.[70] The responsive promise of God further suggests this was an act of mediation, as does the correspondence with Noah's discernment in Gen 7:1–10.[71]

The similarities between God's blessing of Noah and the blessing of humankind in Genesis 1 are obvious and well attested.[72] What is interesting are the variations rather than the similarities between the passages. Where Gen 1:27–31 is entirely positive, Gen 9:2–6 contains implied admonitions

---

64. King, *Realignment*, 79; contra Firmage's suggestion that with Noah God's exclusive sovereignty over life is seceded to humanity. Firmage, "Genesis 1," 102.

65. Orlov, "Heir," 64; Hamilton, *Genesis*, 307; Gentry and Wellum, *Kingdom*, 174.

66. Wenham, *Story as Torah*, 34–35; Mann, *Book of Torah*, 23–24.

67. Blenkinsopp, *Sage, Priest, Prophet*, 105.

68. Rendtorff, *Canonical Hebrew Bible*, 510; Rendtorff emphasizes the altar-building aspect of Noah's action and its "crucial point in cultic life."

69. The strong priestly nature of Noah's sacrifices in Gen 8:20 is even further amplified if Gen 9:8–17 is read as a narrative elaboration of Gen 8:21–22 rather than as a chronologically separate reiteration. The repeated inclusion of all animal life with the covenant to Noah makes it clear that Noah's sacrifice was accepted on all living creatures' behalf. Noah was not acting as a head of household, but as a ruler over Creation.

70. Cf. Orlov, "Heir," 60.

71. Cf. Mathews, *Genesis 1—11:26*, 394.

72. Beale, "Eden," 12; Hamilton, *Genesis*, 313.

against humankind for their failure to steward properly the lives entrusted to them. The presence of fear marks a change in the animals' perception of humanity; however, the responsibility for the animals remains upon humankind.

The divide between humans and animals allows for the consumption of the animals, but with the specific inclusion of the prohibition against blood. The association of blood with life suggests—both here and in the Levitical food laws—that the problem with eating blood is the devouring of life when God is not only a God of order, but also of life. If humanity is to represent him, then they must work to honor life rather than devour it.[73] This ideology explains the natural movement from the fear of the animals, to the eating of animals, to the prohibition against manslaughter in Gen 9:6. Human failure to honor life begins in Genesis 4 and continues until the flood; God's admonition reminds Noah of how humankind has *not* faithfully represented God and therefore failed to uphold the divine image.[74] The admonitions of Gen 9:2–6 reiterate the original purpose of humankind alongside the necessary correctives to human attitude.[75]

What is particularly interesting is that just as Gen 1:27 is the only poetic verse of Genesis 1, so too is Gen 9:6—containing the ascription of the divine צלם to humankind—the only poetic verse of the flood narrative. Notably, Gen 1:27 describes humanity as God's image in a life-giving context while Gen 9:6 uses the description to prohibit life-taking.[76] The invocation of the divine image in Gen 9:6 is not simply a statement against murder, but also a reminder of the role of humanity in the re-Created world: a role identical to the original calling of priesthood and a role that Noah, the righteous man, had already demonstrated.[77]

---

73. Reno, *Genesis*, 56; cf. Hamilton, *Genesis*, 314.

74. Middleton, *New Heaven*, 54; cf. Firmage, "Genesis 1," 103–4.

75. Blenkinsopp, *Sage, Priest, Prophet*, 105; Dempster, *Dominion and Dynasty*, 73; Middleton, *Liberating Image*, 221; Middleton, *New Heaven*, 54.

76. The prohibition against taking human life could be reflective of the general disregard for human life that had preceded the flood as the fear of the animals seems to be, or it could be more specific. The immediate context of sacrifice and the discussion of the interaction between humans and animals suggests that Gen 9:6 may be specifically concerned with prohibiting human sacrifice or the treatment of human beings as if they were animals only fit for sacrifice (an idea contrasting against the interpretation of Nimrod as a man-hunter [Gen 10:8–9]). If this is the case, the priestly overtones of the passage are further amplified and Noah's role as priest elaborated.

77. McKeown, *Genesis*, 64–65. McKeown also notes that Jewish teachings establish Noah as the "lawgiver for the Gentiles" in a manner complementary to Moses' role for Israel, and makes the explicit comparison that "both are saved by an ark . . . ; both have a prophetic ministry, *a priestly role*, and both had key roles in an important building project" (emphasis added).

Cultic Re-Creation and the Priestly Response (Exodus 25–40; 1 Kings 6–8)

Some of the connections between the tabernacle, temple architecture, and Creation have been noted in the present work; however, these few references have been deliberately restricted to specific concerns. This restriction is justified if for no other reason by the preponderance of work on the subject, but also because the broad connections between the structure of Creation and the holy places is secondary to the specific interest in how the temple motifs directly relate to a call to priesthood. The connection between temple and Creation is somewhat irrelevant if they do not demand a priestly presence.[78]

Since there are such strong ties between Creation and the tabernacle/temple, if a priestly response can be seen in one then it may be reasonably inferred in the others. This expectation is magnified when considered in light of the synchronic connections between the formation of Israel and the original Creation.[79] It has been argued that the commissioning of the human in Gen 1:26–30 is a priestly commission, of which the response to the commission was illustrated in the naming ceremony of Genesis 2. Since the primary concern of the present study is to examine the צלם אלהים as a call to priesthood, and since a priestly response to the building of the tabernacle/temple is axiomatic; only the priestly responses to the establishment of the holy places that affirm a priestly reading of Genesis 1–2 will be considered here.

Exodus 25–40 is concerned primarily with the structure of the tabernacle and says little about any sort of priestly response to the building of the tabernacle. That said, it is perhaps notable that the book closes with the cloud of YHWH's glory covering the tabernacle in a manner that would coincide with Walton's suggestion that the idea of Sabbath in Gen 2:1–3 is indicative of the divine inhabitation of the holy place.[80] That this takes place only after the respective holy places have been "completed" (כלה—Gen 2:1–2/Exod 39:32; 40:33) is both logically and theologically necessary.[81] The question then, is whether the inhabitation of the tabernacle shows priestly activity that corresponds with Adam's response in Genesis 2.

There is no immediate connection between priestly activity and the cloud's covering of the tabernacle. Indeed, at first glance it would seem

---

78. Edersheim, *Bible History*, 2:123.
79. Young, *Creator, Creation*, 34; Barr, "Revelation through History," 8.
80. Cf. Stuart, *Exodus*, 792–93.
81. Ross, *Recalling the Hope of Glory*, 88; The logical necessity comes from the temporal sequence. The theological necessity—if Walton's interpretation is accepted—comes from the expectation for the holy place to be complete before God issues his reign from there.

counter to priestly activity, since the presence of the cloud forbade entrance into the tabernacle (Exod 40:35). The conclusion of Exodus with the cloud's presence, however, is not the end of the theological narrative that extends without interruption into Leviticus, which begins immediately with the communication between God and Moses about the proper conduct of sacrifices. While the conduct of the sacrificial system is not directly comparable to the naming ceremony of Genesis 2, it is a very distinct priestly occupation and does show a priestly response to the completion of the holy place's construction.[82]

It could be argued that the priestly instructions on sacrifice in Leviticus 1–8 are divine speech, and therefore not representative of priestly response. However, immediately following the instructions is the narrative of Leviticus 8–9 where not only is the Aaronic priesthood formally ordained but also they immediately conduct sacrifice to YHWH as a response to their calling.[83] Further, after the warning against presumption that the Nadab and Abihu narrative provides, the divine instruction commences in Leviticus 11 with YHWH speaking to both Moses and—for the first time since Exod 6:13 where he was instructed in matters of salvation—directly to Aaron. This is particularly notable considering the strong connection between Leviticus 11 and the categorization of animals in Gen 1:20–25 and the naming ceremony of Gen 2:18–23.[84] These connections form certain parallels between Creation and the completion of the tabernacle:

---

82. Rooker, *Leviticus*, 47–49, 80; cf. Wenham, *Book of Leviticus*, 118.

83. Wenham, *Leviticus*, 129–30; Rooker, *Leviticus*, 138–40. The ordination of Aaron is particularly reflective of the Genesis 1 narrative when one considers the correlation of Adam and Aaron within Jewish thought. The assumption that the high priest was a Second Adam is clearly attested in Sir 49:16—50:1, but also implied in Ezek 28:12–16. While both of these texts are later in the history of Israel, they allow for the possibility of a much earlier tradition from which they were drawing. As Fletcher-Louis states, "Since Ezekiel is taken by some scholars to be closely related in time and theology to the priestly material in the Pentateuch, we should not be surprised to find his theology of God's image worked out in the cultic material of Exodus 25–40."

Blenkinsopp recognizes this connection and actually expands the above observation, noting that the seven day ordination ceremony of Aaron complements the seven-day Creation. While Blenkinsopp's observation does not affirm the צלם אלהים as a priestly calling, it does demonstrate the strong ties between the establishment of the Aaronic priesthood and Genesis 1 and complements the association of Aaron and Adam.

Finally, Gorman suggests that the placement of the sacrificial information prior to the ordination of the priests is logical, and reflects the nature of the priestly task to which Aaron and his sons are being ordained. If this is the case, then Leviticus 1–7 can be considered responsive as well. Fletcher-Louis, "God's Image," 88–91; Blenkinsopp, *Sage, Priest, Prophet*, 69; Gorman, *Ideology of Ritual*, 48–49.

84. Cf. Rooker, *Leviticus*, 170. While Rooker only traces the dietary laws to the clean animals of Genesis 7, the parallels between the flood narrative and Creation suggest

	Creation	Tabernacle
Creation of the Holy Place	Gen 1:1–25	Exod 25–40
Commission of Holy People	Gen 1:26–30	Exod 28–29
Completion and Divine Rest	Gen 2:1–3a	Exod 40:34–38
Priestly Response	Gen 2:15–23	Lev 8–9

While these parallels are not exact, they are legitimate and certainly reflect the reality of not only priestly response to the Creation/tabernacle, but also a similarity in the type of response.[85]

Whether or not the construction of the Jerusalem temple is considered a second reflection of the Creation or a re-creation of the tabernacle, similar theological parallels can be expected.[86] Certainly the building of the holy place is prevalent (1 Kgs 6–8:11 [excluding 1 Kgs 7:1–12]), and the inhabitation of the temple by the glorious cloud of YHWH in 1 Kgs 8:10–11 parallels the inhabitation of Exod 40:34–35.[87] However, the commissioning of the holy people is significantly different in the temple narrative. Where the construction of the tabernacle by Moses led to the ordination of the priesthood, there is no specific charge to the priests in 1 Kings 6–8.[88] There is, however, a very significant implied commission of the nation of Israel as a whole in 1 Kgs 8:22–53, followed by the massive sacrificial activity in which not only Solomon but also "all Israel with him" participated and that served as the completion of the temple dedication by "all the people of Israel" (1 Kgs 8:62–63) and the initiation of a holy feast (v. 65).[89] The sacrifices,

---

that his overlooking of the kinds of animals in Genesis 1 is short-sighted.

85. Cf. Garr, "God's Creation," 89–90; Wenham, *Leviticus*, 129–30. The fact that Moses oversaw the formation of the tabernacle and the ordination of Aaron and his sons can also be considered in light of Exod 4:16 (cf. 7:1). Moses' role as אלהים adequately represents the creative activity of God in the construction of the Tabernacle and the ordination of the priests.

86. Blenkinsopp, *Sage, Priest, Prophet*, 113.

87. House, *1, 2 Kings*, 139.

88. The Chronicler devotes considerable attention to David's cultic activity in 1 Chronicles 23–26, which could reflect a charge to the priests, Levites, and other attendants of the temple. However, while the temple concept is certainly present in the Davidic narrative, the organization of the religious personnel under David serves as a necessary prelude to the temple building rather than a direct function of it. The exact nature of the interaction of 1 Chronicles 22–29 with 2 Chronicles 2–7 is worth considering, but it might be suggested that the primary purpose of the Davidic narrative is to make a messianic statement, while the actual building of the temple is a cultic one.

89. House, *1, 2 Kings*, 150.

the dedication of the holy grounds, and the feast all serve as responses to God that directly relate to the priestly purview.

What is interesting is that Solomon's role in the construction of the temple very much parallels Moses' role in the building of the tabernacle, and Moses' role was itself simply an incarnation of YHWH's work in Creation.[90] It is this parallel that justifies the ostensibly priestly activity of Solomon despite his exclusion from the Aaronic priesthood, and reiterates the national call to priesthood issued in Exod 19:6 that has already been related to the צלם אלהים of Gen 1:26–28.[91] Ultimately, the sequence and types of priestly responses to creative activity in these three narratives are broadly similar and suggest that the natural response to creative work is a response that is not simply worshipful, but distinctly priestly.

Societal Re-Creation and the Priestly Response (2 Chr 36:22–23; Ezra)

The return from exile is consistently portrayed as a second exodus, with the former captives charged to claim their inheritance in the promised land.[92] However, since the Law was already in Israel's possession, there was no direct equivalent to the Sinai event.[93] Instead, the restoration conflates the imagery of Sinai and the establishment of the tabernacle with the motif of the land inheritance—a motif reflective of God's promise to Abraham rather than the war-like conquest that directly followed the exodus from Egypt. This is an important recognition, since it underpins the association of Ezra's

---

90. Morrow, "Creation as Temple-Building," 5; Brueggemann, *Israel's Praise*, 4–5. That all three "temple-building" passages utilize a heptadic structure may also be significant. While a heptadic structure does not in itself indicate a priestly response to temple-building, the possible liturgical significance of heptads suggests that they might be implicitly responsive. Middleton, *Liberating Image*, 83–88.

91. Brueggemann observes that the growth of the temple and its concordant understanding that YHWH reigns was "increasingly an embarrassment to the royal agents" of Israel since it made YHWH a destabilizing influence on the monarchy. However, while the reign of YHWH might destabilize human monarchy (an assertion that can be contested on the basis of the Israelite kingship as a regency rather than an autonomous position) it would be an affirmative statement for the cult. This observation can then be paired with Block's commentary on how the temple "democratizes the experience" of communion with God and "opens fellowship with him to everyone;" a situation that reinforces and restores the calling of the entire nation to come before YHWH as priests in Exod 19:6. Brueggemann, *Israel's Praise*, 59; Block, *Deuteronomy*, 308; Block, "Place for My Name," 221.

92. Thompson, *1, 2 Chronicles*, 392.

93. Cf. Van Houten, *Alien in Israelite Law*, 112.

work on the temple with the tabernacle and the recognition that the land's restoration was predicated on the promise to Abraham rather than the idea of conquest.[94]

The biblical portrait of the restoration is succinctly and directly presented in Cyrus' edict as an expectation that the temple will be rebuilt so that "whoever is among you of all [YHWH's] people" could worship.[95] This frames the entire restoration of the land around the construction of a holy place and the establishment of a holy people in a manner not dissimilar to the Creation, tabernacle, and temple narratives.[96] The book of Ezra then serves to fill in the details of this general call.

Examining Ezra in the received narrative, there seems to be a general accordance with the same pattern that Creation, tabernacle, and temple followed. The construction of the holy place is the first emphasis of the narrative. While there is no specific commission of a holy people during the construction process, the prominent activity of Joshua and the Levites—particularly in their assignment to oversee the temple's construction (Ezra 3:8b)—reasonably substitutes for this lack of commission.[97] The completion of the temple in Ezra 6:14–15 lacks the mention of God's rest upon the structure, but the response to the temple's building is certainly a priestly one: sacrifice and the assignation of the Levites to the temple, followed by the observation of the Passover feast as administered by the priests (vv. 19–22).[98]

While the preceding observations might be enough to establish a priestly context for the reconstitution of a Jewish state, the ongoing

---

94. Dempster, *Dominion and Dynasty*, 49.

95. Ostensibly, this is a reference to the Jewish people spread throughout the Persian Empire; however, it technically could refer to *any* devotee of YHWH (cf. Ezra 6:21), and thereby accord with Exod 12:38 and Abraham's charge for all of the nations (Gen 12:3) as well.

96. Dempster, *Dominion and Dynasty*, 33; cf. Thompson, *1, 2 Chronicles*, 392. This framework further supports the thesis that the צלם אלהים is best interpreted as a priestly calling if its canonical role is considered. Since this passage is the conclusion of the Hebrew Scriptures, it ends the Tanak with an implied invitation to the future readers of the Chronicles to come and participate in the establishment of and worship at the rebuilt temple.

While this theology should not be sustained simply on the basis of canonical placement (which itself is variable), the fact that those who compiled the Scriptures sensed this invitation is significant. It establishes an awareness that every member of the Israelite nation had a calling toward temple service. Brueggemann, *Israel's Praise*, 14; Goswell, "Having the Last Say," 22.

97. Breneman, *Ezra-Esther*, 94–95.

98. The lack of theophany in the restored temple can be explained any number of ways, but it is easily accounted for by hiddenness/disappearance of God theology appropriate for such a late event.

narrative of Ezra serves to further confirm this conception. The suggestion that Ezra is a type of Moses, combined with Ezra's predominant concern of explicating and enacting the Torah, serves to establish a parallel with the Sinai event and the original reception of the Law—a reception by a kingdom of priests.[99] Lest this be dismissed on the basis of the book of Ezra's clear recognition of a distinct priestly and Levitical structure, two observations must be made. First, the Israelite priesthood itself was paradigmatic for the nation; the prominence of priestly and Levitical leadership in Ezra does not detract from a general sense of calling for the nation.[100] Second, and perhaps more importantly, in the concluding chapters of Ezra 9–10 where the Law is actually prescribed and enacted the priests and Levites (with the exception of using כהן as an identifier on an individual) are only mentioned in conjunction with the people of Israel (Ezra 9:1; 10:5; et al.). They have no independent status in the call for purity; neither do they have any special restrictions explicitly mentioned.[101] There is a sense of equivalence despite the paradigmatic role of the priests that is suggestive of the overarching call to be a nation of priests.[102]

SELECTED APOCALYPTIC PASSAGES ON THE NEW CREATION AND PRIESTHOOD

Theologians have long recognized that the end of this Creation is actually the beginning of a New Creation. As such, any connection between priestly activity and the apocalyptic passages of the Old Testament is particularly valuable to the present study.[103] A full analysis of apocalyptic and/or eschatological prophecies would be a work unto itself; however, despite the varying imagery associated with apocalyptic visions, the general tone and theological interests are notably similar. A small sampling of the genre is sufficient to demonstrate that cultic imagery is compatible with the prophecies in question.

---

99. Breneman, *Ezra-Esther*, 149; cf. Brueggemann, *Israel's Praise*, 24–25; Goldingay, *Israel's Life*, 65.

100. Cf. Blenkinsopp, *Sage, Priest, Prophet*, 108–9.

101. This is not to deny the fact that there were specific prohibitions and restrictions on priests' wives in the Law that was being read, but simply observes that in the narrative of Ezra the status of priests is both exalted as a paradigm for the people and equalized alongside the people. While he is not discussing Ezra when he makes the observation, Bordeianu suggests this same phenomenon in the contemporary church. Cf. Bordeianu, "Priesthood," 414.

102. Livingston, *Pentateuch*, 227.

103. Cf. Middleton, *New Heaven*, 106.

It seems reasonable to focus on the Major Prophets with their intertwining themes, influence of or by the Minor Prophets, and larger corpus of work; so Isaiah, Jeremiah, and Ezekiel will be examined first. Further, the distinct apocalyptic language of Daniel and Zechariah demand individual consideration of these two smaller works as well.

The Establishment of the Holy Place and Calendar (Isaiah)

The authorship of the book of Isaiah remains a disputed topic, but this dispute does little to impede an analysis of Isaiah's eschatological portrait. Since little personal information is known about the prophet Isaiah and information on the supposed Isaianic school that carried on his work is purely conjectural, an examination of the eschatological elements of Isaiah must be based wholly upon the extant Scripture, which even critics of Isaianic authorship acknowledge possesses a remarkable theological unity.[104] With this in mind, there is little reason to separate a study of Proto- and Deutero- (or Trito-) Isaiah in the present context.[105]

The primary passages of present concern are Isaiah 24–27, 34–35, and 60–66.[106] Not explicated upon but worth remembering is the title Holy One of Israel. This title has been linked to both the demands of holiness (cf. Lev 19:2 et al.) and the establishment of the nation of Israel in Exod 19:6 This connection with Israel's general calling and the focus on holiness both could be argued to suggest a cultic or priestly context for interpreting Isaiah's prophecies as a whole.[107] Whether or not it should apply to the book as a whole, this implied context certainly accords with the apocalyptic presentations within Isaiah.

Isaiah 24's depiction of judgment begins immediately with the desolation of not only the people, but also the priest (v. 2a). This desolation is, of course, a response to the transgression of תורה (v. 5b) resulting in famine and

---

104. Rendtorff, *Canonical Hebrew Bible*, 168; Oswalt, *Book of Isaiah: Chapters 1–39*, 44; Goldingay, *Theology of the Book of Isaiah*, 15–16.

105. Blenkinsopp, *History of Prophecy in Israel*, 98–99.

106. The Servant Songs could certainly be entered into the discussion as well; however, the controversies and variations of interpretation that surround the songs extend well beyond the present work and do not add enough to the current discussion to warrant the possible distraction from the thesis at hand.

107. Oswalt, *Isaiah 1–39*, 41–42. While Oswalt does not explicitly connect his argument to cult, his repeated assertions that the only acceptable way to holiness is through obedience and righteousness inherently connects to תורה—the instruction in righteousness.

ruination.¹⁰⁸ The proper response to God's action is presented in vv. 14–16a which clearly reflects cultic interests and might expect a temple setting of some kind. By contrast, instead of addressing worship and temple, Isaiah instead addresses the reversal birthed by the treachery of his peers (v. 16).¹⁰⁹

This reversal from the right response of worship to betrayal and persecution is then cast in Creative imagery, where the land is shattered and judged (vv. 18b–20). The opening of the windows of heaven and the shaking of the earth suggests a removal of Creation, while the transgression (פשע) of the inhabitants connects this de-Creation with priestly concerns.¹¹⁰ As the Old Creation is being swept away, YHWH then inhabits Mount Zion with "his glory . . . before his elders" (v. 23b), a reenactment of his glory covering the tabernacle and the temple at their ordination(s). Ultimately, the chapter moves from cultic failure to de-Creation, to the reestablishment not simply of the world but specifically of a holy place in which to worship.¹¹¹ The praise song of Isaiah 25 immediately reinforces this interpretation and leads to the celebration of a feast (v. 6) reflective not of royal ideology but cultic invitation (cf. Isa 2:2; 66:18).¹¹²

Similarly, the warlike imagery of destruction in Isaiah 34 might initially seem to reflect holy war and royal ideology, but it is immediately cast in terms of sacrifice. The fury of God is kindled to devote (חרם) humankind to the slaughter (טבח). The religious connotations of חרם are well attested, but the presence of טבח is particularly interesting. טבח is a general term depicting not simply the killing of an animal, but the killing of an animal specifically for food. This, combined with the explicit sacrificial language of vv. 6–7, suggests that the חרם of the nations is a sort of "anti-feast" that satiates a divine hunger for justice rather than for fellowship.¹¹³ This is further supported by the imperative of v. 16 to "seek and read from the book of the LORD" and the expectation that the faithful of YHWH will do just that and rejoin fellowship with God (v. 17b). The idea of restored fellowship is specifically linked with priestly concerns in the song of Isaiah 35, where joy is found on the דרך הקדש that is barred to any who are unclean and leads directly to Mount Zion, the new Sinai already introduced in Isaiah 24–25.¹¹⁴

---

108. Oswalt, *Isaiah 1–39*, 443.
109. Doyle, *Apocalypse of Isaiah*, 186.
110. Ibid., 199; Gorman, *Ideology of Ritual*, 45; Watts, *Isaiah 1–33*, 325.
111. Oswalt, *Isaiah 1–39*, 456.
112. Doyle, *Apocalypse of Isaiah*, 252–56.
113. Oswalt, *Isaiah 1–39*, 606, 611–12; cf. Goldingay, *Israel's Life*, 148–49.
114. Oswalt, *Isaiah 1–39*, 625–26.

The emphases on fellowship with YHWH and a return to the holy place continue in Isaiah 60–66. Notably, Isaiah 60 begins with distinct Creation language and noting the contrast between the people in חשך and the people of God who would receive אור. In fact, it is the presence of the light that will draw the other nations to come to Zion and behold God's glory.[115] There is clearly no physical intention with Isaiah's use of light in this passage, and its connection with either the Word or the Presence of God duplicates the interpretation of Gen 1:3–5.[116] This is affirmed and repeated in Isa 60:19–20, which prepares for the Jubilee of Isaiah 61—itself a priestly concern.

While the nations' bringing of tribute (Isa 60:5b–13) certainly could reflect royal ideology, it is important to recognize that the tribute is not going to the Israelites alone, but rather to "the City of the LORD, the Zion of the Holy One of Israel." Therefore, the tribute brought to the Israelites is actually an offering to YHWH, and their reception of it is more reflective of priestly facilitation than of royal accumulation (cf. Isa 61:6–7).[117]

The song of Isaiah 61, proclaiming the eschatological Jubilee, must be considered in light of Leviticus 25 where Jubilee was announced at the Day of Atonement.[118] This suggests that the initiator of the Jubilee was the high priest, and as a Sabbath of Sabbath Years it fell fully under priestly auspice. With this in mind, the importance of Isa 61:6 and the designation of all Israel as priests of YHWH cannot be ignored. The declarations of vv. 1–4 and the covenant teaching of vv. 8–9 hinge around this designation, and the attire of v. 10 is not simply wedding attire but priestly attire.

Chapters 62–63 speak of judgment and destruction, which somewhat mutes the cultic imagery, but it is not the people of God who are engaged in vengeance but God alone. The comparison to a royal crown in Isa 62:3 is a statement of YHWH's sovereignty, not Israel's, and the preferred connection between Israel and YHWH is not found in court, but in cult: "They shall be called the Holy people, the Redeemed of the LORD" (Isa 62:12 ESV). Further, after recounting the faithfulness of God and the failure of Israel, Isaiah's prayer pleads for God to return to "the tribes of your heritage" (Isa 63:17b). While inheritance (נחלה) is a common term, it is notable that it is most often used to discuss the people's inheritance of land or property.[119] The idea of a people as an inheritance is far less common, but it is alluded

---

115. Von Rad, *Old Testament Theology*, 2:295; Oswalt, *Book of Isaiah: Chapters 40–66*, 535; cf. Schnabel, "Israel," 41–42.

116. Cf. Oswalt, *Isaiah 40–66*, 538–39; Watts, *Isaiah 34–66*, 297.

117. Von Rad, *Old Testament Theology*, 2:295–96; Middleton, *New Heaven*, 106; Oswalt, *Isaiah 40–66*, 541.

118. Cf. Watts, *Isaiah 34–66*, 303.

119. Cf. von Rad, *Problem of the Hexateuch*, 86.

to in Exod 15:17 where the people are planted into the holy place (a priestly area) and explicitly mentioned in Deut 4:20 and Deut 10:9 where the exodus from Egypt to Sinai (the establishment of the kingdom of priests) and the ordination of the Aaronic priesthood are mentioned. This, combined with the priestly tenor of Isa 62:12 and the connection between the people of Israel and the sanctuary in Isa 63:18, suggests that the redemption of the people is not simply a redemption from slavery but rather a redemption for service in the holy place, a priestly redemption.[120]

Isaiah 64:10–11 continue to emphasize the loss of holy places, while Isaiah 65 begins with a litany of condemnation against a people who violate cult prescriptions in sacrifice (v. 3), diet (v. 4), and presumption (v. 5).[121] While the remainder of Isaiah 65 presents general imagery of restoration, Isaiah 66 immediately begins with YHWH's declaration that his abode is beyond Creation's limits. While this could be read as a royal statement referring to a palace, the fact that dwelling is a place for God to rest lends itself better to a temple image.[122] Further, a temple interpretation better sets the stage for the discussion of false sacrifice and offering in v. 3 and prepares for the announcement in Isa 66:6 that judgment will come not as an edict from a palace, but rather as a sound from the temple.[123] The final judgment that forms the culmination of Isaiah's work is therefore directly tied to the holy place and priestly concerns. Finally, the formation of an eschatological priesthood in v. 21 and the emphasis on the New Creation's adherence to the liturgical calendar (v. 23) cannot be ignored and conclude the work with a focus on priesthood.[124]

Isaiah's eschatological priesthood provides another important consideration for associating the Creation and the image of God with priestly matters. While vv. 20–21 state that God will gather "all of your brothers" from the nations and form the priesthood from them, it is not entirely clear who the brothers in question are. Ostensibly, it might be assumed they are Israelites; however, the immediately preceding discussion addressed the proselytizing of the nations and the rise of God's glory among the whole

---

120. Oswalt, *Isaiah 40–66*, 615; cf. Watts, *Isaiah 34–66*, 334; Goldingay, *Theology of Isaiah*, 84–86.

121. Notably, the presumption of Isa 63:5 is one of cultural superiority that directly impedes the national calling of Israel to serve as a priest for the world and one of the first condemnations explicated in Isaiah's prophecy (cf. Isa 2:2–3).

122. While v. 1 uses מנוחה (a derivative of נוח) rather than a derivative of שבת, a comparison of Gen 2:2–3 and Exod 20:11 suggests that the terms can be used somewhat equivalently.

123. Oswalt, *Isaiah 40–66*, 668–71.

124. Watts, *Isaiah 34–66*, 365.

world.¹²⁵ With this in mind, it is viable to suggest that brothers brought back to the eschatological temple are not necessarily Israelite (cf. Isa 56:7).¹²⁶ This, combined with the very explicit statement that all people (from any land) will worship YHWH in v. 23b, could be argued to connect all of humanity—finally engaged in the occupation for which God has created them—with priesthood, and thereby the צלם אלהים with priesthood as well.¹²⁷

The Dissemination of Priestly Knowledge (Jeremiah)

Any examination of Jeremiah is faced with historical and textual difficulties, as the prophecies are not arranged chronologically and the text itself is marked by the structural divergences between the MT and the LXX.¹²⁸ While these large difficulties impact the discreet exegesis of individual passages, scholars of Jeremiah are in general agreement on the coherence of the theological message of the book and its Deuteronomistic overtones.¹²⁹ Further, while exegetical difficulties do exist the majority of those difficulties have little impact over the present study of priestly concerns in Jeremiah. The text is explicit in associating Jeremiah with the priestly family of Hilkiah (Jer 1:1), and there is no significant contention around Jeremiah's origin. Concerns over whether the prophecy bearing his name originated with Jeremiah or with his students are somewhat overwrought: as noted in the previous section, prophecy originating from a prophet's school might be reasonably assumed to reflect the general theological interests of the prophet unless there is compelling reason to suspect otherwise.¹³⁰ In the case of Jeremiah, the strong interest in covenant mediation that serves as the theological foundation of Jeremiah's individual arguments certainly reflects the priestly role of both intercession and edification and pervades the entire work, whether or not it originated entirely from the prophet himself.¹³¹

---

125. Oswalt, *Isaiah 40–66*, 689.

126. Schnabel, "Israel," 41.

127. Oswalt, *Isaiah 40–66*, 690; Watts, *Isaiah 34–66*, 365–66. This can also be connected with Isaiah 24 and its presentation that *global* destruction is predicated on failure to adhere to the תורה. In his work on this subject, Fischer likens this to violation of the natural revelation of God. Whether violating revealed תורה or natural law, though, the end result is the failure of humanity to properly honor God in worship and service—elements of priestly occupation. Fischer, *Tora fur Israel*, 60–62; Firmage, "Genesis 1," 103.

128. Rendtorff, *Canonical Hebrew Bible*, 201; Thompson, *Book of Jeremiah*, 30–31.

129. House, *Old Testament Theology*, 299.

130. Cf. Block, *Ezekiel 1–24*, 19; Bright, *Jeremiah*, 287.

131. Thompson, *Jeremiah*, 61–62. Adherents of the documentary hypothesis often emphasize the P-source as the culmination of priestly thought; however, this perspective

The majority of Jeremiah's prophecies are directly applicable to his contemporary society and not reserved for any eschatological framework, condemning current and past idolatrous practices.[132] However, when Jeremiah does speak of national restoration, he does occasionally shift into eschatological thought. This thought is more subdued than other prophets', as it focuses almost exclusively on the renewal of a covenant relationship and its internalization. Regardless of its subtlety, though, Jeremiah's concern with covenant internalization reflects priestly theological concerns and in many ways is the apex of the priestly role as paradigm: the priests served to edify the people on the right way of worship, and an internalization of the covenant reflects an ultimate understanding of worship.[133]

This connection between the priestly paradigmatic role and the internalization of the covenant is critical for a proper understanding of Jer 3:15-18. In what initially seems to be a subversive statement, Jeremiah records the elimination of the ark of the covenant that precedes the assembly of nations at Jerusalem. While the removal of the ark might initially seem to run counter to a priestly ideology, this is only true if the removal represents a severance of the covenant relationship. Quite to the contrary, though, Jer 3:15-18 depicts the ark as unnecessary not because of a severed relationship but rather because of the intimacy of YHWH with his restored people.[134] There is no need for a symbolic presence because the divine presence first will be made manifest in the midst of Jerusalem, and the Israelite leaders will then reign with דעה והשכיל as a consequence of that divine presence. Both of these terms (דעה and השכיל) have broad semantic meanings, and cannot be isolated as cultic. The particular form of דעה is relatively rare in the Scriptures, occurring in only five additional verses (1 Sam 2:3; Isa 11:9; 28:9; Ps 73:11; Job 36:4). The occurrence in Isa 28:9 is particularly interesting. In this verse, knowledge is paralleled with proclamation, which then corresponds to the (failed) priests and prophets respectively of v. 7.

---

of P does not change the rather overt priestly interests of D with its concern for a covenant foundation (Deut 4:1-2), the calling of a holy people (Deut 7:6), worship in the proper place (Deut 12:5), proper observance of the liturgical calendar (Deut 15-16), and Levitical oversight of society (Deut 17:8-13, 18). In fact, since Deuteronomy lacks any hard division between its discussion of the Levites and the priesthood, it is very much an essentially priestly document, even if not from the later priestly school associated with P. So while P might be the ultimate representation of priestly theology, the use of D to reinforce priestly thought is both legitimate and, it can be argued, necessary. McConville, "Priests and Levites," 5; Leuchter, "Levite in Your Gates," 435; cf. Sabourin, *Priesthood*, 107; King, *Realignment*, 38-39.

132. Von Rad, *Old Testament Theology*, 2:194.

133. Cf. Blenkinsopp, *History of Prophecy*, 135; Thompson, *Jeremiah*, 67.

134. Rendtorff, *Canonical Hebrew Bible*, 227; Thompson, *Jeremiah*, 69.

Further, while שכל is common, the Hiphil infinitive form (השכיל) is found only in this verse, in Jer 23:5 where it is applied to the Branch, and 1 Chr 28:19 where it is used to describe knowledge of the temple's construction. So while the shepherds' דעה והשכיל is not necessarily an endorsement of priestly knowledge, the association of the terms with priestly activity and the holy place makes it possible. That the redemption of the Israelites—a people called into priesthood (cf. Exod 19:6)—leads directly to the nations gathering before YHWH and accepting the covenant (as implied by v. 17b) only further reinforces the suggestion that Jeremiah's eschatological vision in these verses is priestly.[135]

Regarding the Branch, it must be acknowledged that he is clearly a royal figure. However, the existence of a king does not preclude priestly ideology; particularly when the king in question is also portrayed as a priestly figure.[136] Both Jeremiah 3 and Jer 23:1–6 include discussion of the shepherds of Israel. It should be considered that while the shepherds could be kings or royal figures, they could also be religious leaders as suggested of the shepherds of Zechariah 11–13.[137] Considering Jeremiah's own heritage and the problem of false worship that he decried, the representation of religious leaders as false shepherds is not an unnatural expectation. Similarly, Ezekiel 34:1–6 represents the failed leadership in terms of shepherding, but the context of Ezekiel is even more overtly priestly: the false shepherds ate the fat of God's sacrifices and failed to spiritually nurture the people of Israel.[138] Considering the priestly associations of all three prophets, a consistent use of shepherds to illustrate religious rather than royal rulers is reasonable, and—if accepted—very consistent with a vision of cultic revival and priestly purity in the age to come.

Any idea of eschatological cultic revival must, of course, harmonize with the primary eschatological passage of the book, Jer 31:31–34. The installation of the covenant within has been associated with the prescriptions of Deut 6:4–9 and Deut 10:12–22, and the earlier admonition of the peoples to circumcise their hearts (Jer 4:4). As with Jer 3:16, Jer 31:34 initially

---

135. Thompson, *Jeremiah*, 203; Blenkinsopp, *History of Prophecy*, 174.

136. The Branch, as a Davidic king, is also directly connected with the priesthood of Melchizedek (cf. Ps 110:4). While Israel did not have a full-fledged priest-king mentality, the priesthood of Melchizedek combined with the predominantly priestly context and interest of Jeremiah lends legitimacy to the contention that even when the royal Branch is introduced, the primary focus remains on priestly matters even if not excluding royal concerns.

137. Goldingay, *Israel's Life*, 723.

138. Consider also the end of this illustration, where YHWH serves as the shepherd and judges between the fat sheep and the lean (Ezek 34:20). The evaluation of animals was not a royal task, but rather a priestly duty.

appears to be a subversive statement against the cult. However, examined in light of the wider understanding of vv. 31–33 the statement that there will be no need to teach (למד) one another the covenant is actually expansive of the priesthood.[139] When the entire populace of Israel has inscribed the covenant on their hearts, then they will no longer *need* priestly instructions because they will each have the capability to *be* a priest.[140] This interpretation is supported by the parallel of vv. 31–34 with vv. 38–40 through the introductory phrase הנה ימים באים נאם־יהוה and the description in vv. 38–40 of the restoration of Jerusalem as a sacred space, a temple city, and the subsequent result of the nations' recognition of YHWH (Jer 33:9).[141] With this in mind, the expanding of covenant knowledge serves as an expansion of priesthood: the kingdom of priests will serve as such for the world, a concept fully in keeping with Jeremiah's Deuteronomistic theological foundation (cf. Deut 4:5–8) and possibly hinted at in Jer 31:14.[142] With the inclusion of the nations among the people of God in Jer 3:17, a universal aspect of priestly understanding is established that could reflect the calling of humankind to priestly service in the צלם אלהים.

The Building of the Eschatological Temple (Ezekiel)

If the connection between Jeremiah and a priestly heritage is recognized, the intense priestly perspective of Ezekiel should be even more readily apparent. Aside from his biographical credentials (Ezek 1:3) and personal

---

139. Leuchter, "Levite in Your Gates," 425–26; Thompson, *Jeremiah*, 581; cf. von Rad, *Theology of Israel's Prophetic Traditions*, 213. While למד is a common term in the Old Testament, its distribution favors Deuteronomy and Psalms and suggests that the biblical preference is for teaching that pertains to "the divine-human relationship and the manner of life expected to issue from that relationship" and therefore suggests the covenant mediation and edification entrusted to the priests. Powell, "למד," 108.

140. Thompson, *Jeremiah*, 581; Middleton, *New Heaven*, 106; cf. di Vito, "Alttestamentliche Anthropologie." Incidentally, this reversal of humanity's previous inability to apprehend properly the divine will and live accordingly could be considered a re-initiation of the צלם אלהים not dissimilar from the designation of Noah in Gen 9:6.

141. Thompson, *Jeremiah*, 599. The measuring of that which is to be restored is also found in Ezekiel and Zechariah, once again associating the three priestly writers. The measurements of Ezekiel 40, 42 are specifically temple measurements, while the measurements in Zech 1:16, 2:1–5 apply to Jerusalem as the place where God's glory can be found and where holy fire protects the people (cf. Isa 4:5)—a temple city similar to Jeremiah's vision.

142. Habel, *Land Is Mine*, 96; Greidanus, "Universal Dimension," 39, 50–51.

piety (Ezek 4:14), the elaborate emphasis on the eschatological temple in Ezekiel 40–46 makes his priestly concerns and interests absolutely clear.[143]

While the text of Ezekiel is fraught with literary and semantic difficulties, the extant version generally isolates its discussion of eschatological restoration to the latter chapters of the book.[144] The preparation of Judah for destruction and the fall of Jerusalem in Ezekiel 33 signals a transition into more overtly eschatological thought, as much of the descriptions of restoration in Ezekiel 34–48 cannot reasonably apply to the postexilic reconstruction of Jerusalem.[145] Passages of present concern include Ezek 36:22–38; 37:24–28; 48:30–35. While more could be said of the eschatological temple, the precise measurements of the temple are not the concern so much as its prominence and its movement from or toward these selected passages. Discussions of judgment are not necessary, since the present concern is for the ideal humanity remaining after restoration.[146] Similarly, the eschatological David must be considered, but only—in the present context—in light of how he reveals the overall state of Israel in the eschatological period.

Ezekiel 36:22–28 certainly addresses the vindication of YHWH with the restoration of the people from captivity; however, if the new heart and spirit of vv. 26–28 is read similarly to the new covenant of Jer 31:31–34—which seems to be the best interpretation—then the passage shifts into eschatological expectation beyond what historically occurred.[147] This is important to note, since the next portion of the prophecy is the condemnation of uncleanliness (טמאה, v. 29) and abomination (תועבה, v. 31)—both specific concerns of the priests. It is this cultic rejuvenation that leads to the restoration of the land not to the prominence of the Davidic or Solomonic reigns but rather to the prominence of Eden itself (v. 35).[148] The restoration

---

143. Rendtorff, *Canonical Hebrew Bible*, 232; Kelle, "Dealing with the Trauma," 475–76. The discussion of Ezekiel's relationship to the H source also affirms the strong connections between the prophet and priestly interests. The very fact that the priority or dependency of Ezekiel and H are contested is sufficient to affirm where Ezekiel's primary interests lie. Cf. Lyons, *From Law to Prophecy*, 1, 14.

144. Block, *Ezekiel 1–24*, 14–15.

145. Block, *Ezekiel 25–48*, 268–72.

146. It could be noted that even the judgments of Ezekiel possess priestly overtones. The description of judgment as a sacrifice and a holy feast (Ezek 39:17–20) is certainly explicit. That said, Ezekiel's heritage and background almost demand such imagery; the present concern is not simply whether priestly imagery exists, but rather how it exists in the context of the New Creation and humanity's *telos*.

147. Rendtorff, *Canonical Hebrew Bible*, 255; Block, *Ezekiel 25–48*, 356–57; Petersen, "Creation and Hierarchy," 175.

148. Kelle's study of Ezekiel relates the Edenic connection to the acknowledgment formula ("you will know that I am YHWH"). This is interesting in that it not only

of Israel is then summarized with an illustration directly tied to sacrifice and ritual feasts, and the knowledge of YHWH (v. 38).[149] With this deliberate patterning, Ezekiel explicitly ties ritual purity and observances to not only the eschatological restoration of God's people but also the original Creation, and therefore connects priestly activity to the original man.[150] While the connection with the צלם אלהים is not directly stated, the overall correspondence of the future Israel with Eden provides a strong theological context for the cultic understanding of the divine image.[151]

Similarly, even though beginning with the celebration of the Davidic king, Ezek 37:24-28 focuses on obedience to the Law and the presence of God through the sanctuary of Israel. In fact, while the Davidic king is obviously a royal figure, there is no other royal ideology in this passage.[152] The challenge to perform or walk in God's rules and statutes (משפט and חקות) is one of the primary challenges of both priestly and Deuteronomistic literature for holy living. The covenant of peace that mediates these guides for holiness is then tied directly to the establishment of the sanctuary in the midst of the people. In Ezekiel's eschatology, then, the conduct of the תורה is directly contingent on—or perhaps better said, coexistent with—the presence of God mediated through the sanctuary.[153] Just as the Glory of God's abandonment of the temple indicated the rejection of his people, so too would God's establishment of his sanctuary indicate the redemption of his people.[154]

While there is a strong emphasis on the sanctuary, there is nothing in Ezek 37:24-28 that necessarily elevates all of Israel, much less all of

---

demonstrates the connection between cult and Eden, but also the connection between cult and intimacy with God—a concept originally demonstrated in the garden with Adam (cf. Gen 3:8) and indicative of Adam's priestly nature. Kelle, "Dealing with Trauma," 480.

149. McConville, "Priests and Levites," 15; von Rad, *Theology of Israel's Prophetic Traditions*, 235; Levenson goes so far as to suggest that the Restoration is presented as a New Sinai. If his position is adopted, then Ezekiel deftly conflates Creation, Sinai, and eschatological Restoration into one overarching presentation of Creation theology (and human priesthood). Cf. Levenson, *Theology of the Program of Restoration*, 39.

150. Fletcher-Louis, "God's Image," 88–89; Eichrodt, *Man in the Old Testament*, 44.

151. Beale, "Eden," 8–15, 28–29; cf. Middleton, *New Heaven*, 60. Kelle notes as well that "a deity's name and reputation depend on the deity's people's actions and status"—a concept that may not use the term צלם אלהים but certainly carries the same connotation. Kelle, "Dealing with Trauma," 481.

152. For that matter, Ezekiel avoids using the term מלך at all when not discussing the eschatological David, instead preferring נשא. Rendtorff, *Canonical Hebrew Bible*, 257; Blenkinsopp, *History of Prophecy*, 179; cf. Brueggemann, *Israel's Praise*, 73–74; Block, *Ezekiel 25–48*, 746; Pleins, *Social Visions*, 343.

153. Block, *Ezekiel 25–48*, 421.

154. McConville, "Priests and Levites," 16.

humanity, to a priestly status. In fact, Ezekiel is distinct in ordering eschatological society by their tribes and designating the particular status and fate of the Levites and the priests distinct from Israel at large (Ezek 44:15–31).¹⁵⁵ On the other hand, the shifting between historical and eschatological restoration in the final chapters of Ezekiel does provide some allowance for interpretive variation, and the prophet's description of the restored Israel continues along distinctly priestly lines with its discussions of sacrifice and feast.¹⁵⁶ Perhaps most importantly, the closing passage of Ezek 48:30–35 emphasizes the city's identification as יהוה־שמה. This identification locates the sanctuary of God within Jerusalem but does not necessarily indicate that the city itself is a temple or that its residents are priests. In the earlier vision of the eschatological temple, the presence of the temple building sanctified the entire "territory on the top of the mountain all around" as most holy (Ezek 43:12). Unlike the majority of Ezekiel 40–44 where specific measurements abound, the sanctified area around the temple is left ambiguous. This ambiguity suggests that it was not contained to specific measurements but rather applied to the entire city of Jerusalem. With this in mind, the designation of Jerusalem as יהוה שמה could be interpreted to recognize the entire city was itself a locus of the divine presence and therefore a form of temple.¹⁵⁷ If this is the case, then it could be argued that the people at large, curators of the city, served a priestly role. Notably, while Ezekiel avoids more universalistic statements and focuses his concern on the fate of Israel, there is inclusion of the Gentiles among the Jerusalem residents (Ezek 47:21–23).¹⁵⁸ Those who abide in the presence of YHWH and guard the holy things, obey the divine commands, and indicate the divine presence dwell in the city and come from both native Israelite and converted Gentile peoples.¹⁵⁹ With this, Ezekiel—despite his relatively microcosmic eschatological concerns—affirms a priestly possibility for all humankind.¹⁶⁰

155. Sabourin, *Priesthood*, 110; Petersen, "Creation and Hierarchy," 176–77.

156. Barber would argue that it also emphasizes priestly ideology by making the priesthood the locus of judgment; a position that seems somewhat vindicated by 4QpIsaa 8–10 III, 24–25 and its subjugation of even the messianic king to the priests' authority—an interpretation which serves to validate even further the idea that the dominion of Genesis 1 is a priestly dominion. Barber, "Jesus as the Davidic Temple Builder," 948–50.

157. Block, *Ezekiel 25–48*, 740; Rendtorff, *Canonical Hebrew Bible*, 259; cf. Beale, "Eden," 28–29.

158. Van Houten, *Alien in Israelite Law*, 115–16.

159. Lyons, *From Law to Prophecy*, 133.

160. Cf. Van Wolde, *Stories of the Beginning*, 33; Van Houten, *Alien in Israelite Law*, 118; Block, *Ezekiel 1–24*, 56–57. It could be further argued that Ezekiel, conversant with priestly theology, would have been well aware of Lev 19:34 and its egalitarian approach to

Eschatological Holy People and Place (Daniel)

Any full interpretation of Daniel is immediately met with the difficulty of discerning between futurist and fulfilled interpretations; however, on a smaller scale these distinctions are not necessary. The very nature of apocalyptic language aligned contemporary struggle with eschatological battle, so that the interpretation of any of the passages—past or future—informs the understanding of the other passages in many ways.[161] With this in mind, it is unnecessary to the present study to determine if the rock of Daniel 2 (for example) was Judas Maccabee, the Incarnate Jesus of the past, or the Victorious Jesus who will come. In all three of these cases, the impact on the people of God remains consistent in theme if not in theological grandeur.[162]

Daniel's anthropology in relation to eschatological re-Creation is somewhat discreet, as his greater emphasis is on the fate of nations and the overall glory of God.[163] The opening vision of Daniel 7 addressing the four beasts emphasized YHWH's role as Ancient of Days, but little is said concerning the people of God directly until Dan 7:22 where the kingdom is not established with royal figures, but rather with the holy ones (Aram. קדישׁין). Since God is fully engaged in the dominion of his nation, the absence of a human figure is not problematic. However, it is conspicuous that God's judgment was shared not with kings but rather with people characterized by holiness, the primary concern of the priestly office. Similarly, while the seventy weeks of Dan 9:24–27 mention the coming anointed ruler (v. 25), the larger context of the passage relies on priestly numerology and concern for sin: either in atonement and the establishment of a holy place (v. 24) or in judgment and the abominations of false worship (v. 27).[164] That the messianic ruler is not specifically called a king (מלך) or a prince (שׂר) may be significant: these are cultic concerns.[165] This tone continues in the closing of

---

non-Israelites, leaving open the interpretation that by virtue of their accepting the call to curation and willingly assimilated with the Israelite people, the people of the nations have embraced priesthood. Cf. King, *Realignment*, 139–40; Block, *Ezekiel 25–48*, 741.

161. Von Rad, *Old Testament Theology*, 2:115.

162. Cf. Goswell, "Temple Theme," 517. That the vision of Daniel 2 ends with the uncut stone that becomes a mountain (Dan 2:35b, 45), which could be compared to both the altar regulations (Deut 27:6) and the temple mountain, could be significant as well. The Maccabean rebellion was exemplified by the restoration of the temple, Jesus promised the rebuilding of his temple, and the second coming heralds the new heaven and earth where a temple is unnecessary.

163. Miller, *Daniel*, 50.

164. Cf. Goswell, "Having the Last Say," 26.

165. Cf. also Dan 9:12–15 where the intensity of Jerusalem's punishment is directly linked with their violation of the תורה that other nations lacked. With the greater

the book where purification rituals and proper sacrifice are contrasted with the wickedness of the nations and their desolations (Dan 12:9–13).[166]

Overall there is nothing in Daniel's apocalyptic visions that specifically expects a priestly occupation from Israel in general or humankind at large; but there is significant concern for holiness in person, place, and activity that provides a cultic context reflective of the priestly concerns of Israel.[167]

Jerusalem's Re-Creation into an Eschatological Temple (Zechariah)

Zechariah's apocalyptic vision culminates in the Day of the Lord that re-Creates the world in Zechariah 14. While the Mount of Olives in the Old Testament lacks the significance it later enjoys in the New Testament, its proximity to the temple mount is significant, particularly in light of Ezek 11:23 and Ezekiel 43.[168] More important is the cosmic imagery of Zech 14:6–7 where the very foundations of day and night are eliminated—though significantly the light remains.[169] The reign of YHWH invokes warrior imagery, including the declaration that Judah will engage in the eschatological battle; however, the eschatological battle is not the focus of the passage.[170] Indeed, the greater concern is for justice and—as revealed in vv. 16–21—purification.

The importance of purification is found in v. 16 when the "remnant" (הנותר [יתר]) become faithful worshippers of YHWH and perennial worshippers.[171] Significantly, they will not only go to Jerusalem to worship, but also will specifically observe the Feast of Tabernacles that connects both salvation (the exodus from Egypt) and Creation (the formation of Israel) with the people and God's Presence.[172] This connection leads to further

---

knowledge of YHWH came greater responsibility. The cultic violation of that responsibility is pronounced. Miller, *Daniel*, 247.

166. Goswell, "Having the Last Say," 27.
167. Beale, *Temple*, 58–60.
168. Petersen, *Zechariah*, 142; cf. Beale, "Eden," 8.
169. Keil and Delitzsch, *Commentary*, 10:621.
170. Rendtorff, *Canonical Hebrew Bible*, 308.
171. Cf. von Rad, *Theology of Israel's Prophetic Traditions*, 296; Petersen, *Zechariah*, 155.
172. Keil and Delitzsch, *Commentary*, 10:625. The connection between the Feast of Tabernacles and Creation is often overlooked. However, the nature of festivals as Sabbath events make them inherently connected to Creation and its initial establishment of Sabbath. Further, the association of the Feast of Tabernacles with the Exodus (Lev 23:42–43 et al.) designed to create the nation of Israel (Exod 19:5–6) roots its initial cause in a Creative event. Notably, the transfer of interest from a celebration of

punishment for the recalcitrant (vv. 17–19).[173] But for the faithful, the eschatological worship does not result in a simple statement of reward or blessing, but rather in sanctification and an emphasis on the transformation of the entire city of Jerusalem to a temple environment (vv. 20–21).[174] This final condition of Jerusalem, while not explicitly ordaining the nation to priesthood, effectively makes every inhabitant of Jerusalem an authorized representative of the holy and partaker of the holy things; so while Zechariah does not address all of humanity (and even allows for the continued existence of the theological Canaanite outside of Jerusalem) he does expect that the end result for YHWH's faithful ones is exaltation to a priestly status.[175]

OCCUPATIONAL PASSAGES AND SUGGESTIONS OF AN EXPANDED PRIESTHOOD

While it is important to connect Creation and humankind in mythic and eschatological contexts, if the image of God is truly an assignation of duty to all of humanity, it is reasonable to expect some indication of priestly behavior from a wide spectrum of humankind.[176] The general problem with this expectation is, of course, the exclusivity of the Levitical curation of the holy place and things and of the uniquely Aaronic priesthood. The question of how a general priestly calling can be accepted within this context is important. In the past, this problem was largely avoided by reconstructing the history of the priesthood in Israel and severing the Levites, the Aaronic

---

the exodus—represented by the erection of tents—to the celebration of agricultural splendor (Lev 23:40–41; Exod 34:22b) is connected with the inhabitation of the land, which could itself be seen as a Creative event both on its own (cf. Heb 4, Rev 21 and Mathewson's discussion of the eschatological Sabbath) and especially alongside the exodus (Josh 5 and the completion of the exodus by rededication, circumcision, and celebration of Passover for a new generation; cf. Deut 31:10–13). House, *Old Testament Theology*, 146; Mathewson, *New Heaven and a New Earth*, 199.

173. Petersen, *Zechariah*, 157.

174. Ibid., 159; Keil and Delitzsch, *Commentary*, 10:626.

175. If the paradigmatic nature of the Israelite priesthood is considered, this point becomes even more salient. In Zechariah 3, Joshua the priest is pledged ongoing prosperity and eschatological success for both himself and his descendants if he will properly maintain the new temple. This aligns the holy person with the holy place in the postexilic re-creation of national Israel and sets the stage for the continuation of the priesthood of the holy people in the holy place in the New Creation that Zechariah describes in ch. 14. Cf. Segal, "Responsibilities and Rewards," 733.

176. Cf. Pierce, *Enthroned*, 28, 36–37. Pierce's focus is on the concepts of worship and missions; however, since both worship and missions (or—if other language is preferred—edification and mediation) are cultic activities, the observation that the Creation's assignation of function to humankind necessarily pervades Scriptures is valid.

priests, and the Zadokites from one another completely; and claiming that their synthesis is a late, literary expediency to unite the disparate factions into one organization. While this approach has been widely accepted, it proves inadequate for the present study for two reasons.

First, any conglomeration of multiple priesthoods serves only to further isolate the priestly role and thereby run contrary to the universal aspect of the divine image. This is problematic not only because of the likelihood that the צלם אלהים is a cultic directive but also because the same scholars who suggest that the canonical presentation of the priesthood is an invention rather than a historical reality generally also accept the assignation of Genesis 1 to the P source. If this is the case, then it is illogical to expect that the same editors would both expand the image of God to all of humankind while simultaneously isolating themselves and—by the ever increasing strictness of interpreting the Law with the rise of rabbinic tradition(s)—the Israelite/Jewish people from the rest of humanity. There is a fundamental ambivalence to this approach.

Second, and perhaps more importantly, the present study has relied exclusively on the final canonical context from which to draw its conclusions. Reconstructions are not useful for examining biblical theology, since biblical theology is axiomatically tied to the extant Scriptures.[177] With this in mind, any *historical* divergence that may have existed between the Aaronides, Zadokites, and Levites has no bearing on the *theological* presentation of the Old Testament.[178] Even if the unification of these groups into a singular people is an invention, the canonical context as received relies solely on that invention.[179] As such, it is necessary to determine if a universal calling to priesthood is viable and coherent with the exclusivity of the biblical Levitical priesthood.

To answer this question, it is important to first note that the exclusivity of the Levitical priesthood is relatively well defined and isolated to the tabernacle or the temple.[180] On the other hand, there are a number of passages that suggest that non-Levitical priests not only could but also did perform priestly duties throughout Israel without any particular penalty or condemnation.[181] Examining these passages allows for the discernment of universal priesthood alongside the paradigmatic priesthood that the Levites

---

177. Childs, *Biblical Theology*, 72–73.

178. Habel, *Literary Criticism*, 65–66; cf. Cassuto, *Genesis*, 2; Van Wolde, *Stories of the Beginning*, 4.

179. Cf. Sprinkle, *Book of the Covenant*, 43.

180. Leithart, "Attendants," 19; Blenkinsopp, *Sage, Priest, Prophet*, 87; Sabourin, *Priesthood*, 100–101.

181. Crusemann, *Torah*, 360.

represented. As the Levites ministered at the temple of Israel, an example was established for each person to minister within the temple of Creation. As with the study of Creation theology in the previous section, it is not necessary to analyze every incident that may represent possible priestly activity. A selected group of passages will be sufficient if they can adequately demonstrate legitimate priestly behavior across the spectrum of human society.[182]

Next, the Nazirites and the priesthood of Melchizedek will be examined. These two offices serve to describe either implicitly (the Nazirites) or explicitly (the priesthood of Melchizedek) approved and lasting priesthoods concurrent and synergetic with yet independent of the Levitical priesthood.[183]

Diverse Incidents of Non-Levitical Priesthood

There are two broad categories of non-Levitical priesthoods within the biblical text. The first category includes condemned priesthoods such as Jeroboam's priests of Bethel and Dan (1 Kgs 12:31; 13:33–34) and the syncretic or pagan priests that are found throughout Israel's history (cf. 1 Kgs 16:32; 2 Chr 23:17; et al.). Regarding this first category, there is little need to examine it closely. The condemnation of syncretic worship concerns the blatant disregard for the uniqueness of YHWH and open violation of the covenant (Exod 20:2–3 et al.); no further comment is necessary. On the other hand, the priesthood of Jeroboam could theoretically have been condemned because of its non-Levitical basis. However, while the text clearly notes the non-Levitical *origin* of the priests, the overall context seems more concerned with the *nature* of the priestly activity.[184] First Kings 12 indicates the construction of golden calves and the duplication of the false declaration of Exod 32:4 (v. 28), and the establishment of priests at the high places is specifically designed to prevent worship at the temple and establish non-approved religious festivals (vv. 27, 32) that had been "devised from [Jeroboam's] own heart" (בדא מלבד; v. 33). That this practice continued even after a warning from a prophet is significant as well, as the basis for priesthood was the kings' favor rather than any specific divine calling (1 Kgs 13:33). With this in mind, it seems likely that the problem with Jeroboam's

---

182. Middleton, *Liberating Image*, 64. The term "legitimate" is deliberately chosen. Obviously, the existence of pagan priests is well attested; however, the assignation of priesthood by the צלם אלהים obviously does not intend for these practices, but rather establishes each person as a priest of YHWH. It is only those who perform priestly activity without condemnation that can rightly demonstrate the viability of this interpretation of the divine image.

183. Sabourin, *Priesthood*, 101.

184. Cf. Abba, "Priests and Levites," 5.

priesthood is not simply that they were non-Levitical, but that they were politically expedient rather than holy.¹⁸⁵

The second category is more allusive, and indicates priestly activity outside of the Levitical paradigm but not necessarily considered inherently sinful.¹⁸⁶ This category could theoretically include the patriarchal intercessions; however, the present study will exclude the father-priest and isolate its concern to more formal priesthood(s). Even excluding the Patriarchs, the Nazirites, and the discussion of the priesthood of Melchizedek, the Scriptures still include priesthoods that reflect approved priestly activity from non-Israelites, from women, and from non-Levitical Israelites.¹⁸⁷

The Example of Reuel

Even before he is introduced by name, Reuel (Jethro) is introduced as a priest of Midian (Exod 2:16). While the specifics of Midianite worship are unknown and the particular nature of Reuel's priesthood is largely conjectural, the biblical portrayal of Reuel is consistently positive.¹⁸⁸ Setting aside the unsubstantiated reconstructions that suggest the origin of YHWH as a Midianite tribal god, canonical evidence of Reuel's association with YHWH can be inferred from Gen 25:2 and the connection of Midian with Abraham. It is also worth noting that Moses' father-in-law is first introduced as רעואל ("friend of God") rather than as יתרו. And while אל could be used as a general term for deity and not necessarily referential to YHWH, Reuel's response to the Israelite deliverance in Exodus 18 reveals a reverence for YHWH (vv. 8–12).¹⁸⁹ Finally, Reuel's children—inheritors of his priesthood—are offered equality and honor within Israel (Num 10:29–32), though admittedly they are not explicitly afforded priestly prerogative.¹⁹⁰ Similarly, it must be acknowledged that Reuel's priesthood preceded the inception of the Israelite priesthood and therefore—despite being a formal priesthood—could be compared to the

---

185. House, *1, 2 Kings*, 185.

186. Cf. Sprinkle, *Book of the Covenant*, 44.

187. Cf. Zevit, "Prophet versus Priest," 202–3. Both the Nazirites and the order of Melchizedek also include at least two of these elements each, as the forthcoming analysis of these organizations will demonstrate.

188. McNutt, "Kenites, Midianites, and Rechabites," 115.

189. Bruckner, *Implied Law*, 215; Trimm, "Did YHWH Condemn," 530; Durham, *Exodus*, 240; cf. McNutt, "Kenites, Midianites, and Rechabites," 115.

190. There is conjecture that the Levites are actually the result of the assimilation of the Midianite priests into Israel; however, this theoretical reconstruction is not attested within the canon and therefore undesirable for a proper biblical theology. Sabourin, *Priesthood*, 120; Durham, *Exodus*, 241; King, *Realignment*, 50–51.

patriarchal priestly activity. While Reuel's example does not necessarily establish an ongoing allowance for non-Levitical priesthood, it does demonstrate an acceptance of non-Levitical priests that, because of the acceptance of Reuel's sons in Numbers 10, extends in some form past the establishment of the Levitical priesthood. Overall, then, the portrait of Reuel is both positive and accepting of his priestly office. There is no hint of condemnation, and there is evidence that the god he served was no pagan deity, but YHWH himself.[191]

The Example of Zipporah

While Reuel provides an acceptable example of a non-Israelite priest, Susan Ackerman follows Bernard Robinson's cue and suggests that Zipporah's actions in Exod 4:24-26 seem to be those of a priestess.[192] Robinson suggests that Zipporah is substituting for her father, while Ackerman argues that the activity—including what she perceives as formulaic/liturgical language—is more independent and reflective of Zipporah's own role as a "ritual specialist" of some kind.[193] Ackerman does recognize this as somewhat anomalous, and ascribes it to an overall context of liminality within Exodus as Israel moves from an enslaved people in the opening chapters to an ordained nation in the middle of the book. Since Moses' life is itself a microcosm of Israel's development, the state of flux found in Moses' life does not necessarily support any sort of future for the priesthood of Zipporah (or women in general).[194] Whether or not Ackerman is correct in her assessment of Zipporah's future, the suggestion that the circumcision of Gershom is a liturgical event in both act and language is intriguing. Zipporah's priestly action is not condemned, but instead seems to be absolutely necessary for either Moses' or Gershom's survival.[195]

---

191. Durham, *Exodus*, 244; cf. Stuart, *Exodus*, 413.

192. Ackerman, "Why Is Miriam," 74; Robinson, "Zipporah," 458; Blenkinsopp, *Sage, Priest, Prophet*, 76; Nelson, *Raising Up*, 97-98; McNutt, "Kenites, Midianites, and Rechabites," 122.

193. Ackerman, "Miriam among the Prophets," 74-75.

194. Ibid., 76.

195. Ultimately, whether the second "him" in v. 24 refers to Moses or Gershom is irrelevant. The basic issue remains that before Moses could meet with and intercede for Israel, his own family needed to be in right standing with God (as represented by circumcision). That Zipporah's actions brought about that right standing suggests that this was not simply an act of cultic ritual, but rather human-divine intercession. Stuart, *Exodus*, 156.

The Examples from Judges

While Reuel and Zipporah preceded the installation of the Levitical priests, post-installation examples of non-Levitical Israelite priests can be found in Judges 17–18. The use of Judges to establish an example of legitimacy is difficult to say the least; the book as a whole is a statement about the degeneration of the Israelites without proper leadership. However, if proper caution is applied then legitimate critique of the institutions of Israel can be discerned.[196] So while the story of Judges 17–18 cannot establish on its own a legitimacy for non-Levitical Israelite priests, it can illustrate certain possibilities that can be combined with the other observations of this analysis.

The chapter opens with Micah's admission of theft and his mother's subsequent forgiveness and gift of a silver idol (פסל; מסכה), which Micah then installed in a home shrine before ordaining his own son as a priest over it. This event is immediately followed by the condemning warning of Judg 17:6 that each person did what was "right in his own eyes." This formulaic statement is enough to establish the wickedness of Micah's actions; however, it is unclear if the ordination of his son is the issue at hand. The creation of an idol is an explicit violation of Exod 20:4, and so it certainly is intended. It is less certain whether the problem is with both the idol and the ordination, or the idol alone. Micah's invitation to the Levite in vv. 10–13 lacks—depending on the interpretation of Judg 18:1—a condemnation of the Levite's installation as house priest. The statement of Judg 17:13 that YHWH will prosper Micah because of his Levite priest does not seem to indicate that non-Levite priests were forbidden, but rather that Levite priests were considered particularly auspicious.[197]

The warning that there was no king in Israel—and the implication that people did right in their own eyes, a condemnation—opens Judges 18. This verse could be a hinge that reflects both on the preceding ordination of the Levite and the proceeding story of the Danites, or it could be exclusively proleptic and apply to Judges 18 alone. If the introduction applies exclusively to ch. 18, then the story becomes even more ambiguous as the Danites appear to be successful in their endeavor despite their violent means (vv. 25, 27). Ultimately, Judges 18 is silent on the nature of the Danite attacks on Micah and Laish, and the only definitive things that can be said concerning the chapter are that it demonstrates increased violence or lawlessness (the

---

196. Cf. Nelson, *Raising Up*, 4–5; Goldingay, *Israel's Life*, 49.

197. Nelson, *Raising Up*, 86. Abba's discussion of the priests of the high places, provincial priests, and the temple priests in Ezekiel hints at this as well, though in a later context. Abba, "Priests and Levites," 3–4.

bullying of Micah) and provides historical data on the beginnings of the city of Dan (the capture of Laish).

If Judges is ascribed to the same writer as 1 Kings, then ch. 18 establishes the sinful heritage of Dan and its "appropriateness" as a city for one of the golden calves, as it began with the erection of a silver idol (cf. v. 30a). While the idolatry of Dan is obviously problematic, the capture of Laish is reportedly ordained by God (vv. 5–7, 9–10; cf. Josh 19:47; 23:4–5). Similarly, the establishment of Levitical but non-Aaronic priests in Dan is noted to have lasted "until the day of the captivity of the land" despite the creation of a Levitical role in the temple (1 Chr 23:26–32). That there is no condemnation of the Danite priests prior to the installation of Jeroboam's golden calves, even during the reign of David and the pre-idolatrous reign of Solomon, is interesting.[198]

Obviously, Judges 17–18 cannot argue for the legitimacy of non-Levitical priests; however, it is sufficient presently to note that there is no overt condemnation of them and the ambiguous implications of the chapter are not necessarily concerned with the origin of the priests so much as the idolatry of Micah and the Danites.[199] When this is combined with the recognition that Deut 12:5–7 does not necessarily prescribe a single place (the temple) for Israelite worship but could indicate specific places (ordained by YHWH but not necessarily the temple exclusively), then the service of non-Levitical Israelite priests becomes a viable possibility.[200] The temple priesthood was exclusively Aaronic, but the possibility of non-Aaronic and non-Levitical priests elsewhere in Israel at other worship sites exists.

The Nazirite Vow as Non-Levitical Priesthood

While the presence of acceptable non-Levitical priests in Judges is allusive, the Nazirite vow of Numbers 6 provides a much more practical and specific example of priestly occupation that extends beyond the Levitical

---

198. Indeed, even after the installation of the golden calf, the priests of Dan are not condemned for their non-Aaronic descent, but—as previously noted—for their embrace of the idol of Exodus 32.

199. The overwhelmingly brutal context of Judges 17–21 makes any possible condemnation of the priest's identity or lineage, in the words of J. G. McConville, a mere "sideshow." McConville, "Priesthood," 79; Block, *Judges, Ruth*, 489–90.

200. Cf. King, *Realignment*, 55. Goldingay connects the non-specificity of Deuteronomy 12 with the pilgrimage commands of Exodus 32 and 34, and notes that while there may not have been an exclusive temple in Jerusalem alone, the call for pilgrimage suggests "at least that people were to go to a regional sanctuary." Whatever the case, it can be suggested that even if Deut 12:5–7 intends only the Jerusalem temple there were still religious sites (be they free-standing altars or local chapels) that may have accommodated non-Levitical religious personnel. Goldingay, *Israel's Life*, 122–23; cf. Haran, *Temples*, 17.

priesthood. The Nazirite vow provided a means by which any Israelite from any tribe and gender could dedicate themselves in an extraordinary way to the service of YHWH in a manner not dissimilar from the priests (v. 2).[201]

The precise functions of the Nazirites are not detailed in the Bible, and even Jewish commentaries that expand upon the stipulations of Numbers 6 focus more upon the restrictions of the Nazirites than upon their performance. This lack of detail has led to two difficulties: first, there has been a tendency to focus on the ascetic aspects of the vow rather than the function of it. Second, there has been a tendency—as in the Mishnah—to treat the vow as a simple devotion to YHWH.[202] Approaching the Nazirite vow in this manner may be short-sighted, as it ignores both the canonical placement of the vow stipulations and the biblical emphasis on service and activity.[203]

The rule of the Nazirite is located in the midst of Levitical—not general—instructions. Numbers 1–4 is often treated as one unit and chs. 5–6 as a separate section. This approach originates from the perception that the sundry laws of Numbers 5 seem to address a different topic than the census data of the opening chapters; however, to divide the text in this manner removes the purpose of placing Numbers 5–6 immediately after chs. 1–4. Rather than divide the section between chs. 1–4 and 5–6, it is more useful to examine the first six chapters of Numbers by chs. 1–2 and 3–6. The text should be examined not as two sections of census and mixed laws but as sections of national and Levitical preparations for the consecration that would occur in Numbers 7–9.[204] This structure maintains the integrity of the text

---

201. Chepey, *Nazirites*, 6; Cole, *Numbers*, 119.

202. The assumption that the Jewish works accurately reflect the original purpose and nature of the Nazirite vow is itself problematic. The Mishnah, Talmud, Targums, etc. all arose alongside and intertwined with Rabbinic Judaism and reflect interpretations and accretions that were themselves condemned by Jesus (cf. Matt 15:1–9; 16:5–12). It is useful to examine Jewish sources in the study of the Old Testament, and they certainly lend understanding to aspects of the Nazirite vow, but due caution and discernment is necessary.

203. Cf. Van Wolde, *Stories of the Beginning*, 4; Pierce, *Enthroned*, 3–4.

204. This can be outlined as follows:
I. National Preparations for the Consecration, Num 1–2
   A. Census of the Tribes (with the Exemption of the Levites), Num 1:1–54
   B. Arrangement of the Tribes around the Tabernacle, Num 2:1–34
II. Levitical Preparations for the Consecration, Num 3–6
   A. Duties of the Levites, Num 3:1–39
   B. Redemption of the Levites (in light of their previous Exemption), Num 3:40–51
   C. Specific Duties of the Levitical Lines, Num 4:1–49
   D. Priestly Duties for Consecration, Num 5:1–31
   E. The Nazirite Vow, Num 6:1–21
   F. The High Priest's Blessing, Num 6:22–27
III. Consecration and Ceremonies of the Tabernacle, Num 7–9

without disjoining Numbers 5–6 from the discussion of the priesthood and instead grounding them in that discussion. The census forms the beginning of the discussion of arranging the tribes around the tabernacle, then the Levites are prepared for their own tabernacle roles. Notably, the sundry laws of Numbers 5 designed to purify the people for the tabernacle ceremony do not focus on what confession or restitution might be required or what constitutes adultery. Both of those issues are detailed elsewhere in the Torah. Instead, the laws of ch. 5 emphasize what the priest is to do to purify the community. The priestly activity of ch. 5 unites the entire unit of Numbers 3–5. The high priest's blessing (Num 6:22–27) stands as a final blessing of the Israelites before the consecration of Num 7–9, and naturally belongs to the discussion of Levitical and priestly responsibilities. Recognizing this, the position of the Nazirite vow in the midst of the Levitical material must reasonably influence the purpose of the vow itself.[205]

The position of the Nazirite material associates it with the priesthood—particularly the high priest's blessing—and suggests some priestly aspect to the vow. There is not enough biblical information on the Nazirites to label them as priests, and later events of Numbers 16–18 preclude tabernacle/temple service (though as already addressed, it does not necessarily preclude priestly activity outside of the temple). The three prohibitions of the Nazirites, however, do align strongly with priestly prohibitions and suggest a cultic presence.

The first Nazirite prohibition is against the fruit of the vine in general, but the verbal construction of Num 6:3 emphasized the separation from wine and strong drink and is best considered in light of this emphasis. This abstinence parallels Lev 10:9, including its emphatic preverbal placement of שכר and יין.[206] Similarly, the prohibition against the razor may parallel the forbiddance of tonsure and/or scarification of Lev 19:26–28.[207] The trimming of the priest's hair was prohibited as a reflection of pagan practice; the growing of the Nazirites' hair was a statement of dedication to YHWH.

---

205. Cole, *Numbers*, 120.

206. Ashley, *Book of Numbers*, 141; Cole, *Numbers*, 122; The prohibition in Lev 10:9 was not a general ruling against wine, but was restricted to prohibiting wine when attending to the Tent of Meeting. However, since Nazirites were "before the Lord" for the entire duration of their vow the total prohibition of wine in the Nazirite vow still legitimately parallels priestly prohibitions of appearing before YHWH having imbibed wine. Cf. Wenham, *Leviticus*, 142.

207. There is no statement against scarification in the Nazirite vow, but both Lev 19:26–27 and Lev 21:5 associate the ritual cutting of hair with scarification. It may be significant that the Nazirite vow does not simply preclude cutting hair but actually emphasizes the razor—the same tool for barbering and scarring. It is therefore reasonable to assume that any scarification is prohibited alongside the ban from shaving.

Israelite priests were not to appear the same as pagan priests, but the Nazirites *were* to appear similar to Yahwist priests.²⁰⁸

The final aspect of the Nazirite vow was their absolute separation from death. Leviticus 21:1 explicitly prohibits YHWH's priests from associating with the dead. The absolute separation of the Nazirites was even more restrictive than the priestly rule; unlike priests Nazirites could not even attend to the death of a close relative (Num 6:8; cf. Lev 21:2–3). On the other hand, the high priest was precluded from any mourning whatsoever (Lev 21:10–12). In this, the Nazirites actually parallel the high priest rather than the priests.²⁰⁹

The parallels between the Nazirite prohibitions and the priestly prohibitions closely associate the two offices. While there is insufficient evidence to absolutely designate the Nazirites as priests *per se*, their behavior certainly was priestly. Amos paralleled the Nazirites and the prophets (Amos 2:11–12). Since the prophets themselves were calling for a return to legitimate worship, this parallel only further strengthens the idea that the Nazirites were dedicated to a pure worship of God. So while the Bible contains little direct commentary on the role of the Nazirite, the parallels with the priestly prohibition and the location of Numbers 6 within a priestly block of instruction suggests that the Nazirite vow was a means by which an Israelite—and significantly, *any* Israelite—could become some form of priest, or at least more priest-like. The honor of the Nazirite was to share in the priestly experience.²¹⁰ While the Nazirite vow is only explicitly possible for Israelites, the concept of seeking priestly service that underlies it combined with the exemplary calling of Israel to draw people to YHWH

---

208. Contra Ashley, who fails to see the priestly parallels. Interestingly, there is a possible relationship between the Nazirites and the נתינם of Ezra 2:43–54; 8:20 who served as servants of the Levites, further strengthening the possibility of a priestly character to the Nazarites. Ashley, *Numbers*, 143; Blenkinsopp, *Sage, Priest, Prophet*, 98.

209. Ashley, *Numbers*, 141; Cole, *Numbers*, 123.

210. Cole, *Numbers*, 119, 121. The only indisputable Nazirite in Scriptures is Samson, but since the story of Samson is ultimately a story of his complete failure to uphold his Nazirite calling it is both difficult and ill-advised to use Samson as a template for understanding the Nazirites, and his story fails to contribute either positively or negatively to this study.

On the other hand, Hannah's oath is often interpreted as a dedication of Samuel to be a lifelong Nazirite; a position strengthened by 4QSama's designation of Samuel as a Nazirite at the end of 1 Sam 1:22 and Sir 46:13's affirmation of the same. If 4QSama is adopted, then the suggestion that the Nazirite vow is a form of priestly ordination is strengthened considerably as Samuel's temple service exemplifies this activity. Incidentally, it would also explain the genealogical difficulties of Samuel; born from the tribe of Ephraim (1 Sam 1:1), Samuel's Nazirite calling affiliated him with the Levites (1 Chr 6:27–28). While a full analysis of this possibility is beyond the scope of the current study, the possibility itself encourages the perception that Nazirites were priest-like.

as a kingdom of priests certainly suggests that the ideal person is one who conducts himself in a priestly manner.[211]

The Order of Melchizedek as a Non-Levitical Priesthood

The Order of Melchizedek is both one of the most obvious and at the same time one of the most difficult examples of a non-Levitical priesthood, if for no other reason than the theological development and theories surrounding the exact nature of Melchizedek and his role within the Bible as a whole. On the one hand, the later typological developments elaborate the legacy that Melchizedek left the Israelites; however, on the other hand it would be erroneous to overemphasize the typology of Hebrews in examining the two occurrences of Melchizedek and his priesthood in the Old Testament. With this consideration, the present section's analysis will focus exclusively on Genesis 14 and Psalm 110.

Even isolating a study to the Old Testament passages presents certain difficulties. The introduction of Melchizedek in Genesis 14 is presented as a historical event without commentary on the theology of his priesthood; any understanding of Melchizedek's priesthood in Genesis 14 is therefore implicit. On the other hand, the theoretical elaboration of Melchizedek's legacy is summarized in only one verse in Psalm 110:4 and therefore not particularly helpful either. Despite these difficulties, though, what is clear from the biblical presentation is that Melchizedek entered Israel's consciousness in an honored role and continued to be recognized throughout its history.[212] This fact alone warrants the acknowledgment of a continued appreciation for a non-Levitical priesthood well into Israel's history and after the formalization of the Aaronic ordinations.

Historical Presentation of Melchizedek

Melchizedek's role in Genesis 14, while only briefly addressed, describes the normative activities of an ANE priest: mediation (v. 18) and intercession/blessing (vv. 19–20a).[213] Since he receives an offering from Abram (v. 20b),

---

211. This idea developed further in the intertestamental period, when the revival of priesthood was directly intertwined with the activity of Nazirites (1 Macc 3:46–53). Chepey, *Nazirites*, 43.

212. Mathews, *Genesis 11:27—50:26*, 151–52.

213. Melchizedek does not expressly mediate for Abram; however, the presence of food is suggestive of the table fellowship that served to bond men together or possibly even a form of peace offering (when combined with the tithe of v. 20b) that represents

it could also be argued that Melchizedek serves as custodian of the holy things—the holy gift in this case.²¹⁴ Other than this, Melchizedek's priesthood is defined by the introduction of his person.

Whether or not Melchizedek is a proper name or a title is relatively unimportant, since he is introduced as a king regardless. Not only is he a king, but he is the king of the non-Israelite city of Salem.²¹⁵ These two elements are sufficient to establish his priesthood as one that reflects the common ANE occurrence of priest-kings and one that does not *originate* in Abrahamic/Israelite heritage, though—considering the fact that the priesthood was not only remembered but also celebrated in later Israel—the Israelites obviously did *preserve* this heritage. At a minimum, Melchizedek establishes a biblical precedent for priesthood that not only goes beyond Aaronic bloodlines but also extends beyond Israelite nationality. While it could be argued that אל עליון is not explicitly identified as YHWH, Abram's ready acceptance of blessing in his name and the honoring of the Melchizedek priesthood by David in Psalm 110 clearly imply that as with most occurrences of אל in the Old Testament that are not otherwise designated, God Most High is YHWH himself.²¹⁶

Celebratory Presentation of Melchizedek

The continued reverence for the priest-king Melchizedek may explain some of the activities of David and Solomon that appear to be blatantly priestly. David's assurance in taking the bread of the Presence (1 Sam 21:1–6) could be predicated on his role as king and—as a king after the order of Melchizedek—the inherent priestly authority of that role.²¹⁷ Similarly, the dedication of the Jerusalem temple is obviously a landmark in the cultic history of Israel yet it is Solomon not the priests who officiates the proceedings, including the many sacrifices involved (1 Kgs 8; 2 Chr 5–7). While it is likely that the sacrifices were simply ordered by Solomon and that he did not have a hand in directly performing them, his apparent authority over them is reflective of cultic rather than royal prerogative.²¹⁸ This creates a dialectic

---

the fellowship of Abram and YHWH. In either case, there is a sense of mediation.

214. Moberly, *Old Testament*, 96.

215. That Salem will develop into the Israelite capital in later years is not important for a discreet understanding of Genesis 14, though it does bear mention for the discussion of Psalm 110.

216. Mathews, *Genesis 11:27—50:26*, 150; Boer, *Ember*, 24–25.

217. Cf. Mathews, *Genesis 11:27—50:26*, 155.

218. Thompson, *1, 2 Chronicles*, 227. Brueggemann initially states that it is the king

between the king and the priests—particularly in light of Deut 17:18 and the priestly oversight of the king's education.[219] It is possible that the priests were responsible for ensuring the king was properly trained in the Law, and then the king was authorized to assume his throne and perform appropriate royal *and* cultic activities.[220]

More interesting than the implications of David's and Solomon's activities is the explicit assumption of the role of priest of Melchizedek in Ps 110:4. The context of the psalm certainly has royal connotations (vv. 1–2; 5–7), but the precise ascription of Melchizedek's priesthood in vv. 3–4 seems to bear a different tenor.[221] While David's kingly authority impacts the world outside of Israel, within Israel itself the concern is for cultic matters. The people offer votive offerings (v. 3a) either in the holy place or in holy robes (v. 3b).[222] They are then essentially consecrated with their designation as belonging to YHWH. While this statement is general, it functionally mimics the consecration of the Levites as God's chosen portion. It is only after the people as a whole are both consecrated (the preparation for priestly office) and active in performing sacrifices (the conduct of priestly duties) while wearing priestly garments (the attire of priestly attendants) that the king himself is recognized as being of the order of Melchizedek. This sequence suggests that while the idea of being a Melchizedekian priest may represent a conflation of the priest-king within Israel, it is not distinct or privileged from the overall priestly nature of the people of God—once again hearkening back to Exod 19:6 et al.[223] That the idea of being of Melchizedek's order includes not only a royal heritage but also—and perhaps far more importantly—a non-Israelite heritage suggests that the basis of this priesthood was voluntary submission to the honoring of and obedience to God. The foundational aspect of the order of Melchizedek then becomes the willing

---

who had authority over the liturgy throughout the ANE, including Israel. However, this statement is in error since it fails to recognize the polemical nature of the Israel's calling that reverses this authority and places the king in a liturgically subordinate position to the priests. In a somewhat contradictory fashion, Brueggemann himself notes this reality as he continues his argument. Brueggemann, *Israel's Praise*, 61–63.

219. Craigie, *Deuteronomy*, 257; Horbury, "Aaronic Priesthood," 44.

220. Appropriate being, of course, decided by the prescriptions of the תורה and the observance of the holy boundaries of the tabernacle/temple that bound even the king; cf. von Rad, *Theology of Israel's Historical Traditions*, 42; Renckens, *Israel's Concept*, 15, 31.

221. Allen, *Psalms 101–150*, 85.

222. Depending on which manuscripts are accepted. While the MT and the majority of translators accept הדר, Hebrew fragments found with the Codex Cairensis offer the possibility of הרר. Either word makes sense and provides an identical overall theme to the context. Allen, *Psalms*, 80n3.d.

223. Cf. Sabourin, *Priesthood*, 277; Allen, *Psalms*, 87.

performance of the divine directives. And this aspect is one that is universal in scope, accurately coinciding with and complimenting an understanding of the צלם אלהים as a calling for humankind at large to serve God as priests within the temple of Creation.

REFLECTION ON BIBLICAL PASSAGES FOR PRIESTLY INTENTION

While the specific outworking of each of the previously analyzed passages has differed in nuance, the overall result of this analysis has affirmed the viability of suggesting that the concept of priesthood defined not only God's intention for Israel—both historical and eschatological—but also his design for humankind—the צלם אלהים—as a whole.

Certainly the priestly connections are broad, and it could be argued that too much liberty has been taken with what exactly constitutes priestly ideology. Reverence for the temple, participation in worship, and the sanctification of the nation were keystones in the concept of theological Israel; and it is reasonable to suggest that one need not be a priest to anticipate any of the above.[224] While it may be reasonable to argue that priesthood is not necessarily needed, it is unreasonable to reject the connection between each of these elements and the priestly interest.[225] If anything, the public consciousness of inherently cultic elements such as temple, worship, and sanctification affirms rather than denies the priests' role as the primary ideologues of Israel. The breadth of contact between the biblical norm and the cultic responsibility within the Old Testament text is overwhelmingly synonymous. This synonymy does not demean the priesthood in Israel by making it common, but instead serves to elevate the people of Israel as a whole by expecting greater priest-likeness from them all (cf. Exod 22:31; Lev 19:2; Deut 7:6; et al.).[226] It cannot be accidental that in both the canonically historically earliest (Exodus-Joshua) and latest (the postexilic books) books of Scripture, the leadership of the nation was primarily vested in religious authorities rather than royal figures.[227] While prophecy continued to expect kingly figures in even the postexilic era—as both the development of messianism and the honoring of non-cultic authority figures attest (cf. Hag 2:20–23)—the immediate presence of leadership was spiritual rather

---

224. Cf. Goldingay, *Israel's Life*, 18–20.

225. Blenkinsopp, *Sage, Priest, Prophet*, 79–83.

226. Van Wolde, *Stories of the Beginning*, 29; cf. Brueggemann, *Genesis*, 26; Firmage, "Genesis 1," 108–10; Gronbaek, "Baal's Battle," 36.

227. Habel, *Literary Criticism*, 68.

than political.[228] Further, the increased concern to live the Law properly demanded a movement from secular to spiritual ideology, not only in the leadership but also in the populace as a whole.[229]

Similarly, while there is no explicit demand for all the nations to serve as priests; there is expectation that Israel will bring them under God's dominion, and that there will be faithful members of every nation who will join with Israel as part of God's people (cf. Lev 19:33–34).[230] These expectations were not simply eschatological; provision was established for their historical enactment as well—regardless of whether Israel actually heeded this purpose.[231] Further, the possible acceptance of non-Levitical priests within Israel demonstrates that the exclusivity of the Aaronic priests was not in their general role, but in their specific administration of the tabernacle/Jerusalem temple. This fact alone allows for a broader expectation of and allowance for a general priesthood of some type composed of the faithful from any socio-ethnic background.[232]

Since the צלם אלהים is applied to humanity at large, it cannot be isolated to Israel's unique role.[233] Nevertheless, while the Jerusalem temple was uniquely Israel's charge, all of humankind is expected to properly care for and administer Creation—the temple of the world. Remembering that it is function rather than strict form that provides the primary foundation for ANE reasoning, the reality that all of humankind is charged to administer the world-temple justifies the recognition that the image of God was an assignment of function rather than an ascription of an independent characteristic.[234] Because the function of all of humankind is the proper curation of Creation (already established as a temple), then the suggestion that the

---

228. Eastwood, *Royal Priesthood*, 23; cf. King, *Realignment*, 32.

229. King, *Realignment*, 171; Sprinkle, *Book of the Covenant*, 37; cf. von Rad, *Theology of Israel's Prophetic Traditions*, 283. Of course, the "proper" conduct of the Law was still open to interpretation, particularly with the growth of rabbinism. Further, the fact that priests and other religious authorities benefited from the increased status of priesthood in the nation certainly allows for a degree of self-service in advancing priestly concerns.

That said, the reality that the increased prominence of the priesthood quite possibly led to certain abuses of power or entitled thinking does not detract from the biblical prophecy that expects and affirms the priestly nature of Israel and their calling to facilitate the worship of and service to God. Von Rad, *Old Testament Theology*, 2:282.

230. Schnabel, "Israel," 41–42; cf. Van Houten, *Alien in Israelite Law*, 142.

231. Von Rad, *Old Testament Theology*, 2:283–84; Van Wolde, *Stories of the Beginning*, 29–33; Balentine, *Torah's Vision*, 81, 86–87; Fretheim, "Reclamation of Creation," 363.

232. Von Rad, *Old Testament Theology*, 1:91.

233. Cf. Blenkinsopp, *Sage, Priest, Prophet*, 67.

234. Brunner, *Man in Revolt*, 50; Wolff, *Anthropology of the Old Testament*, 163–64.

צלם אלהים represents a calling for all of humankind to serve as priests is affirmed.²³⁵ The allowance for non-Levitical priesthood within historical Israel allows for this calling to be cultivated and demonstrated by individuals of all backgrounds; and the expectation of temple, worship, and knowledge in eschatology demonstrates this calling will culminate with people of all nationalities assuming their proper place before God in a manner that complements and coincides with the restoration of Eden.

---

235. Von Wolde, *Stories of the Beginning*, 25–31; said another way, priestly service makes a person *more human*. Davies, *Anthropology and Theology*, 151.

Chapter 4

Examination of Theological Compatibility of the צלם אלהים as a Priestly Calling

THE PURPOSE OF AND SELECTION FOR THEOLOGICAL COMPARISON

Since the image of God is the foundation for biblical anthropology, and anthropology directly intersects with every other theological theme of the Scriptures, the proposal that the צלם אלהים reflects a priestly calling or expectation has implications that far exceed the discreet analysis of individual passages.[1] The preceding study demonstrated that a priestly understanding of humanity can be sustained. But considering the ramifications of this for the broader study of the Bible, the next logical step is to examine theological works to determine if there is compatibility or consistency with previously established theories.

The determination of compatibility is necessary for two reasons. First, previous theological proposals have drawn upon the history and tradition of Christian thought. If the suggestion that humankind is inherently priestly is incompatible with or contradictory to major theological works, then it is suspect on the grounds of 2 Pet 1:20. Second, established theological works that espouse a centralized or dominant theme in Old Testament theology will naturally intersect with an understanding of the priestly office by virtue of the widespread duties of the office and the critical importance of the holy place in ancient Israelite theology and practice. To exclude the ramifications

---

1. Erickson, *Christian Theology*, 481.

of or on a priest-person anthropology from the analysis of other Old Testament theologies would be irresponsible and incomplete.

It should be noted—and has already been implied—that the examination of other Old Testament theologies will focus on those theologies that suggest a central or dominant theological theme for the entirety of the Old Testament. Theologies that lack or discount any centralized theme do not need to be examined simply because they cannot attest either for or against a priestly motif. Decentralized theologies accept a multitude of theological tracks within the Old Testament; the addition of a priestly anthropology would simply add one to many. On the other hand, centralized theologies that revolve around a primary theme can pose challenges or offer support for an anthropology of priesthood.

It is beyond the scope of the present work to confer with every centralized theology, so a sampling of theologies that focus on the most widely accepted primary themes of the Old Testament will be examined instead. In many cases, the disparate theologies build upon one another, and so the following analysis will follow them in chronological order.

Centrality of Covenant

Eichrodt's *Theology of the Old Testament* emerged in contradistinction to the atomistic philosophy of religions approach to the Old Testament, which justifies Eichrodt's concern to emphasize the "constant basic tendency and character" of the Scriptures.[2] Eichrodt's emphasis on the role of covenant is well known and important, but it is also necessary to recognize that his approach was very much connected to the broader ANE cosmological and cultural contexts.[3] This latter recognition is of particular importance since while other ANE societies did not necessarily—or even at all—define themselves according to covenant concepts, they very often *did* define their culture in accordance with their theologies.[4] The nature of humankind as a whole and their individual nation in particular was dictated by their own creation stories. This is particularly true for those countries that held to a god-king or priest-king concept.

---

2. Eichrodt, *Theology of the Old Testament*, 1:11; Busenitz, "Introduction to Biblical Covenants," 182.

3. Eichrodt, *Theology of the Old Testament*, 1:25; Miller, "In the 'Image,'" 303; House, *Old Testament Theology*, 30–31; Waltke and Yu, *Old Testament Theology*, 52.

4. Cf. Eichrodt, *Man in the Old Testament*, 14–16; Busenitz, "Introduction to Biblical Covenants," 175.

Further, while Eichrodt is often noted for his covenant-based theology, his treatment of the covenant inherently demands a divine-to-human relay of information and a respect for the overall unity of both Testaments.[5] The exchange between humanity and God demands some degree of mediation. This mediation is found in the covenant, but that covenant still required people to administer it.[6] And those people were the priests.[7] The unity of both testaments demands a recognition of the New Testament's teachings regarding the relationship between God and humankind, which again returns to a mediatory theme. The New Testament administrator of relationship is, of course, the Christ who serves directly as a high priest (Heb 3:1–6; 4:14—5:10; et al.). The resultant affinity between the priesthood and the Christ is neither surprising nor innovative. However, it does synthesize the New Testament calling to be Christ-like with the Old Testament expectation of priestly behavior in a manner not dissimilar to 1 Pet 2:9's use of Exod 19:6 to establish the church as the people of God.

While Eichrodt's approach implicitly draws a priestly connection throughout the Bible—where the covenant exists the mediators must as well—it is not wholly consistent with the present thesis of humankind's inherently priestly calling since Eichrodt follows the modernist trend of considering the priesthood to be a later replacement of charismatic leaders rather than a foundational aspect of the Hebrew faith.[8] Eichrodt's assignation of the priests to a later date is nevertheless still compatible with the present thesis for two reasons. First, while he assigns the Levites a later rise to power, he does so with the suggestion that there must have already been priests within Israelite society, and cannot delimit when those priests might

---

5. Eichrodt, *Theology of the Old Testament*, 1:26–27; House, *Old Testament Theology*, 31; cf. Waltke and Yu, *Old Testament Theology*, 149; Hasel, *Old Testament Theology*, 117.

6. House, *Old Testament Theology*, 88–89, 120. Perhaps even more interesting is the ascription of the Servant of God himself as the embodiment of covenant in Isa 42:6. With this in mind, one might arguably say that to divide between the covenant itself and the People (Person) of God is itself a false dichotomy; the issuance of a divine covenant is the establishment of a priesthood. Middleton, *New Heaven*, 92.

7. Eichrodt, *Theology of the Old Testament*, 1:403–4; Sabourin, *Priesthood*, 227; House, *Old Testament Theology*, 129; Waltke and Yu, *Old Testament Theology*, 448; King, *Realignment*, 68.

8. Eichrodt, *Theology of the Old Testament*, 1:403. The phrase "Hebrew faith" is specifically chosen here to indicate not only the faith of national Israel, but also the faith of the wilderness wandering proto-Israel and the pre-Israelite patriarchal beliefs. While Eichrodt considers cultic elements within the patriarchal stories retrojections, Blenkinsopp's work on the origin of law (and covenant) in ancient tribal ethics demonstrates that it is unnecessary to recant pre-Sinai demonstrations of the Law. Eichrodt, *Theology of the Old Testament*, 1:49; Blenkinsopp, *Wisdom and Law*.

have emerged.⁹ This ambiguity allows for the possibility of a long-standing tradition of priests even in the midst of the supposed charismatic leaders that supposedly predated the priesthood, especially since Eichrodt admits that even the Levitical priesthood (in whatever form one chooses to accept it) "did not emerge as a phenomenon deriving exclusively from within the history of Yahwism itself."¹⁰ Since priesthood and the concepts of a priest-driven society were so widespread in the ANE, the suggestion that humanity has an inherent connection to a priestly calling is sustainable not only for Israel, but also in general.

Of course, the *proper* mediation between God and humankind can only be conducted through the terms of the covenant.¹¹ In his discussion on the role of humanity, Eichrodt notes that the covenant with Israel derived from the natural cosmic order established by the Creator.¹² Respect for the covenant necessitates a certain amount of respect for Creation. But at the same time, if one examines the theological relationship between covenant and Creation then the opposite proposition could be made: properly to respect Creation one must properly honor the covenant.¹³ In either case, the connection between Adam and humankind as a whole is established and affirmed, with the special role of human beings as "accorded a closer association with God than the animals" a foundational aspect of anthropology.¹⁴

Returning again to Eichrodt's overarching emphasis on the covenant as the primary theme of the Old Testament, the question must be asked: if covenant is representative of relationship with YHWH, and humankind is more closely related to him than the rest of the created beings, then does not Creation demand a covenant? Likewise, if there is a covenant at Creation,

---

9. Cf. Eichrodt, *Theology of the Old Testament*, 1:394–95.

10. Ibid., *Theology of the Old Testament*, 1:402.

11. Eichrodt, *Man in the Old Testament*, 13.

12. Eichrodt, *Theology of the Old Testament*, 2:118. It is not the purpose of this study to defend a covenant theme as the center of Old Testament theology; however, it is worth noting that the objections to covenant as a universal theme on the basis of sapiential literature's non-covenantal nature is mitigated if not contradicted by the recognition of covenant and Creation's relationship with one another. While sapiential literature is typically assumed to be rooted in Creation rather than covenant, the connection between the two means of understanding reveal the divergence between sapiential and cultic material to be less distinct than what might be assumed.

13. King, *Realignment*, 68; cf. Rendtorff, *Canon and Theology*, 7; Eichrodt does not state this explicitly, but his observations on the "de-divinization of Nature" effectively make the same point. The proper maintenance of Creation demands a proper understanding of God and divinity; this understanding is found within the covenant. Eichrodt, *Theology of the Old Testament*, 2:119.

14. Eichrodt, *Theology of the Old Testament*, 2:121.

does it not demand administration? Since both of these questions require an affirmative answer (at least under Eichrodt's paradigm), then there is a demand for humanity at large to administer the covenant over themselves.[15] This reflexive administration is not classically priestly, but it does reflect the mediation, intercession, and—assuming the expectations of properly living within Creation are passed down—instruction that highlight the priestly task. So while it is not possible to demand a priestly anthropology to subscribe to a centralized covenant theme, the interpretation of the צלם אלהים as a calling to priesthood is compatible with Eichrodt's work by inference and in many ways bolsters Eichrodt's covenant thesis.[16]

Centrality of Relationship

Following Eichrodt's theology, Vriezen's theology moved away from the specificity of covenant in favor of the broader, yet more intimate, aspects of relationship.[17] In many ways, his movement to a more impassioned relational paradigm is a subversion of Eichrodt's covenant approach. Reflecting on Jesus' contradiction of Jewish theology, Vriezen suggests that the letter of the Old Testament served as a platform from which to build into a greater relational paradigm.[18] To an extent, Vriezen errs in this approach, since a rejection of Judaism is not a rejection of the Old Testament so much as the rabbinic accretions (cf. Mark 7:6–9ff.).[19] On the other hand, his approach does rightly point out that the covenant is an expression of relationship, but that relationship does not necessitate covenant. On the other hand, the entire process of relating to humankind served to engrave the image of God upon humanity. The צלם אלהים, to Vriezen, was entirely about relationship. This relationship is not limited to the simple capacity to form relationships

---

15. Eichrodt, *Man in the Old Testament*, 26–27.

16. Interestingly, Eichrodt's analysis of the individual and community emphasizes the individual's identity as a function of their community; and the community's cultic activity presents "the real self-communication . . . through the priestly proclamation" of God. The necessary connection of individual with community can also be considered to reflect the anthropological truth that it is לא־טוב for a human to be alone (cf. Gen 2:18). Eichrodt, *Theology of the Old Testament*, 2:239.

17. Vriezen, *Outline of Old Testament Theology*, 128–29.

18. Ibid., 3–4; Waltke and Yu, *Old Testament Theology*, 68; Hasel, *Old Testament Theology*, 121.

19. As Vriezen himself notes: the Old Testament was given for Israel's faith, but the religion of Israel was not necessarily restricted (or even obedient) to the Old Testament. Vriezen, *Outline of Old Testament Theology*, 15.

between fellow humans, but rather includes the more important ability to engage in a relationship with the divine.[20]

The relationship between God and Israel was mediated through the covenant; however, the covenant itself is insufficient to reflect properly the relationship.[21] The need for a deeper relationship is exactly what prompted the prophets who demanded "that Israel shall live truly by God's Covenant" nonetheless to condemn the wayward priests of later Israel who approached their covenant obligations mechanistically.[22] Vriezen's approach allows for an understanding of the pre-covenant era without any anachronistic use of the Law. At the same time, however, Vriezen recognizes that a standard of worship existed pre-covenant and that while the form of worship differed from Israel's worship under the covenant, the goal of intimacy with YHWH was consistent.[23] Further, while Vriezen mentions the evolution of religious practice from pre-covenant to covenantal forms, he maintains the importance of covenant in Israel. His concern is not to dismiss covenant, but rather to delve deeper into the underpinning relationship of it.[24]

The critical aspect of the human-divine relationship is the "right relationship of reverence for the holy God and that [human beings] should let [themselves] be guided by this reverence:" the fear of the Lord.[25] It is this key aspect that directly gravitates against making an idol or image of YHWH—such a creation would be irreverent.[26] On the other hand, the creation of humankind as צלם אלהים subverts the irreverence of idolatry and establishes the means by which a proper relationship can be formed. This relationship finds its biblical expression through Israel; even when speaking of humankind in general, all people are judged in terms of Israel's covenant.[27] Further, Vriezen agrees with Eichrodt that "the list of nations in Genesis 10 ... however conscious of its important place in history ... does not claim for Israel a fundamentally different natural ability" than the other nations. Said another way, the ability to relate to God is not fundamentally different

---

20. Ibid., 17; Frost, *In His Image*, 41.

21. Hasel, *Old Testament Theology*, 121.

22. Vriezen, *Outline of Old Testament Theology*, 26.

23. Vriezen acknowledges that it is impossible to reconstruct fully the ancient forms of Hebrew worship, but suggests that the relational emphasis of Israel's faith can be traced regardless of the specific expressions of it. Vriezen, *Outline of Old Testament Theology*, 27–30.

24. Vriezen, *Outline of Old Testament Theology*, 29–30; Hasel, *Old Testament Theology*, 121.

25. Vriezen, *Outline of Old Testament Theology*, 130.

26. Ibid.

27. Ibid., 143; cf. Firmage, "Genesis 1," 103.

between Israel and the nations. The difference in the relationship is in the observance of God's prescribed way(s) of communion.[28] This observation is particularly important, since it leads directly to Vriezen's discussion of the image of God and its foundational importance in the created-Creator relationship. His preference is to suggest that the divine image is representative of a father-child relationship between God and humanity in a manner similar to other ANE anthropologies but more removed from any sort of physical generation.

Unfortunately, much of Vriezen's interpretation of the divine image is based on his modification of pagan myth's god-spawned humans. He seeks to maintain the father-son relationship without any direct father-son language. This is both problematic and unnecessary. It is problematic because it lacks appropriate scriptural support and unnecessary because alternative interpretations of the image of God serve equally well to establish relationship without drawing on that analogy.[29] Vriezen does well, however, in his observation that the image of God reflected humankind's "fundamental vocation."[30] This concept of the image of God as a vocational calling accords with the present thesis that the divine image more fully represents an assignment or calling upon humanity rather than simply a passive inherent characteristic. Further, the entire conceptualization of the Old Testament in general and the covenant in particular around the concept of communion with YHWH virtually corresponds with a priestly theology, since the mediation of that communion was administered through the cult.[31] That the correspondence between humankind and God necessitated the cult is not unique to Israel, but formed the prevailing mentality of the ancient Near East. Certainly the entire basis of charismatic figures allowed for a non-cultic discourse between God and humanity; however, the general practice was nonetheless cultic. Vriezen's overall theological paradigm not only affirms the possibility of an interpretation of the צלם אלהים as an ordination to priesthood but also suggests its primacy.

---

28. Eichrodt, *Man in the Old Testament*, 35; Vriezen, *Outline of Old Testament Theology*, 143.

29. Scripture does support the sonship of Israel, and even the sonship of the king of Israel—though the latter could be deemed an example of synecdoche or personification of Israel; however, it does *not* use such language to describe humankind in general or in more common expressions of anthropology.

30. Vriezen, *Outline of Old Testament Theology*, 208.

31. Brueggemann, "Kerygma of the Priestly Writers," 398; Zimmerli, *Old Testament Theology*, 149.

Centrality of Creeds and Confessions

Gerhard von Rad, like Vriezen, advocates a non-covenantal relationship model; however, unlike Vriezen, von Rad codifies that relationship in specific cultic constructs. He distills the foundational theology of the Old Testament to a small number of credal statements.[32] In many ways, von Rad also adopts a canonical approach to the Scriptures, since his concern is not the discernment of chronological priority but the analysis of the credal statements in the context of the biblical arrangement distinct from the "actual" historic event(s).[33]

The first of the relatively few creed-groups that von Rad relies upon is the exodus tradition of deliverance from Egypt and the crossing of the Red Sea. He suggests that this tradition is the dominant one "around which the whole hexateuchal history was in the end ranged."[34] Whether or not he can properly sustain this statement, the importance of the exodus themes and motifs for the rest of the Old Testament—including the prophets whom von Rad ironically sets apart from credal interests[35]—is well attested. It is hardly accidental that the origination of the tabernacle and the ordination of the Levitical priesthood is directly connected with this dominant theme. If the Exodus is essential to the creeds themselves, the cult is essential to being the people of the creed. The two themes are tightly interwoven, and connected even more on a practical basis by the reality that the priests were curators of not only the holy place, but also through their edificatory role of the holy word.[36]

---

32. Von Rad, *Old Testament Theology*, 1:vi; House, *Old Testament Theology*, 35; Barr, *Concept of Biblical Theology*, 36. Technically, von Rad focuses his argument on the Hexateuch's credal foundation rather than the entire Old Testament's. However, considering the role of the Hexateuch within the Old Testament and its underpinning of the whole of Scripture in canonical interpretations, to argue that the Hexateuch is based on creed is to argue that the Old Testament as a whole is based on and an elaboration of ancient confessional statements.

33. Von Rad, *Old Testament Theology*, 1:vi, 5; Rendtorff, *Canon and Theology*, 9; Rendtorff, *Canonical Hebrew Bible*, 718; House, *Old Testament Theology*, 35.

34. Von Rad, *Old Testament Theology*, 1:13. This is a consistent standard for von Rad, even when he argues that the judge rather than the priest was the primary arbiter of the Law in the earliest days of Israel, for though the judges were not inherently tied to cult the Law was nonetheless sacral even when handled by non-priestly individuals. Ibid., 32–33; cf. p. 40 and its discussion of the persistence of sacral conceptions.

35. Ibid., vii, 63. The irony of this is that while von Rad suggests that the prophets denied the "efficacy of the old divine actions for their contemporaries," the prophets nonetheless utilized the imagery the events foundational to credal formations. Further, the prophetic call to return to the *proper* observance of cult rather than to abandon it completely virtually demands a credal understanding. Ibid., 66.

36. Ibid., 75.

Perhaps more importantly, von Rad understands the development of the nation of Israel as a religious rather than a political consolidation.[37] This has the effect of immediately subverting the secular leadership—whether patriarch, judge, or king—to the religious authorities. This correlates with and reflects the repeated assertions of this study that the foundation of Israel's formation at Sinai is Exod 19:6 and the priestly calling of the nation. Unity is found in the sacral rather than the secular, or even the biological.[38]

Von Rad approaches the creeds as written codifications intended to immerse later Israel into the wonder of YHWH's previous miracle performance on behalf of the nation that had either ceased or significantly reduced.[39] This is important for the present study since it explicitly connects the creeds of Israel, the province of the priests, with God's miraculous works of deliverance and, more tellingly, Creation.[40] The codification of the miracles and their entrustment to the priests mimics the mythic experience of אדם in Genesis 1–2 and the entrustment of the Creation-Temple and the garden to him, further affiliating the original human(s)—and consequently the צלם אלהים—with the priesthood. Von Rad's further assertion that the Old Testament writings are exclusively concerned with presenting the continuing divine activity of YHWH virtually necessitates a priestly interpretation of the whole of the Old Testament: the mediation, interpretation, and celebration of divine activity is the realm of the priesthood.[41]

---

37. Ibid., 17; cf. Nelson, *Raising Up*, 48–49.

38. Cf. House, *Old Testament Theology*, 36. Von Rad would argue that the biological links between the various tribes are an invention. On the other hand, even if the familial connection is a fiction the canonical presentation affirms that the calling of Israel to be YHWH's priestly nation is preeminent over any individual tribal loyalty.

39. Von Rad, *Old Testament Theology*, 1:53, 69–71; Hasel, *Old Testament Theology*, 125–26; Barr, *Concept of Biblical Theology*, 34.

40. Von Rad does not connect the creeds with Creation; however, since he connects them with theologies of deliverance/salvation and the Exodus events—already discussed as a form of (re-)Creation—the assertion that they reflect a form of Creation theology is valid, even though von Rad insists the Creation narrative was a relatively late addition to Hebrew theology. Cf. von Rad, *Problem of the Hexateuch*, 142; Childs, *Biblical Theology*, 109.

41. Von Rad, *Old Testament Theology*, 1:106, 114–15. Von Rad further explains this concept by noting that "never in these testimonies about history, did Israel point to her own faith, but to Jahweh." While von Rad's purpose in this assertion is to emphasize the confessional character of Israel and its basis on the person of God rather than the practice of the cult, the reality is that biblically the cult practices were explicitly designed to emulate or instruct on the person of YHWH. This is most readily seen in the continual refrain of Leviticus to be holy as YHWH himself is holy, but also discernible in the other prescriptions and memorials in the Pentateuch (cf. Exod 12:14–17; Josh 4:1–7; Hos 12:2–14; et al.). Von Rad, *Old Testament Theology*, 1:111, 226; cf. Waltke and Yu, *Old Testament Theology*, 499; Goldingay, *Israel's Faith*, 43.

This context should be recognized as von Rad discusses the creation and uniqueness of humankind in reflecting "so very immediately to God himself."[42] He emphasizes the patterning aspect of the divine image and the resultant glorification of the human creature, before moving to a typical interpretation of the צלם אלהים as a royal imprint.[43] Even in his discussion of the supposedly royal character of the divine image, von Rad emphasizes the human dominion's boundaries more than its benefits—namely, he notes that while the image of God does subjugate Creation to humanity, it also serves to order humanity under God.[44] It should be noted that this arrangement and representation is just as viably priestly as it is royal, though von Rad fails to recognize it. Von Rad also makes no mention of the implications of his understanding of the image of God as an immediate reflection of YHWH: if confessions served to codify the nature of God in history, and the צלם אלהים served as a statement of God's nature for Creation, then the assignation of the צלם אלהים to people makes humankind a sort of living and sentient confession.

Ultimately, constructing biblical theology around the idea of creed and confessional statements does not conflict with the understanding of the divine image as an assignment to priestly duty. Quite the opposite, von Rad's method actually serves to bolster the viability of this interpretation. Confessions, statements of faith, are part of the curation of the priests, and the demand that the whole earth embrace these same confessions (cf. Isa 45:22–25 et al.) parallels the demand that all of humankind properly administer the Creation-Temple. This connection, along with the implications that human beings are created as some form of confession in creature form; suggests that not only is the proposed interpretation of the צלם אלהים as a calling to priesthood compatible with von Rad, but it also may be wholly necessary to properly reflect his creedal emphasis.

Centrality of Testimony

More recently, Brueggemann has reaffirmed the basic relational thesis of Vriezen, though he channels the relationship through the idea of testimony rather than through covenant *per se*. In this respect, he somewhat mirrors the creedalism of von Rad though with an overall more dialogical nature as Brueggemann emphasizes that the biblical record is a record of what is

---

42. Von Rad, *Old Testament Theology*, 1:144.
43. Ibid., 144–46.
44. Waltke and Yu, *Old Testament Theology*, 407.

said about what God said.⁴⁵ The entire endeavor of theology, he notes, is inherently focused not only on God himself (*theos*) but also on the speech of or about him (*logos*).⁴⁶ He therefore patterns his theology on the dialogue between God in his testimony to Israel and Israel's "counter-testimony" response to YHWH.⁴⁷

Brueggemann relies heavily on the nature of legal disputation in his approach, which hinders a predominantly cultic reading of many portions of the Old Testament, but very rightly emphasizes that without testimony/speech then there is no content to the Hebrew Bible.⁴⁸ Since the Old Testament tendency is to emphasize the active work of YHWH, even the narrative portions of Scripture are actually testimonies of God's activity toward humankind—either as protagonist or antagonist.⁴⁹ This is a particularly important observation, since it is precisely the *activity* of God that lends credence to the image of God being an assignment rather than an attribute.

A strictly courtly-legal rendering might seem to hinder some cultic readings, but the opposite is actually true. Since the law of the land was based within (and in some cases explicitly designated from) the Torah, there is—biblically/theologically, even if not practiced historically—a cultic sense to every legal proceeding in the Old Testament.⁵⁰ This is especially true in the case of the prophetic disputations, which rely upon the standing relationship between YHWH and Israel (even if one is hesitant fully to describe the prophetic work as covenant lawsuit) and are therefore based on theonomous rather than [humanly] autonomous principles. Brueggemann's own emphasis on the foundational aspect of תודה in Israel's testimony only serves to affirm the inherent connection between testimony and cult, since "*the beginning point for articulating an Old Testament theology is in the liturgical, public acknowledgment of a new reality wrought by Yahweh*" (emphasis his).⁵¹ Essentially, Brueggemann from the outset established the inherently cultic and priestly nature of the dialogue between humankind and God.

---

45. Brueggemann, *Theology of the Old Testament*, 117–18.

46. Ibid., 117; Waltke and Yu, *Old Testament Theology*, 69.

47. Brueggemann, *Theology of the Old Testament*, 119–20; Middleton, *Liberating Image*, 192; Barr, *Concept of Biblical Theology*, 543–44.

48. Cf. Barr, *Concept of Biblical Theology*, 548–49. Brueggemann's own emphasis on the foundational aspect of תודה in Israel's testimony only serves to affirm the inherent connection between testimony and cult. Cf. Brueggemann, *Theology of the Old Testament*, 126–28.

49. Brueggemann, *Theology of the Old Testament*, 123; cf. Waltke and Yu, *Old Testament Theology*, 70.

50. Cf. Beale, "Eden," 19.

51. Brueggemann, *Theology of the Old Testament*, 128.

With this establishment, it is not inappropriate to conform even charismatic or individual/personal discourse between humans and God to a priestly motif. The subject of this biblical discourse is summarized by Brueggemann as YHWH's righteousness.[52] Remembering that the Hebraic treatment of righteousness is not the possession of an attribute but the performance of "right deeds," Brueggemann's approach affirms the active nature of God in the Old Testament testimony and affirms a performative or even vocational response to God.[53]

Before examining the ramifications of the cultic nature of Israel's dialogue and the vocational response to God's righteousness, one additional aspect of Brueggemann's approach must be properly appreciated: the complete lack of Israelite identity apart from YHWH.[54] This reality forms the foundation for Brueggemann's understanding of the lawsuits of Israel, where the nation was charged with abandoning God and consequently abandoning their very *raison d'etre*. This ultimately is true not only of Israel specifically, but humankind at large, for "*the Old Testament has no interest in articulating an autonomous or universal notion of humanness*" (emphasis his).[55] Of course, Brueggemann excludes a universal aspect of humanness since he ties the humanness of the Old Testament intrinsically to the covenant with Israel. The problem with his assumption, however, is that it ignores the universal applicability of the covenant to all of humanity. If the non-Israelite nations had been faithful to the covenant, they would have shared in the blessings of Israel. The prophetic condemnation of the nations on the basis of covenant affirms the expectation that *all* people were to live in obedience to the covenant—or at the very minimum the basic provisions of it—and/or in honor of Zion, which cannot be assumed to refer to Israel itself so much as the overall aspect of being a holy place in which God's presence abides.[56] Further, just as covenant stipulations can be read anachronistically into pre-Sinai narratives so too can covenant stipulations be read transnationally over the actions of the nations.[57] Brueggemann af-

---

52. Ibid., 130.

53. Cf. Goldingay, *Israel's Life*, 130–31.

54. Brueggemann, *Theology of the Old Testament*, 133–34.

55. Ibid., 450.

56. Brueggemann himself paradoxically makes this same point in discussing the partnership of humanity and God. Brueggemann, *Theology of the Old Testament*, 455–56.

57. Bruckner's work on the implied law in the patriarchal narratives combines with Blenkinsopp's work on the origin of law in tribal culture to suggest a widespread ethical understanding that went well beyond the borders of Israel. While there are many historical or sociological arguments that can be made on this point that could exclude the exclusive and ultimate example of the biblical covenant, the reality is that the canonical

firms Levinas's understanding that "authentically human humanity" only exists in proximity to the throne of YHWH.[58]

The accuracy of Brueggemann's observations on the essential nature of Israel and humanity make his subsequent treatment of the image of God all the more confusing. He directly asserts that *"the notion of humanity in 'the image of God' plays no primary role in the Old Testament articulations of humanity*; it does not constitute a major theological datum of Israel's reflection on the topic" (emphasis his).[59] His statement that the image of God provides no primary foundation for biblical anthropology is only viable, however, if it is only the specific phrase in question that is considered. The *aspects* of the image of God, as already discussed, are critical for any accurate conception of humankind.[60] On the other hand, Brueggemann accepts the royal interpretation of the צלם, and a royal engraving on humanity is indeed inconsistent with his overall thesis on the nature of human identity. If, however, the image of God is interpreted as a priestly motif, then it is not only a viable basis for human nature in Brueggemann's theology but also a necessary basis since access to the holy presence of God is an inherently cultic activity. The idea that human identity is entirely predicated on YHWH cannot dismiss human creation in the divine image. It can—and does—provoke a reevaluation of the meaning and purpose of the divine image.

Brueggemann's earlier theses of a liturgical proclamation of God's righteous deeds now comes back to the fore. There is little need to note the cultic aspects of liturgical proclamations, but the righteous deeds of YHWH can be addressed further. If righteousness is performative, then the call of Israel to righteousness is ultimately an assignment of activity. The activity that Brueggemann first notes is the cultic practice of praise and worship (תודה), but he also emphasizes the need to obey YHWH with the specific idea of *"the courage to assert* and *the confidence to yield"* to YHWH's covenant stipulation.[61] It is hardly coincidental that both the assertion/instruction of the covenant and the proper means of yielding/submitting to the

---

presentation of this universal ethic *can* be traced to YHWH alone, as the sole Creator of humanity and one who was known universally by humankind. Canonically and theologically, the nations apostatized from knowledge of YHWH. Israel's election was to provide a means of redemption, not introduction. Bruckner, *Implied Law*; Middleton, *New Heaven*, 85, 91–92; cf. Brueggemann, *Theology of the Old Testament*, 451; Firmage, "Genesis 1," 103.

58. Brueggemann, *Theology of the Old Testament*, 450–51; Levinas, *In the Time of the Nations*, 124.

59. Brueggemann, *Theology of the Old Testament*, 452.

60. Bray, "Significance of God's Image," 201.

61. Brueggemann, *Theology of the Old Testament*, 459.

Lord fall into the realm of priestly activity. Ultimately, while Brueggemann fails to connect the צלם אלהים with a calling to priesthood, he does—either inadvertently or deliberately though subtly—connect the essential task of humanity with priestly activity. In this it can be safely asserted that Brueggemann's work is not incompatible with the current suggestions regarding the proper understanding of the image of God, and in many ways—though certainly not every way—affirms it.

REFLECTION ON THE COMPATIBILITY OF THEOLOGY WITH A PRIESTLY EMPHASIS

While a brief overview is insufficient to convey fully the nuances of major biblical theological works, the preceding synopses do credibly reflect the broad approaches and understandings of Eichrodt, Vriezen, von Rad, and Brueggemann. The synopses also credibly demonstrate that while none of these theologians explicitly connect priesthood with the central aspect of the Old Testament as they perceive it, there is no disruption of either the proposed theology (theologies) or the priestly concept when the two are merged together.

The relative harmony that can be found in this approach underscores not only the compatibility of a priestly approach to the Old Testament as a whole, but also the viability of interpreting the image of God as a distinctly priestly concept—a viability that remains intact even if the theologian himself, as in the case of Brueggemann, decries the importance or role of the צלם אלהים. The fact that both the importance and the interpretation of the divine image can be paralleled with each of these theologies even in opposition to the author's original intention serves to strengthen rather than weaken the thesis that a priestly conception of humankind is dominant, since it coincides with these works without any intentional authorial accommodation.

With the establishment of complementary possibilities of a primarily priestly anthropology with these theological models, all that remains is to accept the possibility of a primarily priestly interpretation of the image of God. Each of these models relies on a central tenet that reflects the biblical story as a whole and—therefore—the nature of the divine-human relationship as a whole. Since the foundational relationship between YHWH and humanity in Creation is summarized in the צלם אלהים, then the צלם אלהים must be compatible with the central tenet.[62] A priestly interpretation of the image of God provides this compatibility in every case and in some cases, such as von Rad's, augments it by better aligning the role of humanity at large with the

---

62. Wolff, *Anthropology of the Old Testament*, 159.

perceived center of scriptural thought. Considered in this light, there is no reason to disqualify the interpretation of the image of God as an assignment to priestly vocation on the basis of other major theological approaches; quite the contrary, this interpretation correlates with and/or strengthens existing theological models and connects the discreet study of biblical anthropology with the larger study of Old Testament theology as a whole.[63]

---

63. Cf. Davies, *Anthropology and Theology*, 151.

Chapter 5

The Significance of a Priestly צלם אלהים within Biblical Theology

It has been proposed that the image of God is a foundational concept to biblical anthropology, and since the Bible is essentially concerned with the nature and expression of the relationship between God and human beings, an understanding of the nature of humankind cannot help but illustrate or contend with the whole of biblical theology.[1] Themes of deliverance (which even in the Old Testament would include social and spiritual deliverance, and not simply physical ones), community (which relate to land and promise theology, as well as the nature of Israel and/or the church), and edification (which accommodates not only the Torah, but also the Psalms, sapiential materials, and even apocalyptic works) all rely on an understanding of the human need as in the case of deliverance, or the divine provision for humanity through a relationship of some kind.[2] Even the idea(s) of edification rely on this construct: the instructions of the Scripture expect the recognition of the authority and power of God by the human reader/listener and an appropriate response that inherently demonstrates a relationship of some kind, whether it is intimate or simply a mechanical obedience.[3]

---

1. Sherlock, *Doctrine of Humanity*, 17, 31; Van Wolde, *Stories of the Beginning*, 4; cf. Ross, *Recalling the Hope of Glory*, 78; Bird, "Male and Female," 129–30, 156.

2. Van Wolde, *Stories of the Beginning*, 23; Sherlock, *Doctrine of Humanity*, 37.

3. Blenkinsopp, *Sage, Priest, Prophet*, 3–4; Goldingay, *Israel's Life*, 65–70; cf. Knohl, *Sanctuary of Silence*, 128, Renckens, *Israel's Concept*, 17. Reno's statements about Creation in general are applicable here as well. Reno notes that "creation must be the enduring basis for all divine action. The created order is not the first act; it is the enduring stage upon which the entire divine drama unfolds." Since human beings are the apex of that Creation, his general observation logically applies to biblical anthropology as well. It is the connection between humanity and God that forms the entire theological environment of

Considering the proposal that the divine image represents a calling for humankind to serve in a priestly capacity, it seems reasonable to expect a reevaluation of biblical theology as a whole. This reevaluation does not necessarily demand any sweeping changes to theological conclusions, but will likely result in both a broad change of nuance in examining the Scriptures and a discreet shift in focus for select passages.[4] Since biblical scholars already read the Bible with a recognition that it reflects mandates for worship, holiness, and the pursuit of divine understanding; any realignment of thought to include the essential priesthood of humankind remains remarkably compatible with established theologies and often serves to amplify rather than contradict primary theses.[5]

SUMMARY OF THE SIGNIFICANCE OF A PRIESTLY IMAGE OF GOD IN OLD TESTAMENT THEOLOGY

Both the clarity of presentation and the canonical positioning of Genesis 1 establish it as the Creation account *par excellence* within the biblical context. This serves to give a certain theological priority to the chapter that forms the foundation of biblical doctrines of Creation and the nature of humankind.[6] This priority creates a direct impact on canonically later biblical texts and their interpretations.

As far as the Creation itself, there is widespread agreement that Genesis 1 serves as a temple-building account. This context therefore can reasonably expect the role of humankind to be one of priest.[7] Despite this natural expectation, many interpretations of the image of God err in first ascribing a primarily royal character to the image of God, and second in assuming that the divine image is a quality or characteristic rather than recognize that it is

---

the Scriptures. Reno, *Genesis*, 58–59; Humphreys, *Character of God*, 24, 33.

4. Though Bird does not call for this approach, it is a logical consequence of her argument that biblical scholars and dogmatic theologians must form a greater dialogue if a proper understanding of the image of God is to be found. Bird, "Male and Female," 130–32.

5. Cf. Sprinkle, *Book of the Covenant*, 37; Cross, *Canaanite Myth*, 299. There is little reason to limit Cross' statement that "the entire cultic paraphernalia and cultus was designed to express and overcome the problem of the holy, transcendent God visiting his pervasively sinful people" to Israel. It accords to the overall biblical presentation. The question is never whether God uses cultic means to reach his people, but rather who the priests are and where/what is the temple itself.

6. Van Wolde, *Stories of the Beginning*, 1; Middleton, *Liberating Image*, 60; cf. Balentine, *Torah's Vision*, 60–63; Firmage, "Genesis 1," 101.

7. Fletcher-Louis, "God's Image," 84–85; Barker, *Gate of Heaven*, 69–70; Mouroux, *Meaning of Man*, 28; Beale, *Temple*, 81; Eichrodt, *Man in the Old Testament*, 30.

a function or assignment.⁸ The examination of the use of both צלם and דמות within the Hebrew Bible suggests that the natural reading of these terms expects a cultic rather than courtly meaning. Further, the importance on functional designation within God's Creative work reveals that the image of God has a teleological and functional interest.⁹ This interest is best expressed in the form of assignment: by placing the divine image upon humankind, YHWH has essentially assigned them a cultic task, or the role of priest(s).¹⁰

A brief study of various other passages in the Old Testament that interact with Creation theology (and/or eschatology, which is itself a form of Creation theology) or with the role and nature of humanity demonstrates that while this particular theological emphasis has not always been immediately suggested by interpreters, it is compatible with—and in many cases strengthening of—the majority of biblical interpretations. So while the role of biblical anthropology in general and the צלם אלהים in particular is often left without significant comment, it does not intrude upon the interpretations of the examined passages.

Similarly, major theological works—particularly those that have sought a central theme or unifying thread for the Old Testament—have been demonstrated to accommodate an overall priestly context quite well. While themes such as covenant, dialogue, or simply a rather ambiguous statement of relationship might be considered apart from a priestly context, to do so ignores the well-accepted role of the priests as mediators, arbitrators, and curators of the holy things. The divine-human relationship in the ANE was most naturally thought of in terms of cult and priesthood. With this in mind, the generalized central themes espoused by Eichrodt, Vriezen, von Rad, Brueggemann, and others are strengthened by an association with priesthood. So as with the examination of discreet Old Testament texts, so too the examination of Old Testament theologies demonstrates compatibility with the assumption that the nature of humankind and the means of divine-human relationship is found within a God-priest interaction that is presented from the first chapter of the Bible in the form of the צלם אלהים.¹¹

---

8. It should be noted that the error is in assigning a *primarily* royal character to the צלם אלהים. Since God is presented as a sovereign throughout the Scriptures, a certain royal prerogative can rightly be assigned to the divine image. However, in the actual biblical context and the canonical role of Genesis 1, this royal assignment is secondary to a priestly motif. Humankind may *possess* a royal position and sovereignty, but was created *for* a priestly activity and function.

9. Van Wolde, *Stories of the Beginning*, 26–27; Firmage, "Genesis 1," 99; Boer, *Ember*, 3; cf. Garrett, *Systematic Theology*, 1:396.

10. Blenkinsopp, *Sage, Priest, Prophet*, 67–68; Eichrodt, *Man in the Old Testament*, 30; cf. Firmage, "Genesis 1," 111.

11. Cf. Firmage, "Genesis 1," 111–12.

EXAMINATION OF THE IDEA OF A PRIESTLY IMAGE WITHIN NEW TESTAMENT THEOLOGY

Determining the New Testament understanding of the divine image and the concept of priesthood can be quite involved; however, forming a summary of the thought is a relatively simple—though not necessarily easy—process. First, a brief examination of New Testament occurrences of εἰκων (used by the LXX as the Greek equivalency of צלם) will establish a general pattern of usage.[12] Then, a brief overview of the idea of divine imitation and reflection on priestly features in the New Testament will demonstrate the overall use of these concepts and their compatibility with, contrast against, or expansion of the Old Testament use of these concepts. While this will obviously not form a comprehensive statement, it will provide a legitimate New Testament theological context.

Εἰκων in the New Testament

Εἰκων is not particularly common in the New Testament, occurring only twenty-three times in twenty verses, of which half are in the Revelation. It is used only once in each of the synoptic gospels in different accounts of rendering taxes to Caesar (Matt 22:20; Mark 12:16; Luke 20:24). In this context, it is clearly referring simply to a picture, and while the person of Caesar is a royal figure, there is neither a particularly political nor cultic intention of this passage. The note that the image is an inscription (ἐπιγραφη) clearly establishes this as a simple descriptive statement.

Paul uses εἰκων nine times (eight verses) throughout his writings. Romans 1:23 is the only reference to idolatry; each of the other occurrences (Rom 8:29; 1 Cor 11:7; 15:49; 2 Cor 3:18; 4:4; Col 1:15; 3:10) involves the assumption of the image of God in some manner. Romans 8:29 and 1 Cor 15:49 explicitly expect the Christian to adopt the image of Jesus ("the son" and "the [spiritual] man from Heaven"); however, Paul's association of Jesus with the image of God in 2 Cor 4:4 and Col 1:15 expects a juxtaposition of

---

12. The Greek equivalent of דמות, ὁμοιωσις, occurs only one time in the New Testament (Jas 3:9), and that use is clearly reflecting Gen 1:26 as a statement of the foundational nature of humankind. While James' use arguably could suggest that the ὁμοιωσις is a characteristic rather than a calling or ordination, the isolation of this incident makes a sweeping conclusion impossible, particularly since the context is replete with statements of blessing and cursing that would not be unusual in a priestly context. What is notable, however, is the possible inference to original humanity's dominion in v. 7. The connection with Genesis 1 suggests that the way that the people of God speak reflects their position or purpose and does serve to retain a teleological intention to the image/likeness.

the images: to assume the image of the Christ is to assume the image of God, and vice versa.[13]

The remaining three Pauline uses of εἰκων all are distinctly concerned with the conduct of the Christian. Interestingly, 2 Cor 3:18 connects the transformation of the Christian into an image of the glory of God directly to an understanding of not only who Jesus was, but also of the correct reading of Torah (cf. v. 14).[14] There is the implication that the correct reading of the Law allows for or even facilitates the expression of the image of God. Paul does not contrast Jesus with Moses (and therefore the Law) in these passages, but does contrast Jesus with Adam in 1 Cor 15:42–49.[15] This contrast is an important recognition since εἰκων in Col 3:10 explicitly connects the holy life of the Christian with the Creator. There is a clear thought that it is the Christ-follower who seeks to emulate Jesus that expresses the image of God.[16] That this was a performative rather than simply declarative reality is seen in 1 Corinthians 10–11. Paul's discussion of man's role as the εἰκων καὶ δόξα θεοῦ in 1 Cor 11:7 directly follows that call to imitate Jesus through Paul's example (1 Cor 11:1) and an extensive discourse surrounding various cultic principles (1 Corinthians 8–10) and precedes instruction on the ordinance of communion and the ministry of the Christian within the body (1 Corinthians 11–14).[17]

With these considerations in mind, Paul's general view of the image of God can be discerned in his application of εἰκων. The image of God is essentially synonymous with the image of Christ, and so the imitation of Christ (a performative, though not necessarily physical, expression) expresses the divine image. Paul then describes the proper imitation of Christ in terms of righteous living.[18] The taking up of righteousness as an expression of the image of God in Col 3:10 transcends heritage and ethnicity (v. 11) and leads to not only proper lifestyle (vv. 12–13), but also a holy community (vv. 13–15) and explicit worship through both word and deed (vv. 16–17).[19] While Paul

---

13. Guthrie, *New Testament Theology*, 180; Garland, *2 Corinthians*, 212.

14. Harris, *Second Epistle to the Corinthians*, 313–14.

15. Guthrie, *New Testament Theology*, 178.

16. Maloney, *Cosmic Christ*, 46–47; Renckens, *Israel's Concept*, 126–27; Guthrie, *New Testament Theology*, 180.

17. A similar pattern—though lacking the direct use of εἰκων—is seen in Ephesians 5 where the imitation of God (v. 1) is found in Christ-like performance (v. 2). This performance is then specified through both negative (vv. 3–5) and positive (vv. 6–21) prescriptions for living, including specific commentary on the role of community and the conduct of worship in vv. 19–21.

18. Middleton, *New Heaven*, 141.

19. Dunn, *Epistles*, 220–22.

does not describe the Christian in explicitly priestly terms, the use of εἰκων in his epistles coheres with and reflects the same interests with which the Israelite priesthood was charged.

Outside of the Revelation, εἰκων is only used in the General Epistles in Heb 10:1. The writer's use is distinct from Paul's and adds a complexity to the New Testament use of εἰκων that was previously absent. In Hebrews, the Law and the practiced religion of Israel are compared to a σκια ("shadow"), while the true nature of the relationship between humanity and God is described as the εἰκων.[20] By making this distinction, the writer essentially gives the image a substance and higher nature than the Law through which the צלם אלהים had been expressed in the Old Testament.[21] This elevation is consistent with the overall theme of the book, demonstrating that the reality of Jesus was superior to the entirety of the Old Testament witness, yet at the same time affirming that the Old Testament witness was directly concerned with showing (the pre-incarnate) Jesus to the original audience. This affirmation is particularly pertinent to the present topic since it not only connects the divine-human relationship through εἰκων terminology, but also because the remainder of Hebrews 10 is an expansion and realignment of the priesthood in light of the fuller revelation of the Christ.[22]

Εἰκων is used ten times (eight verses) in Revelation, always in connection with the Beast.[23] What is particularly interesting is the distinct lack of a descriptive use. The first occurrence of εἰκων in Rev 13:14 concerns the formation of the image of the Beast, which could be interpreted as a simple instruction to build an idol. In v. 15 the image itself then is given a certain degree of independent existence: it is granted the ability to speak and to compel worship and tribulation. This empowerment of the image suggests that it is best interpreted not as a thing, but rather as a person—a person whose role is the proliferation of the worship of and obedience to the Beast, a sort of priest.[24] The image's success is demonstrated through the "mark" that is placed on either the head or hand of the Beast's followers (v. 16). In the Hebraic context that the apocalyptic materials rely upon, the mark of the

---

20. Lane, *Hebrews 9–13*, 254nb.

21. Ellingworth, *Epistle to the Hebrews*, 490, 494.

22. Cf. Lane, *Hebrews*, 260. It could be argued that Hebrews 10 serves to expand the work of the priesthood in a manner similar to Matthew 5–7's expansion of the Torah. Just as the Sermon on the Mount amplified rather than nullified the Old Testament commandments, Hebrews 10 seems to emphasize the call to priesthood for all Christians rather than excise priesthood from the church.

23. Rev 13:14, 15; 14:9, 11; 15:2; 16:2; 19:20; 20:4.

24. Beale, *Book of Revelation*, 710.

Beast is best seen not as a physical mark, but rather as a comment on living.[25] Just as the Scriptures are "bound" to the hand and between the eyes of the faithful follower of YHWH (Deut 6:8) and the Aaronic priests were marked on their ear, hand, and foot (Lev 8:23–24), so the description of the mark of the Beast is a statement affirming the acceptance of the Beast's perversion of both external (the hand) and internal (the head) life.[26] So through the occurrence of the mark of the Beast, a connection is formed between being an image and doing a task.

This connection is important in the understanding of Rev 20:4, where those who did not worship the image were the ones who received dominion.[27] The contrast between worshiping the image of the Beast and obedience to Jesus is undeniable, and the context expects only one of these two options: either one followed the Beast and received condemnation (v. 15) or they followed Jesus and were granted authority and life, and deemed "blessed and holy" (v. 6).[28] In either case, though, the idea of emulation is not only found in the context of general living but also of sacred worship; and always in the context of performative action rather than simply as an inherent characteristic. The sacred worship of the faithful is then ultimately contrasted with the servants of the Beast in Rev 22:4, where they have the name of God written on their forehead serving not only as a contrast to the false priesthood of the Beast but also as an affirmation of the universal priesthood of the faithful.[29]

Imitation and Priesthood in the New Testament

The use of the specific term εἰκών is infrequent in the New Testament, but the actualization of the divine-human relationship through imitation or emulation is foundational.[30] Similarly, while there are no direct calls to priesthood in the New Testament that resemble the ordination of the Aaronic priests of YHWH, priestly ideology is critical for a proper understand-

---

25. Easley, *Revelation*, 233.

26. Cf. Barker, *Temple Theology*, 26. Barker also notes that the Name of YHWH is inscribed on the heads of the faithful in Rev 22:4, further aligning the idea that Revelation presents two contrasting priesthoods: the priesthood of the Christ and the priesthood of the Beast.

27. It should be noted on the basis of Rev 13:15 that syntactically the image worshiped in Rev 14:9, 11; 16:2; 19:20; and 20:4 could be either the object of worship *or the manner of worship*.

28. Cf. Schnabel, "Israel," 57.

29. Beale, "Eden," 25–26.

30. Guthrie, *New Testament Theology*, 151.

ing of the New Testament—both in terms of Jesus' ultimate high priesthood and in terms of the priesthood of the believers.[31]

Priesthood in the Synoptic Gospels and Acts

The synoptic gospels do not have any overt expressions of Christ-followers' priesthood. While this may be due in part to the Gentile primary audience of Mark and Luke, the more likely explanation is that the gospels' presentation of Jesus as the Christ consistently focuses on his identity and work rather than of his disciples.[32] Generally, emphasis is given to the Christ's kingship; however, there is still ample concern for cultic/priestly matters.[33]

Matthew's gospel is useful in this, as the five-discourse patterning of the book has been likened to the Torah.[34] Further, the close affiliation of Jesus with Israel (Matt 2:15 et al.) inherently connects Jesus not only with the Davidic calling to kingship but also with the Israelite role as priestly mediator between God and humankind.[35] The temptation account ends with an emphasis on worshiping God alone (Matt 4:10), while the Sermon on the Mount is clearly an explication of the Law that reflects rabbinic methodologies, but also addresses vows, tithing, prayer, fasting, etc.—all matters of priestly concern.[36] Further, the concerns to guard over holy things (Matt 7:6) and to demonstrate a right relationship with YHWH through obedience to his Law (Matt 7:21–23) stand out as priestly abjurations.[37] Similarly, Jesus' healing of lepers and other unclean individuals explicitly include the declaration of cleanliness that represents not a royal dictum but a priestly announcement. As a final example, Jesus' concern for the temple—cleansing

---

31. Barker, *Temple Theology*, 13; Eastwood, *Royal Priesthood*, 14.

32. Morris, *New Testament Theology*, 91–92, 120; cf. Guthrie, *New Testament Theology*, 219–20.

33. Further, the association between David and the priesthood of Melchizedek suggests that if Jesus is the Davidic King, then he is also a Melchizedekian priest—a point that is later made explicit in Hebrews. Barker takes this suggestion further. Rather than simply allowing for priestly concerns in the midst of a royal narrative, she asserts that the "original gospel message was about the temple . . . and [the] presentation of Jesus anywhere else than in the temple setting distorts what they were preaching and misrepresents the original gospel." While Barker almost certainly overstates her position, her primary point is significant. Jesus is presented just as much as a priest as he is a king. Barker, *Temple Theology*, 1.

34. Morris, *New Testament Theology*, 115.

35. Cf. von Rad, *Theology of Israel's Prophetic Traditions*, 329, 334–35.

36. Cf. Barber, "Jesus as Davidic," 935; Nolland, *Gospel of Matthew*, 219; Goldingay, *Israel's Life*, 40.

37. Morris, *New Testament Theology*, 181.

it (Matt 21:12–13), ministering healing from it (Matt 21:14), and foretelling its destruction (Matt 24:1–2)—serves to demonstrate his custody of the holy place.[38] It is notable that while on temple grounds in Matt 21:23–27, Jesus reacts to the religious authorities not as an attendant, but rather as an equal (or even as a superior).[39] The emphasis of the gospel is on Jesus' priesthood; the discipleship pattern of imitation suggests that the apostles were expected to assume priestly function as well.[40] This expectation is particularly visible in Matt 10:5–15 with the sending of the twelve and their authorization to deal with the clean and the unclean (vv. 1, 8a). It is also possible to associate Jesus' forbiddance of acquisition (vv. 8b–10) and the blessing or curse that is consequent with honoring the apostles (vv. 12–15) with the Levitical reliance on God as their portion and their role in blessing.

Finally, Jesus concern for the temple was not isolated to the physical Jerusalem temple, but included a concern for the eschatological temple that is the church itself.[41] Peter's confession in Matt 16:16 leads to the proclamation that the Christ would build his church. This proclamation has been identified as a statement of temple-building. If a temple is built, then priestly attendants are necessary. The giving of the keys and the authorization of Peter to bind or loosen are suggestive of priestly edification and/or mediation.[42] With the promise to build the church-temple, Jesus also ordains his followers (particularly—but not exclusively—Peter) into a priesthood.[43] This ordination is actualized in Matt 28:16–20 when the disciples go to a holy mountain (v. 16), engage in worship (v. 17), and then receive a commission of cleansing and edification that is directly predicated upon their presence with Jesus (vv. 18–20).

While Mark does not significantly elaborate the priestly themes and ordinations in Matthew, Luke shows a surprising interest in matters of

---

38. Best, "Spiritual Sacrifice," 291; Garrett, "Biblical Doctrine," 143–45.

39. Beale takes this even further, noting that Jesus is himself the temple in human form. The obedience of those following his high priestly pattern may denote them as priests; however, the idea of "abiding" in Jesus could also be considered a corollary to a priestly calling and an invitation to live and work within the holy place. Cf. Beale, "Eden," 20.

40. Bordeianu, "Priesthood," 406; Middleton, *New Heaven*, 68; cf. Guthrie, *New Testament Theology*, 707.

41. Best, "Spiritual Sacrifice," 291; cf. Barker, *Temple Theology*, 1, 5.

42. Barber, "Jesus as Davidic," 947. Goldingay does not suggest that Matt 16:19 is a priestly portrait *per se*; however, he does note that the "dynamic in the New Testament . . . corresponds to the one that brought into being the collection of rules for life in the Torah" (emphasis added), which considering the priestly custody of the Torah, results in the same understanding. Goldingay, *Israel's Life*, 34.

43. Barber, "Jesus as Davidic," 951–52; Best, "Spiritual Sacrifice," 291.

temple. The presentation of Jesus and his boyhood instruction of the priests in the temple are both unique to Luke's gospel, while the gospel concludes with Jesus' blessing of the apostles as they worshipped and the statement of their relocation from an isolated room to the Jerusalem temple. While the actualization of priesthood within the disciples in Luke is not as succinctly presented as it is in Matthew's gospel, the opening chapters of Acts show the apostles casting lots (Acts 1:26), being cleansed themselves for priestly service (Acts 2:1–4; cf. 1:4–5), and then serving as agents of others' cleansing both metaphorically (cf. Acts 2:37–41) and physically (Acts 3:1–10).[44] This priestly service is then extended beyond the twelve, first implicitly by the Samaritan's reception of the Holy Spirit then explicitly by James' invocation of the prophets and the acceptance of the Gentiles by the Jerusalem church (Acts 15:16–18).[45]

Ultimately, the synoptic gospels and Acts emphasize the identity of Jesus—including his priesthood—rather than the direct call of his followers into a priestly role. It should be noted, however, that the commissioning of the apostles and their reactions, especially in the post-Resurrection accounts, suggests that there is an implicit expectation that just as Jesus was a priest, so too are his followers to serve as priests.[46]

Sanctification and Equality in the Pauline Corpus

Paul does not directly advocate any priestly office within his writings. This obvious fact could reflect awareness of his primarily Gentile audience and their different preconceptions about priesthood in comparison to the Jews,

44. Goldingay, *Israel's Life*, 121; cf. Mouroux, *Meaning of Man*, 28; Middleton, *New Heaven*, 157. Marshall notes that Jewish tradition associated Pentecost with both the renewal of the Noahic covenant (*Jub.* 6:17–18) and the day when the Law was given at Sinai. Not only does this associate the disciples with both a Creation and a covenant event, but also it connects—via rabbinic legend—with the proceeding proclamation in tongues that mimics a tradition that God's word was given in the "seventy nations of the world" and therefore the priest's תורה. This expression of multiple priestly allusions is powerful when considered cumulatively, and leads to a situation where, as Nelson states, "priesthood helps bolster the church's claim to be the heir of Israel's salvation history." Marshall, *Acts of the Apostles*, 68; Nelson, *Raising Up*, 169.

45. Middleton, *New Heaven*, 68–69; Schnabel, "Israel," 51–52. Schnabel also considers the Tent of David to be not a royal dynasty, but rather the eschatological temple, further enhancing the universal priestly tenor of this passage. Cf. Marshall, *Acts*, 252.

46. Bordeianu, "Priesthood," 406. Guthrie discusses the holiness of God "as a pattern for man's holiness." While he does not demand a priestly association for this observation, the priests—as the paradigm for holiness in the Old Testament—would have provided a natural referent for the New Testament calls to holiness. Guthrie, *New Testament Theology*, 99, cf. 60–61; Middleton, *New Heaven*, 148.

the assumption that priesthood as a standard for divine relations was ubiquitous so as not to require declaration, or something altogether different.[47] A thorough reading of the Pauline materials shows that Paul does not explicitly assign any priestly office to the Christian, however, his theology emphasizes both ecclesiology and sanctification and thereby accommodates discussion of both communal and personal priestly interests.[48]

While the entirety of Paul's theology reflects an emphasis on God's gracious justification of the sinner, his discussions of sanctification consistently express sanctification through right behavior, paralleling the connection between the image of God and its performative and priestly expression.[49] This connection is affirmed by Paul's description of sanctification in terms of the imitation of Jesus.[50] This particular approach is made more intriguing by the discussion in 2 Cor 3:12—4:6 where the understanding of God, the righteous life (in both deed and thought), and the image of God are connected in a way that does not look at the divine image as the origination of Christian behavior, but rather as the culmination.[51] The pursuit of godly life transforms the pursuer into an image of God (2 Cor 3:18), or rather makes the believer more Christ-like which is actually the same thing (cf. 2 Cor 4:4–5).[52] Paul's teaching on sanctification therefore serves to simultaneously call the readers to assume the divine image (whether the image of Christ or the image of God) and to live holy lives that comport to and distill Israel's more elaborate list of statutes as supervised by the priesthood.[53]

Sanctification is largely a microcosm of Paul's ecclesiology.[54] The pursuit of Christ-likeness and the lived expression of righteousness are individ-

---

47. Wenham, *Story as Torah*, 131–32.
48. Best, "Spiritual Sacrifice," 288–89.
49. Cf. Guthrie, *New Testament Theology*, 650–53.
50. Middleton, *New Heaven*, 69; cf. Wenham, *Story as Torah*, 131–32; Reno, *Genesis*, 51. Rom 6:4; 15:7; 1 Cor 4:16; 11:1; Eph 5:1–2; Phil 3:17; 1 Thess 1:6; 2:14; 2 Thess 3:7, 9; cf. Rom 12:2; 1 Cor 2:16; Gal 4:14; Eph 5:21—6:9; Phil 1:27; 2:5; 4:7; et al.
51. Berkouwer, *Man*, 100; cf. Guthrie, *New Testament Theology*, 694; Middleton, *New Heaven*, 104.
52. Garland, *2 Corinthians*, 199.
53. Guthrie, *New Testament Theology*, 695–97; cf. Jukes, *Types in Genesis*, 38, 47; Greidanus, "Universal Dimension," 48; Middleton, *Liberating Image*, 17; Thielicke, *Being Human*, 405.
54. The biblical approach to the church, including Paul's teachings, suggests that the common modern understanding of the church as a group of believers is incorrect. Rather than view the church as a group of individual believers, the biblical norm—and its contemporaneous cultural norm—is that the individual believers are parts of the church. This may seem to be a minor correction; however, the shift in emphasis makes a considerable difference in understanding the inherent, insolvable connection between

ualizations of the overall role of the church as the body of the Christ.[55] The use of the physical metaphor suggests that while the identity of the church is found in its election, it is demonstrated in its activity. The church is called to be holy, and it is this idea of a holy people that forms the background to the discussions of Romans 9–11. These discussions are particularly important since, like 1 Corinthians 12–14, they explicitly address the unity of the church and its supersession of racial boundaries. While Paul's concern is to affirm the legitimacy of salvation for all of humankind, his particular method demonstrates that the people of God—whether Jew or Gentile—are identical in purpose.[56] This unification of purpose suggests that just as the nation of Israel was a type of priesthood, so too is the church.[57] And since the church (or True Israel, if that is preferred [cf. Rom 9:6–8]) is open to all humankind, the compatibility with the image of God as a calling toward priesthood is affirmed in Paul's ecclesiology.[58] This affirmation is then amplified by the temple motif in 1 Cor 3:16–18; 6:17–20; 2 Cor 6:14–18; and Eph 2:19–22 with the designation of Christians as both the people and the place of God.[59] That each of these passages speaks toward both sanctification and equality among believers further connects the ideas of righteous living, priesthood, and the image of God within Paul's theology.[60]

New Testament Priesthood in the General Epistles

Where Paul's theology implicitly affirms the priesthood of the Christian and the concurrent opening of the priesthood to Christians of any socio-ethnic background, the General Epistles explicitly address the ideas of priesthood in the Petrine letters and Hebrews.

First Peter associates the church with Israel first through the explicit invocation of Lev 11:44–45; 19:2; et al.[61] This association is then apparently subverted by the condemnation of the "futile ways" (ματαιας ἀναστροφης;

---

the individual and the church.

55. Guthrie, *New Testament Theology*, 667; cf. Goldingay, *Israel's Life*, 607–8.

56. Guthrie, *New Testament Theology*, 177; Morris, *Epistle to the Romans*, 352; cf. Middleton, *New Heaven*, 69.

57. Novenson, "Jewish Messiahs," 366; Fredriksen, *From Jesus to Christ*, 83–86; Childs, *Biblical Theology*, 437.

58. Cf. Berkouwer, *Man*, 45; Sherlock, *Doctrine of Humanity*, 87.

59. Beale, "Eden," 23–24; Guthrie, *New Testament Theology*, 751; Best, "Spiritual Sacrifice," 291.

60. Guthrie, *New Testament Theology*, 672; Schnabel, "Israel," 55.

61. Schreiner, *1, 2 Peter, Jude*, 80.

1 Pet 1:18) that had previously been relied upon; however, the admonition to love from a pure heart in v. 22 suggests that the condemnation is not levied against the Israelite faith so much as the layers of rabbinic explication that had been added to it (cf. Mark 7:6–13).[62] It is this context that leads to the transfer of identity from national Israel to the church in 1 Pet 2:9–10. Peter essentially designates the church as the True Israel (similarly to Paul's argument in Rom 9–11) with a foundation in priesthood (1 Pet 2:4–8).[63] This designation not only serves to expand the concept of Israel, but also opens the possibility of priesthood to all of humanity (cf. 2 Pet 3:8–9). Interestingly Peter connects the priesthood of the church to the movement from darkness into light (1 Pet 2:9b), a movement that New Testament scholars have endorsed as a reference to Genesis 1 and the beginnings of Creation.[64] If this connection with Genesis is accepted, then Peter effectively unites the church, the Creation, and priesthood. Since the church consists of those who not only are elected (a characteristic) but also built up to offer spiritual sacrifices (a calling; 1 Pet 2:4–5), this unification both affirms the inherent priestly calling of humankind and offers scriptural text that affirms that the light of Gen 1:3–5 was not merely a physical light but rather a spiritual manifestation of God that informs the understanding of not only the chapter as a whole but also the nature of humankind and the צלם אלהים.

While Peter's letters are instructive toward the church, the Epistle to the Hebrews is first and foremost an elaborate christological statement. Its primary concern is to identify Jesus the Christ in his superiority.[65] However, while the magnification of Jesus remains the dominant theme of the entire book, the οὖν of Heb 10:19 marks a shift in the Scripture from the demonstration of the Christ's superiority to the reaction and accommodation of that superiority in the lives of the believers.[66] Critically, the writer of Hebrews concluded his demonstration of the superiority of Jesus with cultic matters of high priesthood (Heb 8:1ff.), holy place (Heb 9:11–14ff.), Law (Heb 10:1ff.)

---

62. Cf. Guthrie, *New Testament Theology*, 683. Alternately, one could interpret the ματαιας ἀναστροφῆς apart from Israel entirely and as an indication of the Gentile audience's previous pagan faith. This is a common approach; however, the strong Levitical context of this chapter suggests some relationship between the imperishable sacrifice of Jesus and the transient sacrifices of even the Israelite cult. Schreiner, *1, 2 Peter, Jude*, 84–85; Walls and Anders, *I & II Peter, I, II, & III John, Jude*, 14.

63. Guthrie, *New Testament Theology*, 783; Attridge, "How Priestly," 4; Lea, "Priesthood of All Christians," 17; Nelson, *Raising Up*, 157–58; Schreiner, *1, 2 Peter, Jude*, 105–6; cf. Middleton, *New Heaven*, 70; Garrett, *Systematic Theology*, 2:555.

64. Schreiner, *1, 2 Peter, Jude*, 116; cf. Boer, *Ember*, 11.

65. Sabourin, *Priesthood*, 178; Reno, *Genesis*, 59.

66. Ellingworth, *Hebrews*, 516; Lea, *Hebrews, James*, 185.

and sacrifice (Heb 10:11–14).[67] In the final verses before the proper response of the church in outlined, Jeremiah 31:33–34—a passage marked by priestly character—notes the beginning of the eschatological people.

The writer's immediate understanding of the eschatological people of the Christ is one of priesthood. The natural response to Jesus' superior high priesthood is the priesthood of the believers, ordained as priests by the blood of Jesus and now able to enter into the holy places with confidence (Heb 10:19–22); which quickly leads to the celebration of the holy place of Zion and the assembly at an eschatological feast (Heb 12:22–24) and the expectation of lives that worship properly (Heb 12:28–29) and offer spiritual sacrifices not only praising God but also edifying others (Heb 13:15–17).[68]

Ultimately, Hebrews serves to demonstrate Jesus' identity as the fulfillment of the promises of the Old Testament and the ultimate high priest.[69] In doing so, it naturally expects a reevaluation of one's response to him and provides distinct guidelines for that response.[70] Even as guidelines for reevaluation are given, they are cast in the same priestly framework that the Old Testament response to YHWH utilized.[71] Despite the opportunity to cast the people of God in a new framework, the writer maintains the priestly framework and implicitly affirms the natural priestly emphasis of the Scriptures.[72]

The Nature of Jesus and the Priesthood of the Faithful in Johannine Writings

Like the writer of Hebrews, John's primary concern in his gospel is to present a Christology rather than to direct specific responses despite a clear

---

67. Guthrie, *New Testament Theology*, 213; cf. Ellingworth, *Hebrews*, 517; Nelson, *Raising Up*, 142.

68. Lane, *Hebrews*, 269, 282–85; Best, "Spiritual Sacrifice," 281; Ellingworth, *Hebrews*, 722–24; cf. Lea, *Hebrews, James*, 240; Nelson, *Raising Up*, 151–52. It may also be notable that the call for "acceptable worship" (λατρευω εὐαρεστως) in conjunction with God's nature as a consuming fire may very well be a reference to Lev 10:1–3, further warning that proper Christian conduct is as critical as—and closely associated with—proper priestly conduct.

69. Cf. Barker, *Temple Theology*, 5.

70. Sabourin, *Priesthood*, 185; Best, "Spiritual Sacrifice," 284–86.

71. Eastwood, *Royal Priesthood*, 45–46; Garrett, *Systematic Theology*, 2:555. While the primary concern of her argument is Hebrews 7, Schmitt's work on the interpretation of νομος is useful for seeing both the contrast *and* the connection between what was previously given and what was now possible with the work of the Christ. Schmitt, "Restructuring Views on Law," 193–98.

72. Best, "Spiritual Sacrifice," 283; Carson, *Gospel according to John*, 90; cf. Mouroux, *Meaning of Man*, 34.

expectation that obedience would follow (cf. John 3:36; 8:51; 14:15, 21; et al.).[73] On the other hand, the emphasis on who Jesus was serves as the basis not only for a response, but also for what that response should be.[74] This emulation is implied throughout the gospel, but also forms the explicit basis for the apostle's first epistle (1 John 1:1–7ff.).[75] Similarly, it is faith that is both proclaimed and enacted by the people of God that designate the true follower of Jesus in the Revelation.

While the gospel does not present a specific, systematic response to Jesus' identity, it does contain overt directives and expectations within the various statements of Jesus. Some of the most telling of these statements are found within the prayer of John 17. Often designated as the Christ's "high priestly prayer," the prayer serves to focus attention on the glory of God through the actions not only of the soon to be crucified Jesus but also through the ongoing work of Jesus' disciples.[76] The glorification of God through the disciples actually begins in v. 6 where they are described as having kept God's word.[77] This phrase is important, as the idea of "keeping" (τηρεω) is not simply an idea of obedience, but one of protection. The concept of keeping the word adds a reverence for it and a protectiveness—or custody—over it. This mimics the frequent use of שמר within Leviticus to describe the holiness of Israel (cf. Lev 18:4–5, 26; 19:19; 20:8; et al.) and connects the nature of the disciples to the holy people of God. Similarly, the hope for the sanctification of the disciples (John 17:17–19) serves as a form of consecration or ordination.[78] If Jesus is the high priest in this passage, he very clearly is establishing the disciples as his chosen priesthood.[79] The priesthood is then immediately expanded beyond the disciples to include the church at large—both present and future (v. 20). The ultimate goal of the church is not only the proclamation of Jesus, which serves the priestly functions of edification and mediation (vv. 21–23; cf. John 20:21–23) but also the inhabitation of the holy place (v. 24; cf. John 14:1–3, 20, 23). Jesus explicitly connects his high priestly prayer with the Creation (vv. 5, 24),

---

73. Reno, *Genesis*, 71–72. Even within the stated purpose of the gospel (John 20:30–31), though the expected response of the audience is emphatically one that recognizes the Christ's identity, there is no specific outline of (future) activity prescribed.

74. Morris, *New Testament Theology*, 267–68; Guthrie, *New Testament Theology*, 457–58, 664; Carson, *Gospel according to John*, 87–88.

75. Guthrie, *New Testament Theology*, 642–43.

76. Ibid., 664; Borchert, *John 12–21*, 193; Fisher, "John's Theology," 41.

77. Carson, *Gospel according to John*, 558.

78. Guthrie, *New Testament Theology*, 664; Attridge, "How Priestly," 10; Borchert, *John 12–21*, 202–3.

79. Carson, *Gospel according to John*, 65–66.

which itself had already been connected to the light of the Christ (John 1:1-5) and thereby to the emulation of God (John 1:14-18).[80] In a sense, John 17 serves to tie the multiple theological threads of the book to that point together in a statement that not only declares who Jesus is, but also how it ordains humankind into a priesthood.[81]

This movement from Creation, through the incarnation, to the people of God is repeated in 1 John 1, where sacrificial images of blood and cleansing introduce the epistle (vv. 7, 9). This introduction then moves directly into the task of keeping the commandments (1 John 2:1-6) followed by an extended discourse that does not eliminate divine statutes but instead expands upon them similar to the Sermon on the Mount.[82] The ability to recognize and perform these new commands is predicated on the relationship with Jesus; but that relationship is described in cultic terms of anointing or ordination (1 John 2:20), imitation and consecration (1 John 3:2-3), and mediation and intercession (1 John 3:16-24).[83] The entire letter is then concluded with an admonition against idolatry. So while John does not use a systematic structure to present the priestly calling of the church, the actual content itself is replete with priestly references and concerns. Even the frequently repeated admonitions of love can be interpreted as at least partly priestly in concern: the idea of love in the Old Testament predominantly centers on the concept of covenant obedience rather than personal interaction.

While John's gospel establishes Jesus (and thereby the imitation of Jesus) as the foundation of the Christian calling, and his first epistle outlines practical applications of this calling in what could be considered priestly terms, it is the Revelation that fully connects the nature of Christianity with the ordination to priesthood.[84] Where Daniel's apocalyptic material focuses upon the fates of nations, John's concern in the Revelation is actually closer to Ezekiel's eschatological approach. It certainly addresses the fate of the (unbelieving) world; however, the presentation is actually very much focused on the people of God and their role within and reaction to God's overall plan and purpose.[85] That this purpose is priestly is established immediately: the introduction to the seven letters to the churches, establishing the faith context that will underlie the rest of the book, specifically identifies

---

80. Borchert, *John 12–21*, 203.

81. Attridge, "How Priestly," 11–12; Carson, *Gospel according to John*, 570–71.

82. Kruse, *Letters of John*, 78–80.

83. Akin, *1, 2, 3 John*, 117, 138–39, 158–59; Kruse, *Letters of John*, 100–101, 116–17, 137.

84. Attridge, "How Priestly," 8, 11; Beale, *Revelation*, 176; cf. Garrett, *Systematic Theology*, 2:555.

85. Childs, *Biblical Theology*, 321; Beale, *Revelation*, 174.

the church as a priesthood (Rev 1:5b–6; Rev 5:10).[86] The preservation of the church—or better, the people of God—in the midst of the calamities released from the seven seals is directly connected with their ordination (Rev 7:14) and service as priests (Rev 7:15–17).[87] Further, it is the altar prayers of the saints that precede the blasts of the seven trumpets (Rev 8:1–5 [v. 3]).

Priestly and cultic references continue to appear in the midst of the eschatological judgment: the evils of idolatry and abomination (Rev 9:20–21), the earthly temple of God's desecration (Rev 11:1–2) and the heavenly temple's revelation (Rev 11:19), the perseverance of those keeping the commandments of God (Rev 14:12), and the resurgence of triumphant worship (Rev 15; 19:1–10).[88] After the destruction of the enemies of God and the present Creation, the New Creation that arrives is one that—while lacking a specific temple building (Rev 21:22)—is characterized in terms of both holiness and communion between God and humankind (Rev 21:3).[89] Similarly, the New Jerusalem receives its light not from sun or moon, but rather from the light of God's presence (Rev 21:23). The New Jerusalem is then connected with both Eden (Rev 22:1–2), and with worship (v. 3) and ordination (v. 4).[90] This conclusion both enforces a discontinuity with the present corrupt world and promotes a continuity between not only the original state of Creation and the New Creation to come but also between the priesthood of the churches and the New Creation.[91] The ultimate fate of the people of God in the Revelation is one of priesthood; and with the connection between Original Creation and New Creation, their ultimate purpose until that time—and of the image of God—is also priestly service.[92]

Summary of the Consistency of Priestly Theology with the New Testament Witness

While the preceding study of New Testament themes and theological interests is necessarily brief, it does demonstrate the legitimate and visible presence of priestly themes and theology within each of the major areas of

---

86. Schnabel, "Israel," 57; Attridge, "How Priestly," 8.

87. Guthrie, *New Testament Theology*, 786–87; Beale, *Revelation*, 439; Robertson, *Word Pictures*, "Revelation 7:15."

88. Best, "Spiritual Sacrifice," 280; cf. Childs, *Biblical Theology*, 321.

89. Easley, *Revelation*, 401; Beale, *Temple*, 25; Beale, "Eden," 25.

90. Easley, *Revelation*, 415–16; Beale, *Revelation*, 1103–4.

91. Middleton, *New Heaven*, 152; cf. Barker, *Gate of Heaven*, 64, 78; Beale, "Eden," 9.

92. Beale, "Eden," 25–26; Best, "Spiritual Sacrifice," 294; cf. Middleton, *New Heaven*, 70–71, 170–71.

the New Testament literature.[93] This is hardly surprising, since christological studies have consistently reflected on Jesus' high priestly role. However, despite the acknowledgment of Jesus as the high priest, many New Testament studies have failed to appreciate fully how pervasive the call toward priesthood is within the New Testament and how it is foundational to the nature of the Christian as an image of the Christ. In many cases, the priesthood of the believer is essentially relegated to the relatively small realm of direct communication with God. A closer examination suggests it has a far more profound influence on the Christian calling and is as concerned with external and communal expression of the Christ as it is with internal and personal matters.[94]

CONCLUSIONS ON THE PRIESTLY CALLING OF THE IMAGE OF GOD FOR BIBLICAL THEOLOGY

The examination of each of the Testaments of Scripture individually is prudent, in as much as it allows each part of Scripture its own "discreet witness" that establishes a viable and pervasive priestly theology.[95] Having established both Old and New Testament theologies, however, allows for a synthetic understanding of the priestly calling of humankind that transcends the limitations of either individual testament's presentation.

Old Testament theology provides a foundational understanding of the human role in Creation and the basic depiction of what is expected from the priests of YHWH. Yet at the same time, Old Testament theology also accommodates the reality that the Creation has been corrupted; it is for this reason that the understanding of priesthood was recast through a single paradigm, the Aaronic priesthood. This recasting was not to remove the call of priesthood from humanity at large but rather to illustrate the original demands of God's Creative dicta.[96] The continuous reflection on the covenant and call for holiness among the people of Israel served to codify the divine expectation, but the divine expectation was never to be limited to the covenant and/or the Israelite people.[97]

---

93. Barker, *Temple Theology*, 13.
94. Davies, *Anthropology and Theology*, 145–51.
95. Cf. Childs, *Biblical Theology*, 77–78.
96. Gorman, *Ideology of Ritual*, 42; Bruckner, *Implied Law*, 206.
97. Ross, *Recalling the Hope*, 78–82; Young, *Creator, Creation*, 34; Berkouwer, *Man*, 55; Renckens, *Israel's Concept*, 116; Greidanus, "Universal Dimension," 39.

New Testament theology largely begins where Old Testament theology on priesthood ends.[98] Where the Old Testament approached the priestly role of humanity from the universal call to humankind at Creation to a singular example, the New Testament approach is to begin with the singular example—Jesus the Christ himself—and then extend that example outward to the people of God and call for all people to conform to the priestly image.[99] The mandate to reach all of Creation with the gospel affirms the universality of the calling itself, even if that call is rejected by those eschewing the Christ. It is precisely because some will reject what it is to be human—the call to priesthood—that it is necessary for the present Creation to not only be purified, but also replaced entirely with a New Creation that restores both the environment (a new Eden) and the teleology (service as priests) of Genesis 1–2.[100]

Combining the two theological approaches demonstrates a consistency to a biblical anthropology that connects what it is to be human with the calling toward priesthood. The emphases of each of the theological approaches in each testament are built upon in the other testament, while any perceived gaps or ambiguities are clarified in the same fashion. That the idea of priesthood between the two testaments is so consistent, despite the distinct change in how the Law is explained, affirms that the overall biblical theology of humankind is one that must include concern for the holy (custody), mediation for that/those which are not holy (mediation), discernment and proclamation of what is holy (edification), and dedication to live a life that is holy (ordination). Or said another way, the importance of human priesthood within both Old Testament theology and New Testament theology affirms its nature and importance to a proper biblical theology.

---

98. Cf. Goldingay, *Israel's Gospel*, 27; Childs, *Biblical Theology*, 225–26, 397.

99. Berkouwer, *Man*, 45; Renckens, *Israel's Concept*, 126–28; cf. Childs, *Biblical Theology*, 437.

100. Middleton, *New Heaven*, 71.

Chapter 6

Concluding Matters on the Interpretation of the Image of God as a Commission to Priesthood

FUTURE STUDIES IMPACTED BY THE PRIESTLY DESIGNATION OF THE DIVINE IMAGE

It has been repeatedly asserted that the צלם אלהים is a foundational concept to the understanding of the human being and biblical theology, and therefore impactful on any aspect of the divine-human relationship.[1] The intention of this study has been to affirm that assertion and to reexamine biblical anthropology in light of the interpretation of the divine image as an ordination of priesthood. If the understanding of a foundational concept is changed or expanded, however, then it will naturally have ramifications that go beyond the scope of the present study.

These ramifications can be broadly categorized as exegetical, theological, and methodological, and focused on hermeneutical approaches, theological considerations, and applications within contemporary church culture. Following the natural learning process, perhaps the greatest emphasis should be placed on the exegetical and hermeneutical adaptations, since these considerations form the basis for any theological adjustments, which themselves serve as the underpinnings of church methodology.

---

1. Knohl, *Sanctuary of Silence*, 155; Brunner, *Man in Revolt*, 28, 50; Bird, "Male and Female," 134.

The Impact on Biblical Exegesis

While source critics could argue that Genesis 1, ascribed to the rather late P-document, has little hermeneutical bearing on the majority of the Old Testament that was written prior to the redaction of the P materials this argument is invalidated on two points.

First, assuming that the reconstructed dating proffered by source criticism is valid, then a late dated passage such as Genesis 1 would still be intricately linked to the previous materials, the difference being that it serves as a summation of anthropological thought rather than a foundation of it.[2] So while the צלם אלהים would not form an interpretive basis for the other Hebrew texts, it would represent a culmination of their interpretation and thereby suggest hermeneutical cues for how older Scriptures were interpreted by the biblical redactor.[3]

Second—and connected with the first observation—the canonical approach to both hermeneutics and theology has been consistently upheld in the present work simply because the final canonical form(s) of the Old Testament text is the only verifiable and available material from which to draw conclusions.[4] Scholarly reconstructions of history and religious development can be informative, but their conjectural nature precludes them from rewriting the final authoritative statement of Israelite faith (the Hebrew Scriptures).[5] Whatever the development of inter-biblical interpretations may have been, the final text expects the progression from the Law that is unified in its presentation, to the prophetic works that canonically explicate the Law further, and then to the rest of the writings that monitored the cultic, festal, and (especially in the case of wisdom materials) public activity of the nation in accordance with the Law.[6]

---

2. Rendtorff, *Canonical Hebrew Bible*, 720; Blenkinsopp, "Abraham," 227.

3. Cf. Rendtorff, *Canonical Hebrew Bible*, 3; Middleton, *Liberating Image*, 60–65.

4. Cf. Middleton, *Liberating Image*, 141; Goldingay, *Israel's Gospel*, 20.

5. Rendtorff, *Canonical Hebrew Bible*, 2; Wenham, *Story as Torah*, 7; McConville, "Priests and Levites," 6; Smith, *Priestly Vision*, 176; cf. Sailhamer, *Old Testament Theology*, 198.

6. Leuchter alludes to this, though he does not explicitly state it, when discussing the evolution of the Levitical role that is "no longer cultic, but it is still sacral. Ministering to YHWH and securing divine blessing now take place through administering the law." Leuchter, "Levite in Your Gates," 425.

Recognizing a Broader Priestly Background for Interpretation

Since an understanding of the צלם אלהים as a call to priesthood impacts the very core of divine-human relations, it possibly influences the interpretation of every passage of Scripture. Ironically, if the source critical suggestion that the biblical redactor was influenced by the priests is accepted, then the impact of the priestly nature of the image of God is only bolstered, since it would suggest that the final form of the Scriptures is one distinctly biased toward priestly ideology.[7] Therefore, whether reading Genesis 1 from a foundational or a cumulative perspective, the understanding of the divine image impacts the overall hermeneutics of the Bible by establishing a consistent underlying principle for determining authorial intention.[8]

Obviously a bias for priestly ideology does not automatically override any other ideological concerns expressed in a given passage. However, it does suggest that any interpretation must consider the inherently priestly nature of humankind. The application of this consideration is particularly important when considering passages such as 1 Kings 6–8 where the Levitical priesthood—and even the temple itself—seems to be at least partly subverted to royal ideology and the aggrandizement of Solomon, or Jeremiah 31 and its apparent elimination of the priesthood.[9] But with the acceptance of an inherently priestly aspect to humanity, passages such as these are more easily recognized as not only compatible with priestly ideology but also in many ways expansive of it. Similarly, the supposed conflict between the prophets and the priests can be set aside and focus instead placed on the conflict between faithfulness and apostasy from any given party—a conflict that distinctly reflects priestly concerns of holiness and obedience.[10]

The result of a greater awareness and appreciation of the priestly nature of each passage is the elimination of supposed contradictory ideologies within the Scriptures and a foundation for complementary and synthetic ideologies that pursue various agenda, but always toward the end

---

7. Mann, *Book of Torah*, 4.

8. Or, as Bird phrases it, "a grammar, or grammars, which are fully as essential to the message as the individual terms." Bird, "Male and Female," 155.

9. Habel, *Land Is Mine*, 24.

10. Middleton, *New Heaven*, 103. That YHWH's prophets were as quick to condemn false prophets as they were to condemn any given priest further affirms that their intentions were not anti-cultic. Quite the contrary, the prophetic refrain continuously calls Israel and Judah back to faithful covenant obedience, including proper worship. In fact, it could be argued that had the Israelite priests been faithful to their calling, then there would never have been need for the biblical prophets and their condemnation of presumption and apostasy. Rendtorff, *Canonical Hebrew Bible*, 198.

of promoting the inherent calling of Israel, and humanity in general, to the proper worship and (priestly) service of YHWH.[11]

Considerations of Alternate Interpretive Paradigms

If the Scriptures have a consistent priestly interest, then it is reasonable to expect that interest to influence directly the proper interpretation of not only those passages that are recognized as cultic but also passages normally interpreted apart from a priestly context. This influence does not remove the importance of proper historical-grammatical consideration, nor does it override considerations of genre or the immediate authorial context. It can and should be considered in conjunction with standard hermeneutical practices to further illuminate the theological motivation of a given passage.[12]

Narrative as Priestly Torah

The inclusion of significant narrative portions within the תורה establishes an immediate connection between those stories and the cultic regulations.[13] While exact connections are difficult to ascertain, it is certain that the narratives included are not merely provided as historical accounts. Even if they are read as simple ancestry stories, Blenkinsopp's work connecting both Law and wisdom to patriarchal leadership serves to affirm that the stories of the patriarchs exist to demonstrate a heritage meant to be emulated by the Israelites in conjunction with the תורה.[14] Further, the selection of patriarchal stories and their patterning within Genesis is undeniably deliberate and purposeful. Whether certain stories are intended to admonish, adjure, or encourage behavior can be argued, but the underlying understanding that they exist for one of these reasons is clear.[15]

---

11. Theokritoff, "Creation and Priesthood," 357.
12. Rendtorff, *Canonical Hebrew Bible*, 720–21; Bird, "Male and Female," 157.
13. Pleins, *Social Visions*, 71.
14. Blenkinsopp, *Sage, Priest, Prophet*, 27; Blenkinsopp, *Wisdom and Law*, 84–85; While Blenkinsopp notes the roots of the Law in the patriarchal and pre-patriarchal periods, he fails to fully explicate the reciprocal nature of the relationship between Law and ancestral ethics. Certainly the Law has ancient roots, but the patriarchs did not codify either the Law or their own narratives. That codification came later as the Law itself was being recorded. So while the Law may find its origin in ancient tribal leaders, the narratives about those leaders have been filtered through the lens of the Law when they were selectively recorded in Scripture.
15. Wenham, *Story as Torah*, 3–4, 13; Cross, *Canaanite Myth*, 295; Firmage, "Genesis 1," 112; Bruggemann, "Kerygma of the Priestly Writers," 399.

The foundation of Law in previously known acts of righteousness, combined with anachronistic commentary (cf. Gen 7:1–3 et al.) and implied law (cf. the "ought and ought not" arguments of Genesis 18–20) demonstrates that the particular ancestor stories contained in Genesis serve to provide demonstrations of the Law—either positively to emulate or negatively to avoid.[16] Supposedly neutral stories that do not seem to emphasize either aspect of the Law instead emphasize the providence of God in providing for his people, which in fact serves to bolster the faith to obey since it demonstrates that the righteous person—revealed at Sinai to be the one who obeys the תורה (Lev 18:5)—can trust in YHWH's deliverances.[17] This general pattern should not be reserved for Genesis alone. The fact that the only narrative in Leviticus involves the ordination of the faithful priests (Leviticus 8–9) and the elimination of the presumptuous ones (Leviticus 10) affirms both the celebration and the limitation of the Israelite access to YHWH's presence.

Wenham extends the reading of narrative as תורה into the book of Judges and its dual demonstrations of God's faithfulness to Israel and Israel's failure to maintain their covenant obligations. The cycle of punishment and redemption is predicated on the pursuit of YHWH and well in accord with Deuteronomistic theology.[18] If this is the case—and there is no reason to suggest that it is not—then there is no reason to treat the rest of Dtr differently: Dtr presents the Law in history and the blessing on Israel when it is followed and the nation's condemnation when the Law is violated. Indeed, it is the connection between narrative and Law that makes the history of Israel sensible and provides hope from a story that otherwise ends in death and tragedy.

Similarly, Ezra-Nehemiah is directly and repeatedly connected with cultic interests not only in the rebuilding of the temple building, but in the re-dedication of the holy people. To read these works apart from the Law is nonsensical. At the same time, the Deuteronomistic history provides a demonstration of the problems of which Ezra-Nehemiah warn, tying the three sections of Scripture together into a theological whole guided by the priestly interest of covenant maintenance/obedience to the Law.[19] The sanitized history of Israel in the Chronicles then presents the history of Israel not as it was, but as a limited expression of who they should have been.[20]

16. Bruckner, *Implied Law*, 22–23; Middleton, *New Heaven*, 100–102.
17. Cf. Wenham, *Story as Torah*, 22.
18. Ibid., *Story as Torah*, 45–46.
19. Leuchter, "Levite in Your Gates," 435–36.
20. It should be noted that the Chronicler's expression of this idealized Israel is

THE IMAGE OF GOD AS A COMMISSION TO PRIESTHOOD   177

These connections between the narratives of the Old Testament and the Law demonstrate that the narratives were chosen due to their (positive or negative) relationship to the תורה.²¹ Since this is the case, there seems to be little reason to resist recognizing an underlying theology within the narratives that connects directly with the interests of the priests. Rather than deem pre-Sinai events anachronistic, they can be recognized as a part of the same תורה given at Sinai. It is not a question of historical anachronism so much as theological demonstration.²² Since the theological demonstration of the Old Testament centers on priestly interests, it is reasonable to suggest that priestly interest underlies the narratives of the Old Testament. Rather than focusing on the ethnic heritage or historical events of Israel, the narratives illustrate the priestly imperatives and cultic expectations in light of YHWH's sovereignty that applies not only to Israel but also to all of humankind.²³

Wisdom as Priestly Torah

Wisdom in the Old Testament has often been contrasted with תורה. The universal and often somewhat secular nature of wisdom can seem contrary to the exclusivity of the Law and its emphatic cultic interests. Further, Hebrew borrowing of materials best accounts for the similarity between the biblical sapiential materials and the proverbs and sayings of other ANE nations, further distancing the wisdom materials from the Israelite תורה.²⁴

The secular interest of biblical wisdom is not contradictory to the Law; even within the תורה itself statutes governing both the field and the marketplace abound.²⁵ Since all of Israelite life was—theoretically at

---

limited by the actual history of the nation. While the Chronicler certainly is selective in both the material and the method in which he presents it, he is not writing an actual revisionist history.

21. Cf. Wenham, *Story as Torah*, 7.

22. Goldingay, *Israel's Gospel*, 39; Firmage, "Genesis 1," 103; Durham, *Exodus*, 259.

23. It must be noted that this is not to suggest that the Old Testament narratives do not present historical events or that passages directly applicable to Israel should be universally spiritualized. Rather, it simply affirms that the historical events presented exist to establish and demonstrate the theological relationship between YHWH and humankind. Wenham himself notes this with his observation that the interest of these ethical narratives is not simply in keeping the Law, but actually in serving as "the image of God, his representatives on earth." Wenham, *Story as Torah*, 107; Greidanus, "Universal Dimension," 43.

24. Rendtorff, *Canonical Hebrew Bible*, 363–64; Middleton, *New Heaven*, 96.

25. Blenkinsopp, *Sage, Priest, Prophet*, 38–39.

least—considered an act of worship, there was no truly secular activity.[26] Conducting business with משפט was as much a concern of the cult as of the gate. Further, even in the postexilic era when the scribes and sages rose to prominence the cult was not displaced so much as integrated with the rabbinic approaches to Scripture. The teaching activities of the sages was complementary to the priestly edification rather than oppositional to it.[27]

Further, the very similarity between Israelite and non-Israelite wisdom sayings begs the question of why some materials were accepted and others were rejected. The fact that not all foreign wisdom was accepted itself suggests a selectivity and implies a particular standard for that selectivity. The most reasonable standard of selection is the Law.[28] Wisdom from whatever source that accords with the Law could be reasonably subsumed into the Israelite sapiential tradition. On the other hand, wisdom that contradicted the תורה would be discarded.[29] That the biblical wisdom materials were largely produced in the court rather than the temple is not problematic, since the court scribes—like the king and other legal officials—could easily have been versed in the Law by the Levites (cf. Deut 16:18–20; 17:10–13, 18–19).

If the Law formed the standard by which wisdom was evaluated, and Israel's general call to priesthood is remembered, then it could even be suggested that the sapiential material of the Bible represents some form of "practical תורה."[30] The association between Creation and wisdom only strengthens this suggestion, particularly when Genesis 1 is read with a temple-building context and אדם recognized as a priest-figure.[31] If wisdom materials are based on Creation and Creation itself serves to establish the priestly nature of humankind, then the observations of wisdom—at least

---

26. Middleton, *New Heaven*, 52; King, *Realignment*, 62; Sprinkle, *Book of the Covenant*, 161; Goldingay, *Israel's Life*, 19. This perception is not exclusive to Israel. The idea of a "secular society" was somewhat foreign to the ANE in general.

27. Rendtorff, *Canonical Hebrew Bible*, 362–65; Leuchter, "Levite in Your Gates," 425–28, 434; Blenkinsopp, *Wisdom and Law*, 15–17.

28. Eichrodt, *Man in the Old Testament*, 23. This is certainly the general methodology of Ben Sira, who to some extent redefines both wisdom and Law with his conflation of the two. Berg, "Ben Sira," 140.

29. Middleton, *New Heaven*, 98. That conflicting material was not only discarded, but also by implication designated as תועבה, a well-defined cultic term, is significant as well. Rendtorff, *Canonical Hebrew Bible*, 665.

30. Bullock, "Wisdom," 16. Additionally, Blenkinsopp does not state this point but does inadvertently argue for it. He notes that the Law "is therefore *the* expression of divine wisdom" and ultimately greater than the secular wisdom of the nations while simultaneously arguing for the use of universal wisdom in the codification of the Law. With this in mind, the Law becomes the standard for wisdom, since it stands as the pinnacle of it. Blenkinsopp, *Wisdom and Law*, 151–53, 176.

31. Cf. Middleton, *New Heaven*, 46–47.

when filtered through the תורה revealed at Sinai—become a form of priestly code of conduct.[32] In this sense, the sapiential materials serve as supplements to priestly edification rather than impediments to it.[33]

Prophetic Oracle as Priestly Torah

Despite the frequent antagonism posited between the prophets (and their supposedly more rural and primal ideology) and the priests (with their more sophisticated and urbanized ideology), there is little biblically to support a significant feud between the two religious offices.[34] On the other hand, there is reason to suggest that the prophetic works actually served as a form of ethical תורה.[35]

Much of the proposed antagonism between the prophets and the priests centers on condemnations of both the priests themselves and the religious rites of Israel. Read contextually, however, it is clear that the condemnation of the priests is directly connected with their violation, not their propagation, of the Israelite cultic system (Jer 2:8; 32:31–34; Ezek 22:26; Hos 10:5; Mic 3:11; Zeph 3:4; Mal 2:7–8; et al.).[36] Similarly, the condemnation of ritual observances is tied to the failure to honor the holiness of the observance rather than a simple condemnation of the system as a whole (Isa 1:10–15; 43:22–24; Jer 32:34–35; Ezek 20:31; 23:38–39; Hos 8:11–13; Amos 4:4–5; Zeph 1:4–6; Mal 1:6–10; et al.).[37] It is also notable that the condemnation of the priesthood often occurs in tandem with the condemnation of the

---

32. Bullock, "Wisdom," 17. This is reinforced further from biblical wisdom references observing the behaviors of animals (1 Kgs 4:33; Job 39:13–18; Prov 30:24–28), seeking to understand the natural order of the world according to the animals' actions within their assigned spheres of existence. Neville, "Differentiation," 213.

33. Cf. Childs, *Biblical Theology*, 388–89; Middleton, *New Heaven*, 98.

34. Zevit, "Prophet versus Priest," 208.

35. Blenkinsopp asserts this position explicitly in *History of Prophecy in Israel* where he states that the prophets served as "custodians and tradents of Torah," and more implicitly in *Sage, Priest, Prophet* where he notes that the prophetic conviction of an ethical and responsive relationship with deity for all intents and purposes mimics the תורה. Blenkinsopp, *History of Prophecy*, 14; Blenkinsopp, *Sage, Priest, Prophet*, 145; cf. Bullock, "Wisdom," 6; Middleton, *New Heaven*, 104; Sanders, *Torah and Canon*, 55.

36. Rendtorff, *Canonical Hebrew Bible*, 198; Brueggemann, *Israel's Praise*, 111–12; Zevit, "Prophet versus Priest," 192–93; von Rad, *Theology of Israel's Prophetic Traditions*, 194. Von Rad's observation is focused on Jeremiah's ministry; however, the general observation proves true with all of the prophets—a fact Rendtorff notes in his discussion of Isaiah.

37. Zevit, "Prophet versus Priest," 197–98; cf. Blenkinsopp, *Sage, Priest, Prophet*, 40–41.

prophets (Isa 28:7; Jer 5:31; 6:13; Mic 3:11; Zeph 3:4), rendering the assumption that the priesthood at large was condemned absurdly hypocritical.[38]

On the other hand, while they condemn sinful priests, the prophets envision the restoration of a faithful priesthood and the cleansing of the Sanctuary. The priestly tenor of the Major Prophets' eschatological vision has already been examined, but this general idea of priesthood is not purely eschatological. The condemnation of Hosea 4:4–5 is addressed first to the "children of Israel;" the rejection of the people from being priests is not aimed at the Levites, but at the nation as a whole. All of the people of Israel had rejected their inherent priestly calling (cf. Exod 19:6). This rejection explains the highly cultic imagery and priestly teleology of the prophetic works. The prophetic exhortations for repentance are not simply calls for the people to return to worship of YHWH, but to the priestly service of YHWH. In other words, they are calls to return to the תורה—in both act and spirit.[39]

The frequent association of the prophets with covenant lawsuits serves to reinforce further the idea that the prophetic corpus serves as—if not a distinct תורה—an invocation of the תורה to be applied to the lives of the Israelites.[40] While the תורה is not fully encapsulated within the covenant, it is initiated in a distinct way by the Sinai covenant. A prophetic ריב that notes the failure to maintain the covenant established at Sinai inherently condemns the failure to obey the Law and exhorts a return to the Law with an attitude of both holiness and obedience (cf. Exod 19:7–15).[41]

The ultimate priestly intention of prophetic thought, combined with the number of prophets who either were priests themselves or have been associated with priestly families in some way, allows for the classification of prophetic oracles as a form of priestly edification.[42] If read as priestly

---

38. Ben Zvi, "Observations," 21; Patton, "Layers," 151–52.

39. Or, as Middleton would describe them, the prophetic critiques are not simply antagonisms from charismatic preachers against the cult, but instead are better recognized as "an *internal* ideology critique." Middleton, *Liberating Image*, 195; Bullock, "Wisdom," 5; Thompson, *Jeremiah*, 67–71; Goldingay, *Israel's Life*, 118; cf. Ben Zvi, "Observations," 24.

40. Childs, *Biblical Theology*, 174–75.

41. Young, *My Servants*, 79.

42. Blenkinsopp, *History of Prophecy*, 21–24; Torrance, *Royal Priesthood*, 3–5. Childs is ambivalent on this issue, noting that the prophets "often had an institutional connection with cult and court." While this approach does not isolate the prophetic institution to cultic relationships, it does demonstrate a precedence for interpreting the prophetic works with cultic interests. This is further affirmed by Young's observation that the prophets' "political activity is *always subservient to a religious end*" (emphasis added). Childs, *Biblical Theology*, 170; Young, *My Servants*, 82; cf. Gronbaek, "Baal's Battle," 36.

edification, the prophetic works do not conflict with priestly ideology but instead serve to expand it over the entire kingdom of priests.[43]

THE IMPACT ON THEOLOGICAL THOUGHT

The reinterpretation of the צלם אלהים to emphasize its priestly character impacts theology both discreetly and broadly. Much of the discreet impact comes from the new exegetical considerations that the interpretation offers: as the exegesis of individual passages is addressed, new theological observances and cues can be developed. The broad theological application of the priestly image is found in considerations of what a primarily priestly anthropology entails for the larger disciplines of biblical and systematic theologies.

At its broadest, a theological anthropology that emphasizes the call of humankind to a priesthood can arguably provide a consistent theme through the entirety of Scriptures.[44] While this possibility has been proffered earlier in this study as a supplemental theme to other theological constructs, it is equally possible that it is the theme of priesthood that is central with other theological formulations serving secondarily to it.

Similarly, if the nature of humankind is considered from the perspective of function—as a call to priesthood establishes—then theological anthropology must be reexamined to focus not on the nature or character of human beings but on their teleological role and activity.[45] This approach fits the functional approach to Creation from Genesis 1 as well as the New Testament applications of Matt 28:19–20 and Acts 1:8 in preparation for the temple activity of the Revelation.[46]

The Viability of a Consistent Central Theme to Biblical Theology

The question of whether there is a central theme to the entirety of either testament, much less the Bible as a whole, is a persistent one. Depending on a given scholar's interpretive approach, the question can be considered irrelevant; those emphasizing source criticism or a history of religions approach would deny any centralized theme since they have relegated the Bible to an amalgamation of differing—often contradictory—ideologies and religious

---

43. Ben Zvi, "Observations," 26–29.

44. Davies, *Anthropology and Theology*, 151; cf. Waltke and Yu, *Old Testament Theology*, 49.

45. Frost, *In His Image*, 85; Augustine, *Summa Theologica*, Q.93, 8; Theokritoff, "Creation and Priesthood," 357; Cairns, *Image of God*, 30; cf. Thielicke, *Being Human*, 407.

46. Cf. Middleton, *New Heaven*, 70.

agenda. However, with the increase in canonical and narrative approaches to the Scriptures and the rise of literary criticism, the emphasis has shifted to the final redaction of the Bible and reinvigorated the possibilities of a central theological principle.[47]

Nonetheless, the primary difficulty of determining a central theological point has remained unchanged. Generally, the problem in determining any primary theme has been the tendency toward one of two poles: either the theme is sufficiently broad to account for the diversity of the Scriptures but—in achieving that breadth—also too vague to be of any appreciable use; or provide an adequate framework for part, often even the majority, of the Bible but be unable to account for specific sections or genres without some degree of misapplication.[48] In order for a central theme to be viable, it needs to be comprehensive enough to apply to all of the scriptural genres yet specific enough to apprehend and apply in a functional manner.[49]

It is universally recognized that the Bible is written as a presentation of God (either in fact or as he was perceived). Similarly, if the Bible is written to human beings then it necessarily serves as a message about the relationship between YHWH and humankind.[50] While this is universally recognized, the human-divine relationship must be clarified constantly for any significant theological insights to occur.[51] The idea of "people of God" is too vague; but more codified examples of how humanity interacts with YHWH, such as "covenant," typically fail to account for genres such as wisdom that do not rely on any direct human-divine dialectic.[52]

The priesthood of humanity as offered through the proposed understanding of the צלם אלהים does seem viable as a centralized theme.[53] It is built upon the foundational concern of the human-divine relationship and accords with both the Law and the Prophets.[54] Since the function of the priesthood included edification and recognition of the natural order of Creation, it also accommodates the sapiential materials of the Old Testament. The Psalms

---

47. Habel, *Literary Criticism*, 116, Goldingay, *Israel's Faith*, 17.

48. Cf. Hasel, *Old Testament Theology*, 139–40. Even setting aside other considerations, the diversity of the scriptural materials themselves is daunting enough that Waltke summarized the idea of a central biblical theme as impossible: "the material is too unruly and extensive to be tamed to develop that theme systematically." Waltke and Yu, *Old Testament Theology*, 51.

49. Cf. Childs, *Biblical Theology*, 521–23.

50. Brunner, *Divine-Human Encounter*, 31; Scobie, *Ways of Our God*, 469.

51. Middleton, *New Heaven*, 39–41.

52. Childs, *Biblical Theology*, 441–46.

53. Cf. Theokritoff, "Creation and Priesthood," 345–46.

54. Cf. Sabourin, *Priesthood*, 181.

and the Megilloth are already associated with the priests through their use in worship and religious ritual, while Ezra-Nehemiah and other narratives emphasizing the need for holiness and distinction from the world exemplify the application of Lev 10:10–11 to the postexilic society.[55] Further, the priesthood of humanity prevents an overly nationalistic or exclusive character to the overall message of the Bible, and particularly accommodates the New Testament emphasis on the evangelism of the entire world.[56]

While the priesthood of humanity is broad enough to accommodate the entire canon of Scripture, it remains functionally applicable. The basic tenets of priesthood—ordination, curation, mediation, edification, and sanctification—are adaptable to a variety of texts and situations without the need to change their basic meanings or essential functions.[57] In this sense, they provide the specific application framework that is necessary for the broader understanding of the Bible as a book on the priesthood of humanity.

Before any application of the priesthood of humanity as the central theme in the Bible can be made, considerable examination is still required. The present study, however, has established a starting point for those examinations and suggests that the theory is viable.

The Recognition of the Teleological Function of Biblical Anthropology

Christian teleology is often relegated to philosophical and eschatological studies, and considered only tangentially in other theological branches. However, a functional understanding of biblical anthropology that emphasizes the commissioning rather than the condition of the human creature is inherently teleological.[58] While a certain purposefulness to humankind is

---

55. Livingston, *Pentatuech*, 150, 227. It must be acknowledged that the use of a text in a worship context does not demand that the audience—be it Israel, the church, or humanity as a whole—be deemed priestly; however, in the Old Testament context it does demand, or at least expect, a priestly presence and interest that accords with an overall theology of the priesthood of humanity.

56. Cf. Middleton, *New Heaven*, 71.

57. King, *Realignment*, 72.

58. Brunner, *Man in Revolt*, 28; Eichrodt, *Theology of the Old Testament*, 2:109; Theokritoff, "Creation and Priesthood," 356–57; cf. Kallenberg, "Positioning MacIntyre," 62–63. Goldingay suggests that the Old Testament "never talks about God having a plan for the world ... [but God] works out a purpose in the world in interaction with the human beings who are designed to be key to the fulfilling of those goals." It should be noted that this discussion of humanity's role in God's plan is focused not on the grand scheme of eschatology, but instead on the nature and activity of humankind. While Goldingay's assertion is certainly disputable, the fact that he essentially subverts eschatology to anthropology is distinct. Goldingay, *Israel's Gospel*, 60.

well noted (the rather vague task of bringing glory to God), the interpretation of the צלם אלהים as an ordination to priesthood provides a specific structure and direction for understanding the human condition and moves teleology into a central position within biblical anthropology that accords with the overall functional concerns of the Genesis 1, the ongoing work of the people of God, and the redemption of this Creation/entrance of the New Creation in the *eschaton*.[59]

A teleological approach to biblical anthropology serves to provide both an individual and a corporate purpose to humankind.[60] Since each person is called to priestly performance, each person has an inherent purposefulness in life. This recognition allows for a starting point of meaning and structure and shifts the conversation from "why" to "how."[61] The existential concern for the individual is recognized without severing the individual from the inherent corporate identity of all humanity.[62] In fact, if the question of how to live a priestly life rather than what is the purpose of life is the primary consideration, then human self-determination is balanced with divine ordination. Individual contexts and relationships can be evaluated, but never apart from the overall orderliness of Creation and the human responsibility to curate and cultivate their environment according to the principles of the Creator.[63]

A greater focus on the τέλος of biblical anthropology also serves to emphasize the connection between anthropology and eschatology. That both disciplines have the same ultimate intention—the glory of God—is hardly accidental.[64] Nevertheless, in many discussions biblical anthropology is used

---

59. Sexton, "*Imago Dei* Once Again," 187–88. Eichrodt's observation that the will of God over humankind essentially installs "both a content and a goal" to human existence coincides with this observation. Humans do not simply exist; they have purpose. Eichrodt, *Man in the Old Testament*, 27; cf. Middleton, *New Heaven*, 49, 60; Goldingay, *Israel's Gospel*, 109.

60. Sherlock, *Doctrine of Humanity*, 87; Eichrodt, *Man in the Old Testament*, 27; Goldingay, *Israel's Faith*, 560.

61. The suggestion that צלם אלהים possesses an adverbial character further suggests this, as it makes the quality of the image wholly dependent upon the activity of the dominant verb. Interestingly, Goldingay notes that the discussion of wisdom at Creation in Proverbs 8 is likewise focused on the "how" of Creation rather than the "why." The purposefulness of God at Creation expects an inherent purpose to the existence of humanity as well. Bird, "Male and Female," 139–40; Goldingay, *Israel's Gospel*, 48.

62. Cf. Guthrie, *New Testament Theology*, 896; Goldingay, *Israel's Life*, 18; Grenz, *Social God*, 162.

63. Hall, *Imaging God*, 61; Dempster, *Dominion and Dynasty*, 56; Renckens, *Israel's Concept*, 61; Eichrodt, *Theology of the Old Testament*, 2:109–12; cf. Middleton, *New Heaven*, 49; Smith, *Priestly Vision*, 114; Thielicke, *Being Human*, 407; cf. Goldingay, *Israel's Gospel*, 60; Goldingay, *Israel's Faith*, 565–66.

64. Cf. Renckens, *Israel's Concept*, 104. Brueggemann describes the "ultimate vocation"

to serve eschatology; recognizing the essential teleology within the creation of humans affords the possibility that it is actually eschatology that serves or expands upon biblical anthropology.[65] Humankind and their assignment of duty is the culmination of Genesis 1, which is then recognized in the Sabbath of YHWH. Similarly, the New Creation that gathers the saints before the direct presence of God with the express purpose of worship is the culmination of Christian eschatology that enters into the Eternal Sabbath.[66]

CONTEMPORARY APPLICATIONS OF THE IMAGE OF GOD AS A PRIESTLY CALLING

The vast diversity found among the Christian community prevents any singular application of a theological principle; different churches already apply any given point in various ways that cannot be comprehensively evaluated. However, while specific applications are beyond the scope of the present work, certain guiding principles can be affirmed and should be expected.

The intense need to recognize the holiness of God is germane to every church. The calling of God's people—whether called "Israel" or "the church"—is the pursuit of holiness (Lev 11:44–45 et al; 1 Pet 1:14–16).[67] Biblically, the priests were expected to maintain their own holiness and ensure that their society as a whole became holy, whether through mediation or edification.[68] Ironically, however, in many cases the incorrect application of the "priesthood of the believer" has served to diminish a high view of the holiness of God. Many evangelical churches emphasize the priesthood of the believer in terms of each Christian's individual access to God without

---

of all of Creation in terms of praise; however, he clarifies that praise as an act not only of petition or celebration, but also as an intercession and duty that serves to connect earth with heaven—a clearly priestly vocation. Brueggemann, *Israel's Praise*, 1–3, 6.

65. Cf. Goldingay, *Israel's Gospel*, 60. In many ways understanding of the צלם אלהים as a priestly calling suggests that Moltmann's famous statement that all theology is actually eschatology should be adjusted to "all theology is anthropology." While both statements are incorrect—in truth all theology is reflective of theology proper (the doctrine of God)—the recognition that eschatology is a discussion of the ultimate climax of the human-divine relationship affords the argument that every genre of theology that serves an eschatological purpose also serves to further explain not only who God is, but what humankind is and how it relates to the Creator, both of which are anthropological concerns. Cf. Erickson, *Christian Theology*, 481.

66. Skillen, "Seven Days," 126–32; cf. Middleton, *New Heaven*, 49, 60, 125–26.

67. Smith, *Priestly Vision*, 70; cf. Goldingay, *Israel's Faith*, 22.

68. Sabourin, *Priesthood*, 101; Firmage, "Genesis 1," 104–6; Goldingay, *Israel's Life*, 621–22.

the need for a human mediator.[69] The problem with this arises when the emphasis on access to God is not paired with an equal emphasis on the fear of God.[70] By promoting access to God without a proper admonition toward humility, the church allows for presumptive behavior that assumes access to the holy is a right rather than a revered—and fearful—honor.[71] If, however, the church emphasizes the priestly nature of the Christian, then circumspection becomes integrated with action.[72]

Similarly, before the priests could enter into the holy place they were to take steps of repentance and cleansing. Applied to all of humankind through the צלם אלהים, the need for consecration prior to unfettered access to the Lord reinforces the need to call for repentance from sin in evangelistic efforts. Contemporary evangelistic approaches that favor minimizing the discussion of sin do not accord with the importance given to holiness in the Bible. This observation about evangelism is not to suggest that people must purify themselves prior to accepting the lordship of Jesus, but it does recognize that the first steps of accepting a priestly commission include confession (through the bringing of sin offerings) and cleansing (the washing and re-clothing of the prospective priest[s]), followed by commissioning to holy service (the ordination not only of oil but of the blood on the ear, hand, and toe). To demand access to God before submitting to the purification that he has ordained is presumptuous, and to evangelize in that manner is spiritually irresponsible and dangerous.[73]

The recognition that humankind was created as a priesthood over the Temple of Creation should also impact the church's role in contemporary discussions on geo-ethics and bio-ethics.[74] The church should enter into these discussions with a mindset of the holiness of God and note that the curation of the earth is not important merely because human beings are stewards entrusted with dominion, but because the treatment of the planet—a temple structure—demonstrates reverence for and understand-

---

69. Middleton, *Liberating Image*, 207.

70. Cf. Goldingay, *Israel's Life*, 76–78; Sprinkle, *Book of the Covenant*, 196. Sprinkle notes that Exodus 19–24 is patterned as a chiasm, with the Fear of God as the central element. The calling to be a kingdom of priests is directly intended not only to allow Israel a special access to YHWH, but also to establish the proper recognition of his holiness.

71. Brueggemann, *Israel's Praise*, 124–52; Middleton, *New Heaven*, 110.

72. Lea, "Priesthood of All Christians," 21; cf. Goldingay, *Israel's Life*, 59.

73. Middleton's observation that—biblically—salvation is never completed with justification alone but rather with sanctification is pertinent. If sanctification does not follow the justification of an individual, there is ample reason to doubt the initial justification itself was sincere. "Obedience . . . is itself a crucial component of salvation." Middleton, *New Heaven*, 88.

74. Sherlock, *Doctrine of Humanity*, 36; cf. Estes, "Creation Theology," 40.

ing of the God of the temple.⁷⁵ In many ways, the failure of the church to interact with environmental and zoological concerns is a failure to maintain the holiness of God.⁷⁶

Ultimately, however, the greatest impact that the צלם אלהים and its priestly character should have on the church is in evangelism.⁷⁷ The church, like Israel, is a kingdom of priests. Priests were curators of the holy—including the Holy Word.⁷⁸ They were also mediators between God and humans, both through the application of holy ritual and through their role in edification.⁷⁹ The reality of biblical priesthood is that it was externally focused. While ordination and consecration (internal aspects of God's calling) were critical, they served as the foundation for the curation, mediation, and edification of the Israelite society (external aspects of the priestly task) that would consume the majority of the priests' time. This connection between evangelism and priestly character, and the צלם אלהים is further strengthened when humankind's role in tending to the garden, and specifically the Tree of Life, is considered. Mesopotamian parallels of mythical trees that produced reproductive power establish the king as the sole owner of the tree(s), but allowed him to dispense the tree's power through cultic ritual. With this in mind, if God is the King who owned the Tree of Life, the curation of the tree and the mediation of its power to and within Creation—assigned to humanity— becomes both a priestly and an evangelistic calling to mediate life.⁸⁰

---

75. Gorman, *Ideology of Ritual*, 42; cf. Inglis, "Kinship of Creation," 171–74.

76. Cha, "Theological and Ethical Implications," 99; cf. Dempster, *Dominion and Dynasty*, 57–62; Bruckner, *Implied Law*, 226. Beale takes this connection further. He notes that Adam's original role would have been to cultivate the earth and have mastery over all the creatures upon it—including the Serpent! However, with the fall, the concern of humanity's dominion shifted to "reign[ing] over unregenerate human forces arrayed against it." So while Beale does not directly claim this, his argument largely associates the preservation of the Creation with the evangelization of the sinner. Both activities are demanded of the church, and the failure of either is a failure to enact the צלם אלהים for which humankind was created. Beale, *Temple*, 113–21.

77. Cf. Cross, *Canaanite Myth*, 299.

78. Barber, "Jesus as Davidic," 948–50.

79. Leuchter, "Levite in Your Gates," 426.

80. Livingston, *Pentateuch*, 140; cf. Reno, *Genesis*, 56–58. This mediation of life— and the evangelistic task in general—should not necessarily be limited to verbal proclamation. Liberation theology and the social gospel, marked by concern for the tangible needs of life, hold a legitimate place in the evangelistic endeavor when properly applied and parallel the stewardship of Creation well. Humankind is not simply to watch over the planet or to announce salvation, but they are also to work to manifest the signs of that salvation in tangible ways. Cha, "Theological and Ethical Implications," 92–94; cf. Middleton, *New Heaven*, 52.

The church, as a body of priests, is entrusted with the Holy Word and mediates between God and the rest of humanity. Rather than apply sacrifices, the church shares the sacrifice of Jesus with the world through prayer, preaching, and discipleship.[81] But in all of this, the development of individual Christians exists to serve external needs—whether those external needs are horizontal (the evangelization and administration of the world) or vertical (the honoring and worship of God).[82] These things are only successful when the church takes seriously its priestly role and strives for the imitation of the Christ and the enactment of the צלם אלהים. The performance of these priestly duties is the reason that the church was commissioned.[83] It is also the reason that all of humankind was created.[84] The biblical question and the basis of evangelism is not whether or not everyone created in the צלם אלהים is called into the priesthood of YHWH, but whether each individual will accept that calling, be cleansed by the Christ for priesthood, and curate the things of God in lives of service and obedience (2 Pet 3:9–14).[85] Ultimately, the missional mandate of both Israel and the church demonstrates the identities of the ideal people, but also demonstrates the ideal priestly identity of all people.[86]

---

81. Beale, "Eden," 31; Bordeianu, "Priesthood," 409–10. Walvoord states this directly: "The fulfillment of his priestly responsibilities is integral in any vital Christian experience and effective witness for God." Walvoord, *Jesus Christ Our Lord*, 250.

82. Nelson, *Raising Up*, 173–74; cf. Estes, "Creation Theology," 38; Theokritoff, "Creation and Priesthood," 359; Block, "Place for My Name," 235–36. While Block is speaking of the Israelite conduct at the temple, his outline of consecration before YHWH, edification in the Word, and communion in the feasts followed by outreach to the marginalized remains a valid reflection not only of the ideal religious conduct of Israel but also of the expected conduct of the church.

83. Middleton, *New Heaven*, 85.

84. Eichrodt, *Man in the Old Testament*, 30; Mann, *Book of Torah*, 16; Middleton, *New Heaven*, 60; cf. Brueggemann, *Israel's Praise*, 160.

85. Bordeianu, "Priesthood," 407–8; Lea, "Priesthood of All Christians," 18; cf. Skillen, "Seven Days," 139; Brunner, *Man in Revolt*, 105; Block, "Place for My Name," 236–37. Block notes that the prescriptions for the pilgrimage feasts of Deuteronomy can be read as an invitation rather than an imperative. If this is the case, then it reflects nicely the consideration that people can be issued a priestly calling, but they are still responsible to accept that calling and act upon the invitation. The reward of such a response is priestly service. The consequence of a non-response is a lost opportunity for communion with both God and human.

86. Middleton, *New Heaven*, 25; Beale, *Temple*, 121; cf. Middleton, *Liberating Image*, 297; Balentine, *Torah's Vision*, 81; Balch and Pryor, "Jesus' Creation Theology," 287–89. Beale also inadvertently makes this point in noting that the restoration that Ezekiel describes "repeatedly speaks of God 'welcoming' Israel back from captivity." The call to all of humankind to serve in the holy place as a holy people (priests) is not a new ideal, but rather a foundational aspect of what it is to be human—the צלם אלהים. Beale, "Eden," 22; Goldingay, *Israel's Faith*, 527.

Selected Bibliography

Abba, Raymond. "Priests and Levites in Ezekiel." *VT* 28 (1978) 1–9.
Ackerman, Susan. "Why Is Miriam Also among the Prophets? (And Is Zipporah among the Priests?)" *JBL* 121 (2002) 47–80.
Akin, Daniel L. *1, 2, 3 John*. NAC 38. Nashville: Broadman & Holman, 2001.
Alden, Robert L. *Job*. NAC 11. Nashville: Broadman & Holman, 1993.
Allen, Leslie C. *Psalms 101–150*. WBC 21. Waco: Word, 1983.
Andersen, Francis I. *The Hebrew Verbless Clause in the Pentateuch*. JBLMS 14. Nashville: Abingdon, 1970.
Ashley, Timothy R. *Book of Numbers*. NICOT. Grand Rapids: Eerdmans, 1993.
Astell, Ann W. "Biblical Images of God and the Reader's 'I' as *Imago Dei*: The Contribution of Edith Stein." *Interpretation* (2005) 382–91.
Attridge, Harold. "How Priestly Is the 'High Priestly Prayer' of John 17?" *CBQ* 75 (2013) 1–14.
Atwell, James E. "An Egyptian Source for Genesis 1." *JTS* 51 (2000) 441–77.
Bacon, Benjamin Wisner. *Genesis of Genesis: Bibles within the Bible*. Hartford: Student, 1892.
Balch, David L., and Adam Pryor. "Jesus' Creation Theology and Multiethnic Practice." *Currents in Theology and Mission* 39 (2012) 279–89.
Balentine, Samuel E. *The Torah's Vision of Worship*. OBT. Minneapolis: Fortress, 1999.
Barber, Michael Patrick. "Jesus as the Davidic Temple Builder and Peter's Priestly Role in Matthew 16:16–19." *JBL* 132 (2013) 935–53.
Barker, Margaret. *The Gate of Heaven*. London: SPCK, 1991.
———. *Temple Theology: An Introduction*. London: SPCK, 2004.
Barr, James. *The Concept of Biblical Theology: An Old Testament Perspective*. London: SCM, 1999.
———. "The Image of God in the Book of Genesis: A Study of Terminology." *BJRL* 51 (1968) 11–26.
———. "Revelation through History in the Old Testament and in Modern Theology." In *New Theology*, edited by M. E. Marty, 1:4–14. New York: Macmillan, 1964.
Barth, Karl. *The Doctrine of Creation*. Pt. 1, vol. 3.1 of *Church Dogmatics*. Translated by J. W. Edwards et al. Edinburgh: T. & T. Clark, 1958.

Beale, G. K. *The Book of Revelation: A Commentary on the Greek Text*. NIGTC. Grand Rapids: Eerdmans, 1999.

———. "Eden, the Temple, and the Church's Mission in the New Creation." *JETS* 48 (2005) 5–31.

———. *Temple and the Church's Mission: A Biblical Theology of the Dwelling Place of God*. NSBT 17. Edited by D. A. Carson. Downers Grove: InterVarsity, 2004.

Ben Zvi, Ehud. "Observations on Prophetic Characters, Prophetic Texts, Priests of Old, Persian Period Priests and Literati." In *The Priests in the Prophets*, edited by L. L. Grabbe and A. O. Bellis, 19–30. London: T. & T. Clark, 2004.

Berg, Shane. "Ben Sira, the Genesis Accounts, and the Knowledge of God's Will." *JBL* 132 (2013) 139–57.

Berkouwer, G. C. *Man: The Image of God*. Studies in Dogmatics. Grand Rapids: Eerdmans, 1962.

Berry, R. J., ed. *Care of Creation: Focusing Concern and Action*. Downers Grove: InterVarsity, 2000.

Best, Ernest. "Spiritual Sacrifice: General Priesthood in the New Testament." *Interpretation* 14 (1960) 273–99.

Betts, Terry. *Ezekiel the Priest: A Custodian of Torah*. Studies in Biblical Literature 74. New York: Lang, 2005.

Bille, Mikkel, and Tim Flohr Sorenson. "An Anthropology of Luminosity: The Agency of Light." *Journal of Material Culture* 12 (2007) 263–84.

Bird, Phyllis A. "Male and Female He Created Them: Gen 1:27b in the Context of the Priestly Account of Creation." *HTR* 74 (1981) 129–59.

Blenkinsopp, Joseph. "Abraham as Paradigm in the Priestly History in Genesis." *JBL* 128 (2009) 225–41.

———. *History of Prophecy in Israel*. Rev. ed. Louisville: Westminster John Knox, 1996.

———. *Sage, Priest, Prophet: Religious and Intellectual Leadership in Ancient Israel*. Library of Ancient Israel. Louisville: Westminster John Knox, 1995.

———. *Wisdom and Law in the Old Testament: The Ordering of Life in Israel and Early Judaism*. Rev. ed. Oxford Bible Series. Oxford: Oxford University Press, 1995.

Block, Daniel I. *Book of Ezekiel: Chapters 1–24*. NICOT. Grand Rapids: Eerdmans, 1997.

———. *Book of Ezekiel: Chapters 25–48*. NICOT. Grand Rapids: Eerdmans, 1998.

———. *Deuteronomy*. NIVAC. Grand Rapids: Zondervan, 2012.

———. *Judges, Ruth*. NAC 6. Nashville: Broadman & Holman, 1999.

———. "'A Place for My Name': Horeb and Zion in the Mosaic Vision of Israelite Worship." *JETS* 58 (2015) 221–47.

Boer, Harry R. *An Ember Still Glowing: Humankind as the Image of God*. Grand Rapids: Eerdmans, 1990.

Bonhoeffer, Dietrich. *Creation and Fall: A Theological Exposition of Genesis 1–3*. Edited by M. Rüter, I. Tödt, and J. W. de Gruchy. Translated by D. S. Bax. Vol. 3 in *Dietrich Bonhoeffer Works*. Minneapolis: Fortress, 2004.

Borchert, Gerald L. *John 12–21*. NAC 25b. Nashville: Broadman & Holman, 2002.

Bordeianu, Radu. "Priesthood Natural, Universal, and Ordained: Dumitru Staniloae's Communion Ecclesiology." *Pro Ecclesia* 19 (2010) 405–33.

Braken, Joseph A. "Images of God within Systematic Theology." *Theological Studies* 63 (2002) 362–73.

Bratcher, Robert G., and William D. Reyburn. *A Translator's Handbook on the Book of Psalms*. UBS Handbook Series. New York: United Bible Societies, 1991.

Bray, Gerald. "The Significance of God's Image in Man." *TynBull.* 42 (1991) 195–225.
Breneman, Mervin. *Ezra, Nehemiah, Esther.* NAC 10. Nashville: Broadman & Holman, 1993.
Bright, John. *Jeremiah.* AB 21. New York: Doubleday, 1965.
Bruckner, James K. *Implied Law in the Abraham Narrative: A Literary and Theological Analysis.* JSOTSS 335. Sheffield: Sheffield Academic, 2001.
Brueggemann, Walter. *Genesis.* Interpretation 1. Atlanta: John Knox, 1982.
———. *Israel's Praise: Doxology against Idolatry and Ideology.* Philadelphia: Fortress, 1988.
———. "The Kerygma of the Priestly Writers." *ZAW* 84 (1972) 397–414.
———. *Theology of the Old Testament: Testimony, Dispute, Advocacy.* Minneapolis: Fortress, 1997.
Brunner, Emil. *The Divine-Human Encounter.* London: SCM, 1944.
———. *Man in Revolt: A Christian Anthropology.* Translated by O. Wyon. London: Lutterworth, 1939.
Bullinger, E. W. *Number in Scripture: Its Supernatural Design and Spiritual Significance.* Grand Rapids: Kregel, 1967.
Bullock, C. Hassell. *Introduction to the Old Testament Prophetic Books.* Chicago: Moody, 1986.
———. "Wisdom, the 'Amen' of Torah." *JETS* 52 (2009) 5–18.
Burns, J. Patout, ed. *Theological Anthropology.* Sources of Early Christian Thought. Philadelphia: Fortress, 1981.
Busenitz, Irvin A. "Introduction to the Biblical Covenants; the Noahic Covenant and the Priestly Covenant." *The Master's Seminary Journal* 10 (1999) 173–89.
Cairns, David. *The Image of God in Man.* London: SCM, 1953.
Calloud, Jean. "A Few Comments on Structural Semiotics." In *Beyond Form Criticism: Essays in Old Testament Criticism,* edited by P. R. House, 118–42. Sources for Biblical and Theological Study 2. Winona Lake, IN: Eisenbrauns, 1992.
Calvin, John. *Genesis.* Crossway Classic Commentaries. Edited by J. I. Packer. Wheaton, IL: Crossway, 2001.
Cameron, Charles. "Introduction to 'Theological Anthropology.'" *Evangel* 23 (2005) 53–61.
Carson, D. A. *The Gospel according to John.* PNTC. Grand Rapids: Eerdmans, 1991.
Cassuto, Umberto. *Commentary on the Book of Genesis.* Vol. 1, pt. 1, *From Adam to Noah (Genesis 1—6.8).* Translated by I. Abrahams. Jerusalem: Magnes, 1961.
Cefalu, Rita F. "Royal Priestly Heirs to the Restoration Promise of Genesis 3:15: A Biblical Theological Perspective on the Sons of God in Genesis 6." *Westminster Theological Journal* 76 (2014) 351–70.
Cha, Young Seok. "Theological and Ethical Implications of Creation Care." *Journal of Applied Christian Leadership* 6 (2012) 88–106.
Chaney, Charles. "Martin Luther and the Mission of the Church." *JETS* 13 (1970) 15–41.
Chepey, Stuart. *Nazirites in Late Second Temple Judaism.* Ancient Judaism and Early Christianity 60. Netherlands: Brill, 2005.
Childs, Brevard. *Biblical Theology of the Old and New Testaments: Theological Reflection on the Christian Bible.* Minneapolis: Fortress, 1992.
Ciulinaru, Costel. "The Anthropology of the Holy Fathers." *Scientific Journal of Humanistic Studies* 3 (2011) 182–89.

Clifford, Richard J. *Creation Accounts in the Ancient Near East and in the Bible*. CBQMS 26. Washington, DC: Catholic Biblical Association of America, 1994.
Cole, R. Dennis. *Numbers*. NAC 3b. Nashville: Broadman & Holman, 2000.
Collins, C. John. *Genesis 1–4: A Linguistic, Literary, and Theological Commentary*. Phillipsburg, NJ: P&R, 2006.
Craigie, Peter C. *The Book of Deuteronomy*. NICOT. Grand Rapids: Eerdmans, 1976.
———. *Psalms 1–50*. WBC 19. Waco: Word, 1983.
Cross, Frank Moore. *Canaanite Myth and Hebrew Epic: Essays in the History of the Religion of Israel*. Cambridge: Harvard University Press, 1973.
Crusemann, Frank. *The Torah: Theology and Social History of Old Testament Law*. Translated by A. W. Mahnke. Minneapolis: Fortress, 1996.
Dahood, Mitchell. *Psalms I: 1–50*. AB 16. New York: Doubleday, 1965.
Daly, Robert J. "Images of God and the Imitation of God: Problems with the Atonement." *Theological Studies* 68 (2007) 36–51.
Davidson, A. B. *Theology of the Old Testament*. International Theological Library. Edited by S. D. F. Salmond. Edinburgh: T. & T. Clark, 1904.
Davies, Douglas J. *Anthropology and Theology*. Oxford: Berg, 2002.
Davies, Philip R. *Memories of Ancient Israel: An Introduction to Biblical History— Ancient and Modern*. Louisville: Westminster John Knox, 2008.
Deist, Ferdinand. "Genesis 1–11, Oppression and Liberation." *Journal of Theology for Southern Africa* 73 (1990) 3–11.
Dempster, Stephen G. *Dominon and Dynasty: A Theology of the Hebrew Bible*. NSBT 15. Edited by D. A. Carson. Downers Grove: InterVarsity, 2003.
Di Vito, Robert A. "Alttestamentliche Anthropologie." In *Der Mensch im Alten Israel*, edited by B. Janowski and K. Liess, 213–41. Herders Biblische Studien. Frieburg: Herder, 2009.
———. "Old Testament Anthropology and the Construction of Personal Identity." *CBQ* 61 (1999) 217–38.
Doyle, Brian. *The Apocalypse of Isaiah Metaphorically Speaking: A Study of the Use, Function and Significance of Metaphors in Isaiah 24–27*. Leuven: Leuven University Press, 2000.
Dumbrell, W. J. *Covenant and Creation*. Carlisle, PA: Paternoster, 1984.
Dunn, James D. G. *The Epistles to the Colossians and to Philemon: A Commentary on the Greek Text*. NIGTC. Grand Rapids: Eerdmans, 1996.
Durham, John I. *Exodus*. WBC 3. Waco: Word, 1987.
Easley, Kendell H. *Revelation*. HNTC 12. Nashville: Broadman & Holman, 1998.
Eastwood, Cyril. *Life and Thought in the Ancient World*. Philadelphia: Westminster, 1964.
———. *The Royal Priesthood of the Faithful*. London: Epworth, 1963.
Edersheim, Alfred. *Bible History: Old Testament*. Grand Rapids: Eerdmans, 1975.
Eichrodt, Walther. *Man in the Old Testament*. Translated by K. and R. Gregor Smith. Studies in Biblical Theology 4. London: SCM, 1951.
———. *Theology of the Old Testament*. OTL 1–2. Translated by J. A. Baker. Philadelphia: Westminster, 1961–1967.
Eissfeldt, Otto. *The Old Testament: An Introduction*. Translated by Peter R. Ackroyd. New York: Harper & Row, 1965.
Ellingworth, Paul. *The Epistle to the Hebrews: A Commentary on the Greek Text*. NIGTC. Grand Rapids: Eerdmans, 1993.

Erickson, Millard J. *Christian Theology.* 2nd ed. Grand Rapids: Baker, 1998.
Estes, Daniel J. "Creation Theology in Psalm 148." *BS* 171 (2014) 30–41.
Firmage, Edwin. "Genesis 1 and the Priestly Agenda." *JSOT* 82 (1999) 97–114.
Fischer, Irmtraud. *Tora fur Israel—Tora fur die Volker: Das Konzept des Jesajabuches.* Stuttgart: Verlag Katholisches Bibelwerk GmbH, 1995.
Fisher, Fred L. "John's Theology and Gospel Structure." In *New Testament Studies: Essays in Honor of Ray Summers in his Sixty-fifth Year,* edited by H. L. Drumwright and C. Vaughan, 29–42. Waco: Baylor University Press, 1975.
Fleming, Daniel. "By the Sweat of Your Brow: Adam, Anat, Athirat, and Ashurbanipal." In *Ugarit and the Bible,* edited by G. J. Brooke et al., 93–100. Munster: Ugarit-Verlag, 1994.
Fletcher-Louis, Crispin. "God's Image, His Cosmic Temple and the High Priest: Towards an Historical and Theological Account of the Incarnation." In *Heaven and Earth,* edited by T. D. Alexander and S. Gathercole, 81–99. Waynesboro, GA: Paternoster, 2004.
Fredriksen, Paula. *From Jesus to Christ.* New Haven: Yale University Press, 1988.
Fretheim, Terence E. "Reclamation of Creation." *Interpretation* 45 (1991) 354–65.
———. *Suffering of God.* Philadelphia: Fortress, 1984.
Frevel, Christian. "Gottesbildlichkeit und Menschenwürde: Freiheit, Geschöpflichkeit und Würde nach dem Alten Testament." In *Anthropologische Aufbrüche,* edited by Andreas Wagner, 255–74. FRLANT 232. Göttingen: Vandenhoeck & Ruprecht, 2009.
Frost, Bede. *In His Image: A Study of Man's Relation to God.* London: A. R. Mowbray, 1941.
Furfey, Paul H. "Social Action in the Early Church." *Theological Studies* 2 (1941) 171–97.
Gage, Warren Austin. *Essays in Biblical Theology.* Fort Lauderdale: Gage, 2010.
Garland, David E. *2 Corinthians.* NAC 29. Nashville: Broadman & Holman, 1999.
Garr, W. Randall. "God's Creation: ברא in the Priestly Source." *HTR* 97 (2004) 83–90.
Garrett, James Leo, Jr. "The Biblical Doctrine of the Priesthood of the People of God." In *New Testament Studies: Essays in Honor of Ray Summers in His Sixty-Fifth Year,* edited by H. L. Drumwright and C. Vaughan, 137–49. Waco: Baylor University Press, 1975.
———. *Systematic Theology: Biblical, Historical, and Evangelical.* 2 vols. Grand Rapids: Eerdmans, 1990–1995.
Gentry, Peter J., and Stephen J. Wellum. *Kingdom through Covenant: A Biblical-Theological Understanding of the Covenants.* Wheaton, IL: Crossway, 2012.
Gesenius, Wilhelm. *Gesenius' Hebrew Grammar.* Edited by E. F. Kautzsch. Translated by A. E. Cowley. Oxford: Clarendon, 1910.
Giere, S. D. *New Glimpse of Day One: Intertextuality, History of Interpretation, and Genesis 1:1–5.* Berlin: de Gruyter, 2009.
Girdlestone, Robert B. *The Grammar of Prophecy: An Attempt to Discover the Method Underlying the Prophetic Scripture.* London: Eyre and Spottiswoode, 1901.
Gogarten, F. "Das Problem einer theologischen Anthropologie." *Zwischen den Zeiten* 7 (1929) 493–511.
Goldingay, John. *Old Testament Theology.* 3 vols. Downers Grove: InterVarsity, 2003–2009.
———. *Psalms 1–41.* Vol. 1 of *Psalms.* Baker Commentary on Old Testament Wisdom and Psalms. Grand Rapids: Baker Academic, 2006.

———. *The Theology of the Book of Isaiah*. Downers Grove: IVP Academic, 2014.
Gorman, Frank H., Jr. *The Ideology of Ritual: Space, Time and Status in the Priestly Theology*. JSOTSS 91. Edited by D. J. A. Clines and P. R. Davies. Sheffield: JSOT, 1990.
Goswell, Gregory. "Having the Last Say: The End of the OT." *JETS* 58 (2015) 15–30.
———. "The Temple Theme in the Book of Daniel." *JETS* 55 (2012) 509–20.
Greidanus, Sidney. "The Universal Dimension of Law in the Hebrew Scriptures." *Sciences Religieuses* 14 (1985) 39–51.
Grenz, Stanley J. "Jesus as the *Imago Dei*: Image-of-God Christology and the Non-Linear Linearity of Theology." *JETS* 47 (2004) 617–28.
———. *The Named God and the Question of Being: A Trinitarian Theo-Ontology*. Matrix of Christian Theology. Louisville: Westminster John Knox, 2005.
———. *The Social God and the Relational Self: A Trinitarian Theology of the Imago Dei*. Louisville: Westminster John Knox, 2001.
———. "The Social God and the Relational Self: Toward a Theology of the *Imago Dei* in the Postmodern Context." *Horizons in Biblical Theology* 24 (2002) 33–57.
Gronbaek, Jakob H. "Baal's Battle with Yam—a Canaanite Creation Fight." *JSOT* 33 (1985) 27–44.
Grunlan, Stephen, and Marvin Mayers. *Cultural Anthropology*. Grand Rapids: Zondervan Academic, 1979.
Guthrie, Donald. *New Testament Theology*. Downers Grove: InterVarsity, 1981.
Habel, Norman. *The Land Is Mine: Six Biblical Land Ideologies*. OBT. Minneapolis: Fortress, 1995.
———. *Literary Criticism of the Old Testament*. Guides to Biblical Scholarship. Philadelphia: Fortress, 1971.
Hall, Douglas J. *Imaging God: Dominion as Stewardship*. Grand Rapids: Eerdmans, 1986.
Hamilton, Victor P. *Book of Genesis: Chapters 1–17*. NICOT. Grand Rapids: Eerdmans, 1990.
Handy, Lowell K. "Dissenting Deities or Obedient Angels: Divine Hierarchies in Ugarit and the Bible." *Biblical Research* 35 (1990) 18–35.
Haran, Menahem. *Temples and Temple-Service in Ancient Israel*. Winona Lake, IN: Eisenbrauns, 1985.
Harris, Murray J. *The Second Epistle to the Corinthians: A Commentary on the Greek Text*. NIGTC. Grand Rapids: Eerdmans, 2005.
Harrison, R. K. *Introduction to the Old Testament*. Peabody, MA: Hendrickson, 2004.
Hartley, John E. *The Book of Job*. NICOT. Grand Rapids: Eerdmans, 1988.
Hasel, Gerhard F. *Old Testament Theology: Basic Issues in the Current Debate*. 3rd ed. Grand Rapids: Eerdmans, 1972.
———. "The Polemic Nature of the Genesis Cosmology." *Evangelical Quarterly* 46 (1974) 81–102.
Helm, Paul. "Calvin (and Zwingli) on Divine Providence." *Calvin Theological Journal* 29 (1994) 388–405.
Hochstrasser, T. J. *Natural Law Theories in the Early Enlightenment*. Ideas in Context 58. Cambridge: Cambridge University Press, 2000.
Horbury, W. "The Aaronic Priesthood in the Epistle to the Hebrews." *JSNT* 19 (1983) 43–71.

Hornung, Erik. *Conceptions of God in Ancient Egypt: The One and the Many*. Translated by J. Baines. Ithaca, NY: Cornell University Press, 1982.
House, Paul R. *1, 2 Kings*. NAC 8. Nashville: Broadman & Holman, 1995.
———. *Old Testament Theology*. Downers Grove: InterVarsity, 1998.
Humphreys, W. Lee. *The Character of God in the Book of Genesis: A Narrative Appraisal*. Louisville: Westminster John Knox, 2001.
Inglis, Nathanael L. "The Kinship of Creation: An Anabaptist Ecological Anthropology." *Conrad Grebel Review* 30 (2012) 162–87.
Jacobson, Richard. "The Structuralists and the Bible." In *Beyond Form Criticism: Essays in Old Testament Literary Criticism*, edited by P. R. House, 101–17. Sources for Biblical and Theological Study 2. Winona Lake, IN: Eisenbrauns, 1992.
Jauhiainen, Marko. "Turban and Crown Lost and Regained: Ezekiel 21:29–32 and Zechariah's Zemah." *JBL* 127 (2008) 501–11.
Jewett, Paul K. *Man as Male and Female: A Study in Sexual Relationships from a Theological Point of View*. Grand Rapids: Eerdmans, 1975.
Johnson, Aubrey. *The Cultic Prophet in Ancient Israel*. Cardiff: Univ. of Wales Press Board, 1944.
Jukes, Andrew. *Types in Genesis*. 8th ed. Grand Rapids: Kregel, 1976.
Kaiser, Walter C., Jr. *Back Toward the Future: Hints for Interpreting Biblical Prophecy*. Grand Rapids: Baker, 1989.
Kallenberg, Brad J. "Positioning MacIntyre within Christian Ethics." In *Virtues and Practices in the Christian Tradition: Christian Ethics after MacIntyre*, edited by Nancey Murphy et al., 45–81. Harrisburg, PA: Trinity Press International, 1997.
Keil, Carl Friedrich, and Franz Delitzsch. *Commentary on the Old Testament*. 10 vols. Peabody, MA: Hendrickson, 1996.
Kelle, Brad E. "Dealing with the Trauma of Defeat: The Rhetoric of the Devastation and Rejuvenation of Nature in Ezekiel." *JBL* 128 (2009) 469–90.
Kessler, John. *Old Testament Theology: Divine Call and Human Response*. Waco: Baylor University Press, 2013.
King, Thomas J. *Realignment of the Priestly Literature: The Priestly Narrative in Genesis and Its Relation to Priestly Legislation and the Holiness School*. Princeton Theological Monograph Series 102. Eugene, OR: Pickwick, 2009.
Knohl, Israel. *Sanctuary of Silence: The Priestly Torah and the Holiness School*. Minneapolis: Fortress, 1995.
Kraut, Judah. "The Birds and the Babes: The Structure and Meaning of Psalm 8." *Jewish Quarterly Review* 100 (2010) 10–24.
Kruse, Colin G. *The Letters of John*. PNTC. Grand Rapids: Eerdmans, 2000.
Laffey, Alice L. "The Priestly Creation Narrative: Goodness and Interdependence." In *Earth, Wind, and Fire*, edited by C. J. Dempsey and M. M. Pazdan, 24–34. Collegeville, MN: Order of St. Benedict, 2004.
Lane, William L. *Hebrews 9–13*. WBC 47b. Dallas: Word, 1991.
Lea, Thomas D. *Hebrews, James*. HNTC 10. Nashville: Broadman & Holman, 1999.
———. "The Priesthood of All Christians according to the New Testament." *SWJT* 30 (1988) 15–21.
Leithart, Peter J. "Attendants of Yahweh's House: Priesthood in the Old Testament." *JSOT* 85 (1999) 3–24.
Leuchter, Mark. "The Levite in Your Gates." *JBL* 126 (2007) 417–36.

Levenson, J. D. *Theology of the Program of Restoration of Ezekiel 40-48*. Harvard Semitic Monographs 10. Missoula: Scholars, 1976.

Levinas, Emmanuel. *In the Time of the Nations*. Translated by M. B. Smith. New York: Continuum, 2007.

———. *Sinai and Zion: An Entry into the Jewish Bible*. San Francisco: Harper & Row, 1985.

Lightfoot, J. B., and J. R. Harmer. *Apostolic Fathers*. 2nd ed. Edited by Michael W. Holmes. Grand Rapids: Baker, 1989.

Livingston, G. Herbert. *Pentateuch in Its Cultural Environment*. 2nd ed. Grand Rapids: Baker, 1987.

Lohfink, Norbert. *Das Siegeslied am Schilfmeer*. Frankfurt: Knecht, 1965.

Lyons, Michael A. *From Law to Prophecy: Ezekiel's Use of the Holiness Code*. New York: T. & T. Clark, 2009.

Luther, Martin. *Commentary on Romans*. Translated by J. T. Mueller. Grand Rapids: Kregel, 1976.

Maloney, George A. *Cosmic Christ: From Paul to Teilhard*. New York: Sheed & Ward, 1968.

Mann, Thomas W. *The Book of the Torah: The Narrative Integrity of the Pentateuch*. Atlanta: Westminster John Knox, 1988.

Marshall, I. Howard. *The Acts of the Apostles*. TNTC. Grand Rapids: Eerdmans, 1980.

Mathews, K. A. *Genesis 1—11:26*. NAC 1a. Nashville: Broadman & Holman, 1996.

———. *Genesis 11:27—50:26*. NAC 1b. Nashville: Broadman & Holman, 2005.

Mathewson, David. *A New Heaven and a New Earth: The Meaning and Function of the Old Testament in Revelation 21.1—22.5*. Library of New Testament Studies 238. Bloomsbury: T. & T. Clark, 2003.

Mayes, A. D. H., and R. B. Salters, eds. *Covenant as Context: Essays in Honour of E. W. Nicholson*. Oxford: Oxford University Press, 2003.

McConville, J. Gordon. "Priesthood in Joshua to Kings." *VT* 49 (1999) 73-87.

———. "Priests and Levites in Ezekiel: A Crux in the Interpretation of Israel's History." *TynBull*. 34 (1983) 3-31.

McKeown, James. *Genesis*. Two Horizons Old Testament Commentary. Grand Rapids: Eerdmans, 2008.

McNutt, Paula M. "The Kenites, the Midianites, and the Rechabites as Marginal Mediators in Ancient Israelite Tradition." *Semeia* 67 (1994) 109-32.

Merrill, Eugene H. *Deuteronomy*. NAC 4. Nashville: Broadman & Holman, 1994.

Middleton, J. Richard. *The Liberating Image: The Imago Dei in Genesis 1*. Grand Rapids: Brazos, 2005.

———. *A New Heaven and a New Earth: Reclaiming Biblical Eschatology*. Grand Rapids: Baker Academic, 2014.

Miller, J. Maxwell. "In the 'Image' and 'Likeness' of God." *JBL* 91 (1972) 289-304.

Miller, Stephen R. *Daniel*. NAC 18. Nashville: Broadman & Holman, 1994.

Moberly, R. W. L. *The Old Testament of the Old Testament: Patriarchal Narratives and Mosaic Yahwism*. OBT. Minneapolis: Fortress, 1992.

Morgenstern, Julian. "The Sources of the Creation Story—Genesis 1:1—2:4." *American Journal of Semitic Languages and Literatures* 36 (1920) 169-212.

Morris, Leon. *The Epistle to the Romans*. PNTC. Grand Rapids: Eerdmans, 1988.

———. *New Testament Theology*. Grand Rapids: Zondervan, 1986.

Morrow, Jeff. "Creation as Temple-Building and Work as Liturgy in Genesis 1–3." *Journal of the Orthodox Center for the Advancement of Biblical Studies* 2 (2009) 1–13.
Mostert, Christiaan. "The Human Person in Recent Protestant Theology." *Theological Anthropology: A Collection of Papers Prepared by Faith and Unity Commissioners of the National Council of Churches in Australia, 2005.* http://www.ncca.org.au/index.php/faith-and-unity-resources/36-theological-anthropology/file.
Mouroux, Jean. *The Meaning of Man*. Translated by A. H. C. Downes. London: Sheed & Ward, 1948.
Mowinckel, Sigmund. *Erwagungen zur Pentateuch Quellenfrage*. Oslo: Universitetsforlaget, 1964.
Murphy, Bryan. "The Trinity in Creation." *The Master's Seminary Journal* 24 (2013) 167–77.
Nachmanides. *Ramban (Nachmanides): Commentary on the Torah*. Translated by C. B. Chavel. New York: Shilo, 1971.
Nelson, Richard D. *Raising Up a Faithful Priest: Community and Priesthood in Biblical Theology*. Louisville: Westminster John Knox, 1993.
Neville, Richard. "Differentiation in Genesis 1: An Exegetical Creation *ex nihilo*." *JBL* 130 (2011) 209–26.
Newsom, Carol A. "Models of the Moral Self: Hebrew Bible and Second Temple Judaism." *JBL* 131 (2012) 5–25.
Niehaus, Jeffrey J. *God at Sinai: Covenant and Theophany in the Bible and Ancient Near East*. Studies in Old Testament Biblical Theology. Grand Rapids: Zondervan, 1995.
Niskanen, Paul. "The Poetics of Adam: The Creation of אדם in the Image of אלהים." *JBL* 128 (2009) 417–36.
Nolland, John. *The Gospel of Matthew: A Commentary on the Greek Text*. NIGTC. Grand Rapids: Eerdmans, 2005.
Novenson, Matthew V. "The Jewish Messiahs, the Pauline Christ, and the Gentile Question." *JBL* 128 (2009) 357–73.
Olson, Dan. "What Got the Gatekeepers into Trouble?" *JSOT* 30 (2005) 223–42.
Orlov, Andrei. "The Heir of Righteousness and the King of Righteousness: The Priestly Noachic Polemics in 2 Enoch and the Epistle to the Hebrews." *Journal of Theological Studies* 58 (2007) 45–65.
Ortlund, Gavin. "Image of Adam, Son of God: Genesis 5:3 and Luke 3:38 in Intercanonical Dialogue." *JETS* 57 (2014) 673–88.
Oswalt, John N. *Book of Isaiah: Chapters 1–39*. NICOT. Grand Rapids: Eerdmans, 1986.
———. *Book of Isaiah: Chapters 40–66*. NICOT. Grand Rapids: Eerdmans, 1998.
Overstreet, R. Larry. "Man in the Image of God: A Reappraisal." *Criswell Theological Review* 3 (2005) 43–70.
Patton, Corrine. "Layers of Meaning: Priesthood in Jeremiah MT." In *The Priests in the Prophets*, edited by L. L. Grabbe and A. O. Bellis, 149–76. London: T. & T. Clark, 2004.
Petersen, David L. "Creation and Hierarchy in Ezekiel: Methodological Perspectives and Theological Prospects." In *Ezekiel's Hierarchical World*, edited by S. L. Cook and C. L. Patton, 169–78. SBL Symposium Series 31. Boston: Brill, 2004.
———. *Zechariah 9–14 and Malachi*. OTL. Louisville: Westminster John Knox, 1995.

Pierce, Timothy M. *Enthroned on Our Praise: An Old Testament Theology of Worship.* NAC Studies in Bible & Theology. Edited by E. R. Clendenen. Nashville: B&H Academic, 2008.

Pleins, J. David. *Social Visions of the Hebrew Bible: A Theological Introduction.* Louisville: Westminster John Knox, 2001.

Polk, Timothy. *The Prophetic Persona: Jeremiah and the Language of the Self.* JSOTSS 32. Sheffield: JSOT, 1984.

Rad, Gerhard von. *Old Testament Theology.* 2 vols. Translated by D. M. G. Stalker. New York: Harper & Row, 1957–1965.

Renckens, Henricus. *Israel's Concept of the Beginning: The Theology of Genesis 1–3.* Translated by C. Napier. New York: Herder and Herder, 1964.

Rendtorff, Rolf. *Canon and Theology: Overtures to an Old Testament Theology.* OBT. Minneapolis: Fortress, 1993.

———. *The Canonical Hebrew Bible: A Theology of the Old Testament.* Tools for Biblical Study. Translated by D. E. Orton. Dorchester: Deo, 2005.

Reno, R. R. *Genesis.* Brazos Theological Commentary on the Bible. Grand Rapids: Brazos, 2010.

Reyburn, William David, and Euan McG. Fry. *A Handbook on Genesis.* UBS Handbook Series. New York: United Bible Societies, 1998.

Robertson, A. T. *Word Pictures in the New Testament.* Nashville: Broadman, 1933.

Robinson, Bernard. "Zipporah to the Rescue: A Contextual Study of Exodus IV 24–6." *VT* 36 (1986) 447–61.

Rooker, Mark F. *Leviticus.* NAC 3a. Nashville: Broadman & Holman, 2000.

Ross, Allen P. *Recalling the Hope of Glory: Biblical Worship from the Garden to the New Creation.* Grand Rapids: Kregel, 2006.

Routledge, Robin. *Old Testament Theology: A Thematic Approach.* Downers Grove: IVP Academic, 2008.

Rowley, H. H. *Worship in Ancient Israel: Its Forms and Meanings.* Philadelphia: Fortress, 1967.

Rudolph, David J. "Festivals in Genesis 1:14." *TynBull.* 54 (2003) 23–40.

Ryle, Herbert E. *The Book of Genesis in the Revised Version with Introduction and Notes.* Cambridge Bible for Schools and Colleges. Cambridge: Cambridge University Press, 1921.

Sabourin, Leopold. *Priesthood: A Comparative Study.* Studies in the History of Religions 25. Leiden: Brill, 1973.

Sailhamer, John H. *Genesis Unbound.* 2nd ed. Colorado Springs: Dawson, 2011.

———. *Introduction to Old Testament Theology: A Canonical Approach.* Grand Rapids: Zondervan, 1995.

Sanders, James A. *Torah and Canon.* Philadelphia: Fortress, 1972.

Sarna, Nahum. *Genesis.* JPS Torah Commentary. Philadelphia: Jewish Publication Society, 1989.

Schachter, Lifsa. "The Garden of Eden as God's First Sanctuary." *Jewish Bible Quarterly* 41 (2013) 73–77.

Schmitt, Mary. "Restructuring Views on Law in Hebrews 7:12." *JBL* 128 (2009) 189–201.

Schnabel, Eckhard J. "Israel, the People of God, and the Nations." *JETS* 45 (2002) 35–57.

Schreiner, Thomas R. *1, 2 Peter, Jude.* NAC 37. Nashville: Broadman & Holman, 2003.

Schroer, Silvia, and Thomas Staubli. "Bodily and Embodied: Being Human in the Tradition of the Hebrew Bible." Translated by M. E. Biddle. *Interpretation* 67 (2013) 5–19.

Scobie, Charles H. H. *The Ways of Our God*. Grand Rapids: Eerdmans, 2003.

Segal, Michael. "The Responsibilities and Rewards of Joshua the High Priest according to Zechariah 3:7." *JBL* 126 (2007) 717–34.

Seiss, Joseph A. *Holy Types—or the Gospel in Leviticus*. Houston: St. Thomas, 1972.

Sexton, Jason S. "The *imago Dei* Once Again: Stanley Grenz's Journey toward a Theological Interpretation of Genesis 1:26–27." *Journal of Theological Interpretation* 4 (2010) 187–205.

Sherlock, Charles. *The Doctrine of Humanity*. Contours of Christian Theology. Downers Grove: InterVarsity, 1996.

Skillen, James W. "The Seven Days of Creation." *Calvin Theological Journal* 46 (2011) 111–39.

Skinner, John. *Critical and Exegetical Commentary on Genesis*. 2nd ed. ICC. Edinburgh: T. & T. Clark, 1930.

Smith, Mark S. *The Priestly Vision of Genesis 1*. Minneapolis: Fortress, 2010.

Speiser, E. A. *Genesis*. AB 1. Garden City: Doubleday, 1964.

Sprinkle, Joe M. *"Book of the Covenant": A Literary Approach*. JSOTSS 174. Sheffield: JSOT, 1994.

Steinmann, Andrew E. "אחד as an Ordinal Number and the Meaning of Genesis 1:5." *JETS* 45 (2002) 577–84.

Stevens, Marty E. *Temples, Tithes, and Taxes: The Temple and the Economic Life of Ancient Israel*. Peabody: Hendrickson, 2006.

Strine, C. A. "Ezekiel's Image Problem: The Mesopotamian Cult Statue Induction Ritual and the *Imago Dei* Anthropology in the Book of Ezekiel." *CBQ* 76 (2014) 252–72.

Stuart, Douglas K. *Exodus*. NAC 2. Nashville: Broadman & Holman, 2006.

Theokritoff, Elizabeth. "Creation and Priesthood in Modern Orthodox Thinking." *Ecotheology* 10 (2005) 344–63.

Thielicke, Helmut. *Being Human . . . Becoming Human: An Essay in Christian Anthropology*. Translated by G. W. Bromiley. Garden City: Doubleday, 1984.

Thomas, Matthew A. *These Are the Generations: Identity, Covenant and the "Toledot" Formula*. LHBOTS 551. New York: T. & T. Clark, 2011.

Thompson, J. A. *The Book of Jeremiah*. NICOT. Grand Rapids: Eerdmans, 1980.

———. *1, 2 Chronicles*. NAC 9. Nashville: Broadman & Holman, 1994.

Torrance, T. F. *Royal Priesthood*. Scottish Journal of Theology Occasional Papers 3. Edinburgh: Oliver and Boyd, 1955.

Towner, W. Sibley. "Clones of God: Genesis 1:26–28 and the Image of God in the Hebrew Bible." *Interpretation* 59 (2005) 341–56.

Trimm, Charlie. "Did YHWH Condemn the Nations when He Elected Israel? YHWH's Disposition toward Non-Israelites in the Torah." *JETS* 55 (2012) 521–36.

Van Gemeren, Willem A., ed. *New International Dictionary of Old Testament Theology & Exegesis*. Vol. 1. Grand Rapids: Zondervan, 1997.

Van Houten, Christiana. *Alien in Israelite Law*. JSOTSS 107. Sheffield: Sheffield Academic, 1991.

Van Wolde, Ellen. *The Problem of the Hexateuch and Other Essays*. Translated by E. W. Trueman Dicken. London: SCM, 1984.

———. *Stories of the Beginning: Genesis 1–11 and Other Creation Stories.* Translated by J. Bowden. Ridgefield, CT: Morehouse, 1997.

Vogels, Walter. "And God Created the Great *Tanninim*." *Science et Esprit* 63 (2011) 349–65.

Vos, Geerhardus. *The Eschatology of the Old Testament.* Edited by James T. Dennison Jr. Phillipsburg, NJ: P&R, 2001.

Vriezen, T. C. *An Outline of Old Testament Theology.* Oxford: Blackwell, 1958.

Walls, David, and Max Anders. *I & II Peter, I, II & III John, Jude.* HNTC 11. Nashville: Broadman & Holman, 1999.

Waltke, Bruce K. *Genesis: A Commentary.* With Cathy J. Fredricks. Grand Rapids: Zondervan, 2001.

Waltke, Bruce K., and Charles Yu. *Old Testament Theology: An Exegetical, Canonical, and Thematic Approach.* Grand Rapids: Zondervan, 2007.

Walton, John H. "A Historical Adam: Archetypal Creation View." In *Four Views on the Historical Adam*, edited by M. Barrett et al., 89–118. Grand Rapids: Zondervan, 2013.

———. *Lost World of Genesis One: Ancient Cosmology and the Origins Debate.* Downers Grove: IVP Academic, 2009.

Walvoord, John F. *Jesus Christ Our Lord.* Chicago: Moody, 1969.

Ware, Kallistos. "'In the Image and Likeness': The Uniqueness of the Human Person." In *Personhood: Orthodox Christianity and the Connection between Body, Mind and Soul*, edited by J. T. Chirban, 1–13. Westport, CT: Bergin & Garvey, 1996.

Watts, John D. W. *Isaiah 1–33.* WBC 24. Waco: Word, 1985.

———. *Isaiah 34–66.* WBC 25. Waco: Word, 1987.

Weiser, Artur. *Psalms: A Commentary.* OTL. Translated by H. Hartwell. Philadelphia: Westminster, 1962.

Wenham, Gordon J. *The Book of Leviticus.* NICOT. Grand Rapids: Eerdmans, 1979.

———. *Story as Torah: Reading the Old Testament Ethically.* Old Testament Studies. Edited by D. J. Reimer. Edinburgh: T. & T. Clark, 2000.

Wolff, Hans Walter. *Anthropology of the Old Testament.* Mifflintown, PA: Sigler, 1996.

Xintaras, Zachary C. "Man—the Image of God: According to the Greek Fathers." *Greek Orthodox Theological Review* 1 (1954) 48–62.

Young, Edward J. *My Servants the Prophets.* Grand Rapids: Eerdmans, 1952.

Young, Norman. *Creator, Creation, and Faith.* Philadelphia: Westminster, 1976.

Zachman, Randall C. "Jesus Christ as the Image of God in Calvin's Theology." *Calvin Theological Journal* 25 (1990) 45–62.

Zevit, Ziony. "The Prophet versus Priest Antagonism Hypothesis: Its History and Origin." In *The Priests in the Prophets*, edited by L. L. Grabbe and A. O. Bellis, 189–217. London: T. & T. Clark, 2004.

Zimmerli, Walther. *Old Testament Theology in Outline.* Translated by D. E. Green. Edinburgh: T. & T. Clark, 1978.

www.ingramcontent.com/pod-product-compliance
Lightning Source LLC
Chambersburg PA
CBHW051737230426
43670CB00012B/2053